From Poli
to
Administra

Essays in Honour of
William A. Robson

From Policy to Administration

Essays in Honour of William A. Robson

EDITED BY J. A. G. GRIFFITH
Professor of Public Law,
London School of Economics and Political Science

London
GEORGE ALLEN & UNWIN LTD
Ruskin House Museum Street

First published in 1976

ISBN 0 04 350050 1

Printed in Great Britain
in 10 point Times New Roman type
by The Aldine Press
Letchworth, Herts

Preface

The idea of this book came from conversations between Bernard Crick, Peter Self and myself. We all wished to acknowledge with gratitude and affection the great debts that we and so many others owed to William Robson, and to write something that would interest him. To render a detailed account of that indebtedness – Item this and Item that – would be fulsome and he would not wish it. His shadow, during the last thirty years, has come to lie hugely across five great fields of personal endeavour and distinction: that of public law – as witnessed by his vastly influential work of 1928, *Justice and Administrative Law*; that of political science – as witnessed by his numerous writings, particularly on nationalised industries and on the Civil Service; that of London government – as witnessed by his founding and continued direction of the Greater London Group whose work was so influential in the transformation of the LCC into the GLC; that of public affairs – as witnessed by his founding with John Maynard Keynes, Kingsley Martin and Leonard Woolf of *The Political Quarterly* and of his being joint editor of it since 1930; that of consultancy on urban problems to many foreign governments – as witnessed, for instance, by his large and influential report of 1969 on the problems of metropolitan Tokyo.

The book is not a conventional *Festschrift* written by many hands on many subjects. It is a collection of essays on a theme which gives them some unity. It does not try to cover all William Robson's interests. It is a mark of the versatility of his genius that no book could do that and remain unified. Some future biographer may resolve that dilemma, but not in a few score thousands of words.

As editor, I am grateful to those who contributed so willingly and who responded so remarkably to my bullying demands for the delivery of their typescripts by the agreed date. Those who contributed did so on behalf of the very many scholars who would also have written had we tried to cover all aspects of Robson's interests.

J. A. G. GRIFFITH
31 December 1974

Contents

Contributors

BERNARD CRICK	*Professor of Politics, Birkbeck College, University of London*
C. D. FOSTER	*Head of the Centre for Urban Economics, London School of Economics and Political Science, University of London*
CARL J. FRIEDRICH	*Eaton Professor of the Science of Government (emeritus), Harvard University*
J. A. G. GRIFFITH	*Professor of Public Law, London School of Economics and Political Science, University of London*
G. W. JONES	*Reader in Political Science at the London School of Economics and Political Science, University of London*
JOHN P. MACKINTOSH	*Member of Parliament, Visiting Professor of Politics, Birkbeck College, University of London*
J. D. B. MITCHELL	*Salvesen Professor of European Institutions, University of Edinburgh*
PETER SELF	*Professor of Public Administration, London School of Economics and Political Science, University of London*
L. J. SHARPE	*Fellow of Nuffield College, Oxford*

1

The Prime Ministers' Secretaries: Politicians or Administrators?

G. W. JONES

INTRODUCTION

A minister is the hinge between politics and administration. Simultaneously he is a party and parliamentary leader and head of a department; business flows to his desk both from within the department and from the public arena, and in reaching his conclusions he takes into account political and administrative considerations. His closest advisers link him with the world of political activity as well as with the administrative machine. Yet the functions of these advisers cannot be clearly distinguished into either political or administrative components: the leading officials of a minister are deeply involved in the formulation of policy and have to be sensitive to political factors, while the political advisers of a minister have to be aware of the administrative consequences of their proposals. At the top of a department administration is not an activity that is separate from politics, nor is politics an activity separate from administration.

A minister in Britain has had more experience of politics than administration. His career has been spent in speaking in public, fighting elections and winning a reputation inside his party and in Parliament. When he becomes a minister he enters an area he has not previously known and is dependent on his top officials to keep him in touch with his department, to inform him of the views of the

I wish to thank Elly Shodell and Steven Conway for their help while preparing this essay.

administration and to see that his decisions are implemented. The minister has to take care that he is not cut off from his political origins and the political forces that sustain him; and to assist a minister in reconciling political and administrative pressures there has evolved in Britain the private office of departmental officials as well as a looser network of personal and political advisers.

The Prime Minister is the one minister who stands on the peaks of both politics and administration. He too needs assistants to make his daily life run smoothly, to act as links and mediators with a variety of individuals and groups, to think about issues and give him advice, to expedite his decisions or to ensure that they are expedited, and to be just there when he wants to talk to them. But in his role as Prime Minister he has, unlike most other ministers, no department to back and brief him. The nearest equivalent is his private office of private secretaries, those civil servants assigned to serve him. The essence of their work is contained in the title 'private secretary', which embraces the notions of secrecy and writing. They work behind the scenes; they are entrusted with secrets; they are confidential advisers; they are the depository of his records; they write and speak on his behalf and transact business for him. Their tasks are diverse, but their main responsibility is to be of service to him, to enable him to carry out his functions.

GENERAL TRENDS

Prime Ministers at least from the period of the Duke of Newcastle (1757–62) have had private secretaries.[1] During the eighteenth century he was a single secretary, appointed from outside the Treasury, although occasionally a clerk already on the establishment was selected. They received no salary from public funds, and their recruitment and remuneration were entirely at the discretion of the Prime Minister. They were his personal adherents. On leaving office the Prime Minister usually rewarded his private secretary with a place in the Treasury or with an office under the patronage of the Treasury and its First Lord which was the official position held by the Prime Minister. In 1806 for the first time a salary of £300 out of public funds was paid for one private secretary to the First Lord, Lord Grenville, and in 1812 when Lord Liverpool became Prime Minister a salary of the same amount was made available for a second private secretary.[2]

The systematic selection of a private secretary, the payment of a salary from public funds and the appointment of an additional secretary, all reflect the firm establishment of the office of Prime Minister by the early nineteenth century. From then to the 1870s the Prime Minister's responsibilities, both controlling the Government and handling parliamentary and legislative business, were making more demands on his time. His need for assistance in both administrative and political spheres meant that one of his private secretaries was usually chosen from amongst Treasury clerks and the other from outside the Civil Service. If the latter was a member of the House of Commons, as he sometimes was, he received no salary from public funds. He was similar to what was later to be called the Prime Minister's 'parliamentary private secretary'. The official private secretary received his salary in addition to his remuneration as a Treasury clerk, in recognition of the extra duties he had to carry out as the Prime Minister's private secretary.

Numerically, the size of the Prime Minister's private secretariat has not increased greatly since the mid-nineteenth century, despite the increasing amount and complexity of government business, soaring public expenditure, and the rising number of civil servants, which have placed on Prime Ministers an ever-growing burden of work. In the 1870s the number of paid private secretaries was increased to three. It remained at three until the 1920s, when it went up again by one; after the Second World War it rose to five and in the 1960s to six. However, at various points during the period the number of secretaries was higher than was normal: during the two wars, for instance, when more help was needed. Also whenever the Prime Minister combined being First Lord with another portfolio he became entitled to more secretaries. This applied to Gladstone who was at times also Chancellor of the Exchequer and Lord Privy Seal, Rosebery who was Lord President of the Council, and Winston Churchill who was Minister of Defence. Despite these deviations, between the 1870s and the 1960s the number of private secretaries of the Prime Minister rose from three to six.[3]

One explanation for the relatively small increase in the number of private secretaries is that some of their duties have been allocated to new institutions, especially to the Cabinet Office and Secretariat, the press and information division at No. 10 Downing Street, and the miscellaneous political and personal aides who from time to time have served Prime Ministers outside the private office. In addition, many of the more routine chores, personally carried out by the private secretaries in the eighteenth and nineteenth centuries, have been taken over by the clerical and executive staff who support them.

Opening letters, filing, taking dictation, typing, copying, and generally keeping the office running smoothly are the responsibility of junior civil servants, often females. These officials, and their office machines and equipment, were simply not available for Prime Ministers until the turn of the century. The first time that separate provision was made in the estimates for a shorthand writer and a typewriter specifically for the Prime Minister was in 1903–4 when £100 was allocated. By 1905–6 this figure had grown to £250, including clerical assistance. By 1951 there were fifty-two clerks, typists, messengers and cleaners for the Prime Minister and his private secretaries, by 1964 there were fifty-nine, and in 1974 seventy-seven.[4]

The development of the Prime Minister's private office between 1868 and 1975 can be divided roughly into three periods. Up to the 1900s its composition was a mixture of personal and political appointees and officials, but the latter had often entered the Civil Service under the patronage of a politician, their party allegiances were well known, and they were selected personally by the Prime Minister. From the 1900s to the 1920s the personal and political element declined, career civil servants became more prominent, less partisan and less personally attached to the Prime Minister. These trends were apparent before the First World War, but they suffered a setback during the premiership of Lloyd George (1916–22) who surrounded himself with an increased number of personal and partisan secretaries. However, during the 1920s, in reaction to his regime, the personal and partisan elements were reduced and by the 1930s excluded altogether from the private office. From the 1930s to the 1970s the Civil Service monopolised the private office, and personal and political appointees had to be located elsewhere. However, since Prime Ministers always take a great interest in the advisers closest to them, they have occasionally influenced appointments even of their civil service private secretaries.

Between 1868 and 1975 there have been thirty-four men who can be described as the Prime Minister's principal private secretary.[5] Their average age on being first appointed to the position was just over thirty-nine years. Only two were in their fifties, J. A. N. Barlow (1933) aged fifty-two, and M. Halls (1966) aged fifty-one, both civil servants. The youngest was (Sir) Schomberg K. McDonnell (1888) aged twenty-seven. The trend has been for the age to rise slightly: up to 1922 the average age was thirty-six, between 1922 and 1950, forty, and since 1950, forty-three. Since the other private secretaries who work under them have usually been younger than the principal private secretaries, the private office has as a whole consisted of men from their late twenties to their early forties.

The average length of time served as principal private secretary is just over three years: up to 1922 it was four years, between 1922 and 1950 two years, and since 1950 three years. McDonnell served the longest, eleven years, and A. Isserlis the shortest, three months in 1970. When the principal private secretary was a personal appointee of the Prime Minister, the length of his term of office was precisely that of his master: for example, J. T. Davies, principal private secretary to Lloyd George, served for the six years of the Lloyd George premiership. When the principal private secretary was appointed from within the administration, his term of office was not so closely linked to that of the Prime Minister. However, the Civil Service has not been able to lay down an accepted period of service for principal private secretaries. Between 1950 and 1970, three served for five years, two for four years, one for three years, one for two years, one for a year and one for three months. The present principal private secretary, Kenneth Stowe, was appointed in 1975. The varying periods reflect many factors: the wishes of the Prime Ministers, the views of the private secretary, whether they suit each other, the opinions of the head of the Civil Service, and the availability of opportunities for the promotion of the principal private secretary within his department.

Of the thirty-four principal private secretaries, eleven had previously been in the Prime Minister's private office. Since 1955, however, every principal private secretary has come from outside it, and only one had served the Prime Minister in a previous department. Instead their experience has been in the private offices of other ministers or permanent secretaries. Indeed, of the thirty-four only four appear never to have been a secretary to anyone previously. This previous experience was not brief: seventeen had served for over four years elsewhere and another three for over ten years. The career pattern of the principal private secretary since the 1930s is clear. He was at an early age recognised as able and was appointed private secretary to a minister or permanent secretary. Here he made a favourable impression and was later chosen either by the Prime Minister, or by the leading officials of the Treasury (since 1968 the Civil Service Department) in consultation with the Prime Minister, to be the principal private secretary. When a principal private secretary left the private office, and did not remain with his master in opposition or retirement, he usually advanced rapidly into positions of eminence and influence either within the Civil Service or more rarely in business.

1868–1902: SHIFTING PATTERNS

Since the development of the Prime Minister's private office has been to a large extent influenced by the Prime Ministers themselves, as well as by the men who served in it, a chronological analysis of the composition of the office since 1868 will illustrate the changing nature of the secretariat.[6] During 1868 both Disraeli and Gladstone had periods as Prime Minister, and each had a private secretary and an assistant from the Treasury. Disraeli's principal private secretary was Montagu Corry (Lord Rowton). A barrister, he had been noticed by Disraeli whilst entertaining guests at a country house party. Disraeli invited him to be his private secretary, and he remained Disraeli's aide and confidant from 1866, both in and out of office, until his master's death in 1881. His commitment was solely to Disraeli. Gladstone's principal private secretary was (Sir) Algernon West. In his teens he had entered the Civil Service as a clerk in the Admiralty where he became private secretary to its First Lord who later took him to the India Office. West was Gladstone's principal private secretary from 1868 to 1872, when he was appointed a Commissioner of the Board of Inland Revenue and later its chairman. In 1892 after retirement from the Civil Service West, out of loyalty and fondness for his chief, returned to Gladstone as his informal and unpaid principal private secretary until 1894. West was a civil servant, but he owed much of his personal attachment to Gladstone.

Disraeli's Treasury private secretary in 1868 was (Sir) Charles Fremantle. He had entered the Treasury in his teens and had acted as private secretary to a number of Chancellors of the Exchequer, including in 1866 Disraeli. When Disraeli became Prime Minister in March 1868 he took Fremantle with him, and when he fell from office after the general election of 1868 appointed him Deputy Master and Controller of the Royal Mint. Gladstone's Treasury clerk was William Gurdon. He had entered the Treasury in his twenties and had been a private secretary to the Chancellor of the Exchequer. In 1868 Gladstone appointed him a private secretary, and on West's departure in 1872 Gurdon took over most of the former principal's responsibilities. In 1874 on the defeat of the Gladstone Government Gurdon returned to the Treasury until retirement in 1899. Gurdon, like Fremantle, was a civil servant, but one whose political allegiances were well known. In 1884 he was a parliamentary candidate, but had to withdraw when told that 'candidature for Parliament is inconsistent with employment in the permanent Civil

Service'.[7] He was eventually elected a Liberal MP after retiring from the Civil Service.

After West left in 1872 Gladstone used Lord Frederick Cavendish, a Liberal MP, very much as a parliamentary private secretary: he kept Gladstone in touch with developments in Parliament, relayed gossip and spoke on behalf of his master. As an MP he received no salary for his secretarial duties. With Gurdon performing the main work of private secretary Gladstone appointed as his assistant J. A. Godley (Lord Kilbracken). In 1872 Godley was reading for the Bar when Gladstone, going outside the Civil Service, appointed him at the age of twenty-five. When Gladstone's Government fell in 1874 Godley became a private secretary to the leading Liberal politician and friend of Gladstone, Lord Granville. In 1880 when Gladstone next formed an administration Godley became his principal private secretary, until in 1882 he was appointed a Commissioner of Inland Revenue: a year later he was selected as Permanent Under Secretary for the India Office, where he remained until 1909. The personal and political appointee had been transformed into a permanent civil servant. Godley, Gurdon and Cavendish were the secretaries to the First Lord of the Treasury from 1872 to 1874, but Gladstone managed to obtain two others from 1873 to 1874. In 1873 Gladstone became also Chancellor of the Exchequer and so was entitled to the services of another two paid private secretaries. One was (Sir) Edward Hamilton. He joined the Treasury in his twenties and had been private secretary to the Chancellor in 1872–3 when he was taken over by Gladstone. On Gladstone's fall in 1874, he went back to the Treasury, only to be with him again as a private secretary during 1880–5. He then returned to the Treasury, becoming its Permanent Secretary from 1902 to 1907. He was clearly a civil servant, but one whose allegiance to Gladstone and attachment to the Liberal Party were never hidden. The other secretary was Spencer Lyttleton, brother-in-law of Lord Frederick Cavendish. Neither a politician nor a civil servant, he was rather a personal assistant to Gladstone who seems to have appointed him, almost as a favour, to perform a variety of routine clerical tasks in 1872–4, 1882–5, 1886 and 1892–1894. Lyttleton never distinguished himself elsewhere.

On Gladstone's defeat in 1874 Disraeli did not take the Chancellorship as well as the First Lordship, but still appointed three, and not two, private secretaries, in view of the increase of work falling on the Prime Minister who was also Leader of the House of Commons. Corry continued as principal private secretary, and his two assistants were both Treasury clerks. The first was Algernon Turnor. He had joined the Treasury in his late twenties, and was private secretary to the Permanent Secretary in 1871–4 when he was chosen to serve Disraeli. When Disraeli's Government ended in 1880 Turnor was appointed Financial Secretary to the Post Office, retiring in 1896. The second was J. F. Daly (Lord Dunsandle). He had been transferred from the Admiralty to the Treasury and was private secretary to the Patronage Secretary when he was selected to serve Disraeli. In 1880 he returned to the Treasury and ended his public career as Assistant Comptroller of the National Debt Office. Disraeli's private office remained exactly the same throughout his administration from 1874 to 1880. Unlike Gladstone he liked stability in the people around him and was not periodically appointing and promoting his secretaries. He also relied more on his principal private secretary, because unlike Gladstone he was not so involved in handling business himself, nor was he as disciplined and efficient in the dispatch of his work, for instance his correspondence.

As was customary when a new Prime Minister came into office, the secretaries of the old moved elsewhere. Gladstone became Prime Minister again in 1880, and was again Chancellor of the Exchequer until 1882. He increased the size of the paid secretariat to four, and used unpaid secretaries, such as his son Herbert, who was his parliamentary private secretary from 1880 to 1882 when he became a junior whip, and George Leveson-Gower, nephew of Lord Granville, who was unpaid at first (1880–2); then he received a salary until 1885 when he was elected as a Liberal MP. Between 1880 and 1885 Gladstone employed three of his previous secretaries. Godley was principal private secretary until his appointment to the Commission of Inland Revenue in 1882, when Hamilton took over most of his responsibilities until 1885. Lyttleton was still around, and there were two Treasury clerks who alternated as secretaries to the Prime Minister: Henry Primrose (1880, 1885 and 1886) and Horace Seymour (1880–5). Both had entered the Treasury in their twenties, had served as private secretaries to Treasury ministers and the Permanent Secretary, and both were later appointed to the Board of Customs, Seymour as deputy chairman (1890–4) and Primrose as chairman (1895–9). The latter, a cousin of the Liberal leader Lord Rosebery, became chairman of the Board of Inland Revenue from 1899 to 1907, while Seymour replaced Charles Fremantle as Deputy Master and Controller of the Royal Mint in 1894. Both were civil servants; both received promotion under Liberal and Conservative administrations; and neither served as private secretary any Prime Minister but the Liberal Gladstone.

In his brief administration of 1886 Gladstone seemed to have no principal private secretary. Primrose, Lyttleton and a newcomer, (Sir) James Carmichael, were his three secretaries. Carmichael illustrates a trend that other private secretaries sometimes followed: a movement from the Civil Service through the private office into a career in politics. He had been a clerk in the Admiralty, and after transfer to the Treasury had been private secretary to the Chancellor of the Exchequer from 1882 to 1885. Gladstone used him in 1886, and must have inspired him with the delights of politics, for he left the Civil Service and was eventually elected as a Liberal MP in 1892.

In 1892 Gladstone drew informally on Sir Algernon West as his principal private secretary. West brought in his own private secretary from the Board of Inland Revenue, H. G. L. Shand, who was possibly the first Prime Minister's private secretary to write shorthand. Lyttleton was back yet again, and the new man was a Treasury official, (Sir) George Murray. He had joined the Foreign Office in his twenties, transferred to the Treasury and served as Gladstone's private secretary until 1894. When Rosebery, also a Liberal, took office, he retained and promoted Murray to be his principal private secretary. As such he was the first since 1865 to have served consecutive terms under two Prime Ministers. Rosebery appointed three other secretaries, Lord Drumlanrig, an unpaid assistant, who had served Rosebery when Foreign Secretary and killed himself soon after switching to Downing Street, and two officials, one a Treasury clerk, E. G. Harman. When the Government fell in 1895, Murray returned to the Treasury, became chairman of the Board of Inland Revenue (1897–9), Secretary to the Post Office (1899–1903), and joint Permanent Secretary to the Treasury (1903–11).

Although Murray was the first example of a private secretary remaining in the secretariat through a changeover of Prime Ministers since 1865, J. F. Daly was the first secretary since 1855 to serve one Prime Minister, Disraeli 1874–80, and then to be chosen again some years later to serve another, when Salisbury formed his second administration, 1886–7. Salisbury's unusual choice of an earlier Prime Minister's secretary was just one of his innovations. He was the first Prime Minister since the eighteenth century not to hold the office of First Lord of the Treasury while being Prime Minister. Instead Salisbury combined the prime ministership with the offices of Foreign Secretary (1885–6, 1887–92, 1895–1900) and of Lord Privy Seal (1900–2). He was First Lord of the Treasury briefly in 1886–7, and only then did he have a Treasury official, Daly, as a private secretary. For the rest of the time he ousted the Treasury from its position as sole provider of 'official' private secretaries and used Foreign Office officials. The most important of these, acting as Salisbury's principal private secretary for foreign affairs, was (Sir) Eric Barrington. He had entered the Foreign Office at the age of twenty and spent most of his career as a private secretary to Foreign Office ministers, including Salisbury in 1878–80; indeed he served in this capacity all Conservative foreign secretaries between 1874 and 1905 when he became Assistant Under Secretary of State for Foreign Affairs. Other members of the Foreign Office who were Salisbury's private secretaries in the last two decades of the nineteenth century included George Curzon (Lord Curzon) and (Sir) Arthur Hardinge. Even one of Salisbury's parliamentary private secretaries, (Sir) Ian Malcolm, had been a member of the diplomatic service until elected as an MP in 1895.

The two men who were Salisbury's principal private secretaries were Henry Manners (Duke of Rutland) in 1885–6 and 1886–8, and (Sir) Schomberg K. McDonnell in 1888–92 and 1895–1902. Manners was a landowner in Leicestershire and an army officer. In 1888 he was elected as a Conservative to Parliament. McDonnell, son of the Earl of Antrim, became a private secretary soon after leaving Oxford, first to Lord Carnarvon and then to the Duke of Buccleuch. Salisbury appointed him in 1888 and he remained Salisbury's private secretary, both in and out of office, until 1902, when he was appointed Secretary to the Office of Works. He was also a soldier, serving briefly in the Boer War and as a chief intelligence officer 1914–15. He was killed in action in Flanders ten days after arriving at the front in 1915.

Salisbury also used as private secretaries youthful members of his family and fellow peers. Robert Cecil (Lord Cecil of Chelwood) was an unpaid private secretary to his father in 1886–8, as was Evelyn Cecil (Lord Rockley) to his uncle during the 'nineties to 1902. He was also served by Lord Walter Gordon-Lennox (1886), son of the Duke of Richmond, (Sir) Sidney Greville (1888–92, 1896–8 and 1900–1), son of the Earl of Warwick, and Lord Newport (1898–1900), son of the Earl of Bradford.

Salisbury's period as Prime Minister indicates that the style and requirements of the Prime Minister determined the composition of the private office. He did not draw his secretaries from the Treasury, but from the Foreign Office; for a principal private secretary he depended on a personal adherent, McDonnell, who was neither a politician nor an administrator; and he used a cluster of young aristocrats for more routine tasks. There was as yet no bureaucratic private office.

1902–16: THE PATTERN EMERGES

When Balfour succeeded Salisbury as Prime Minister in 1902 he reverted to the pre-Salisbury system. As principal private secretary he appointed his confidant of long standing, a Corry-like figure, J. S. Sandars (1902–5). He had been a barrister until in 1886 he had become the private secretary of the Home Secretary. In this position he had to have frequent contact with the Irish Secretary, A. J. Balfour, who was so impressed with him that he appointed him his private secretary. Sandars served Balfour in this position, both in and out of office, from 1892 to 1915. A subtle intriguer, Sandars was probably the most influential of the Prime Ministers' private secretaries, insinuating his views whilst engaged in his liaison work and acting as a confidential adviser to Balfour. Certainly he is the one who aroused most hostility as a shaper of policy behind the scenes. Balfour took over Lord Newport from Salisbury, and employed in the traditional way a Treasury clerk, first (Sir) Frederick Parry in 1902, replaced by (Sir) Malcolm Ramsay (1902–5). Parry had joined the Treasury in his twenties, served as a private secretary to the Chancellor of the Exchequer, and between 1897 and 1902 was private secretary to Balfour as First Lord of the Treasury. Balfour when Prime Minister used him briefly, before appointing him to the Board of Customs. From 1909 to 1925 Parry was deputy chairman of the Board of Customs and Excise. Ramsay had been a clerk in the Foreign Office before transference to the Treasury. When Balfour's Government resigned in 1905, he went back to the Treasury, eventually becoming its Controller of Establishments (1919–21) and Comptroller and Auditor-General (1921–31).

When Balfour's Government was replaced in 1905 by Campbell-Bannerman's Liberal administration, the Prime Minister's private secretaries were entirely new. There were three private secretaries: one principal private secretary, a personal and political appointee; a Treasury clerk; and another, who might be either a personal and political appointee or a civil servant. This pattern persisted until the fall of Asquith in 1916. Campbell-Bannerman's principal private secretary during 1905–8 was Arthur Ponsonby (Lord Ponsonby). The son of a former private secretary to Queen Victoria, he had joined the Foreign Office and had reached the status of second secretary when he retired in 1902. He worked in the Liberal Central Office, was adopted as a Liberal parliamentary candidate and in 1905 was selected by Campbell-Bannerman as his private secretary.

On election to Parliament in 1908 he left the secretariat. He later joined the Labour Party and was a minister in 1924 and 1929–31. As principal private secretary he was replaced by Vaughan Nash, who had joined the private office with him in 1905. Nash, a former radical journalist, continued to serve under Asquith as principal private secretary until 1912 when he was appointed vice-chairman of the Development Commission. Nash was replaced by (Sir) Maurice Bonham Carter. Like Nash he had been an assistant private secretary to the Prime Minister before being appointed the principal. He had been a barrister before joining the private office in 1910 and was so closely involved with Asquith that he married his daughter Violet. He remained Asquith's principal private secretary until the fall of the Prime Minister in 1916, when he became an assistant secretary in the Ministry of Reconstruction and later in the Air Ministry. He left the Civil Service at the end of the war and pursued a career in business. Thus the three principal private secretaries of the Liberal Prime Ministers of 1905–16 later followed different careers: Ponsonby became a politician, Nash a civil servant, and Bonham Carter, after a brief flirtation with the Civil Service, a businessman.

The rest of the private secretaries between 1905 and 1916 were career civil servants, except for the parliamentary private secretaries whose status and functions were now established. They were back-bench MPs, unpaid, who were responsible for keeping the Prime Minister in touch with the currents of opinion in the Commons and for representing his interests and views there. Campbell-Bannerman had two, and Asquith one. The Treasury continued to provide most of the Prime Ministers' Civil Service private secretaries, but its position, already weakened under Salisbury, suffered a further set-back under Campbell-Bannerman. In 1907 he replaced a long-time career Treasury official, Henry Higgs (once secretary to Algernon Turnor, Disraeli's former private secretary), with a member of the Foreign Office, (Sir) Hubert Montgomery. This reflected the increasing involvement and interest of Prime Ministers in foreign affairs and their need for intimate and continuous contact with the Foreign Office. Montgomery had been private secretary from 1904 to 1907 to successive Under Secretaries of State for Foreign Affairs, and after Campbell-Bannerman left office in 1908 he rose through the Diplomatic Service, becoming Minister at the Hague (1933–8). When Asquith became Prime Minister the Treasury reasserted itself for a while, since he brought to his private office two Treasury clerks who had served as his private secretaries while he was Chancellor of the

Exchequer. (Sir) Roderick Meiklejohn had been, before joining Asquith, private secretary to Sir Edward Hamilton when he was Permanent Secretary to the Treasury and to a Treasury junior minister. He returned to the Treasury divisions in 1911 and eventually became First Civil Service Commissioner (1928–39). (Sir) Mark Grant-Sturgis did not return to the Treasury when he left Asquith in 1910, but was appointed a Special Commissioner of Income Tax. Later he became a joint Assistant Under Secretary for Ireland. Between 1910 and 1914 Asquith had only one Treasury clerk in his private office. From 1911 to 1913 this Treasury man was (Sir) Frederick Leith-Ross, who in the 1930s and 1940s was one of Britain's leading financial experts at international conferences; and from 1913 to 1914 it was Gerald Pinsent, who ended his career as Comptroller General of the National Debt Office (1946–51). Asquith's other Civil Service private secretaries came from other departments, indeed from 1914 to 1916 he had no Treasury man as a private secretary. The Foreign Office provided Eric Drummond (Earl of Perth) (1912–15), who had been a private secretary to Foreign Office ministers from 1906 to 1912, and later became Secretary General to the League of Nations (1919–33) and British Ambassador to Italy (1933–9). He was replaced in 1915 by (Sir) Edward Marsh, a private secretary to colonial secretaries since 1900. After Asquith left office, Marsh continued to serve in the Colonial Office in the same capacity, achieving fame as the right-hand man of Sir Winston Churchill and as a patron of the arts. The final Civil Servant private secretary of Asquith was (Sir) David Davies (1914–16). An official from the Board of Trade, he replaced Pinsent in 1914. He later went to the Bar, took silk, became a county court judge and a National Insurance Commissioner.

In 1916 on the eve of his fall Asquith had three private secretaries: Bonham Carter his principal, Marsh and Davies. The period of Liberal Government of 1905–16 seemed to witness a stabilisation in the nature of the Prime Minister's private office. Its size was constant, and the departure of each private secretary was followed by the appearance of another. A hierarchy within the office itself was apparent, so that when the principal moved out the rest moved up, and a newcomer entered at the bottom. It was also clear that the position of private secretary was filled by men at the start of their careers; except for Marsh, who was forty-three, all the assistant private secretaries were in their twenties or thirties on their first appointment to the private office.

1916–22: THE LLOYD GEORGE INNOVATIONS

This apparently stable situation was shattered on the accession of Lloyd George. He radically changed the system of prime ministerial advisers. His dynamic inventiveness, his ambition to dominate each situation, his lack of a sure basis of support from a party and the need in war time to simplify, speed up and concentrate decision-making, all contributed to produce a revolution in the machinery of government at the top between 1916 and 1922.

Although of the same party as Asquith, Lloyd George removed all his predecessor's private secretaries and appointed three cronies. He had as principal private secretary (Sir) John T. Davies, a Welsh-speaking teacher. He had caught the eye of Lloyd George who as Chancellor of the Exchequer made him his private secretary (1912–1915). He used him in the same capacity when Minister of Munitions (1915–16) and as Secretary of State for War (1916). Davies remained with Lloyd George until 1922 when he was rewarded with a government directorship of the Suez Canal Company. This appointment, like Corry's peerage almost half a century earlier, was called the worst appointment since Caligula made his horse a consul. Frances Stevenson (Lady Lloyd George) had been employed by Lloyd George in 1911 to coach his daughter Megan during school holidays. In 1912 he asked her to be his private secretary at the Treasury. She accepted, became his mistress, later his wife, and remained with him until his death. The third member of the private office, from 1916 to 1918, was (Sir) William Sutherland, used mainly to manage the Press and distribute honours. 'Bronco Bill' was possibly the most sinister of the Prime Minister's secretaries, vanishing from public life after the fall of his master in 1922. His career began as a civil servant in the Board of Trade where he impressed Lloyd George, who as President in 1905–8 used him to prepare many Bills. He followed Lloyd George to the Treasury as a private secretary and, like Davies and Miss Stevenson, served him in his succeeding ministerial positions. In 1918 he was elected to Parliament, acted as Lloyd George's parliamentary private secretary, and later as a junior whip and as Chancellor of the Duchy of Lancaster. In 1918 he was replaced in the private office by a Welsh-speaking lawyer, Ernest Evans, who remained until 1920 when he was elected a Liberal MP. He later became a county court judge. Evans was replaced by Geoffrey Shakespeare from 1921 to 1922: another non-civil servant, a lawyer who was elected to Parliament in 1922 as a National Liberal and held various ministerial posts in the 1930s. In 1921 Lloyd George acquired as a private secretary A. J.

Sylvester, who had been the private secretary to Maurice Hankey (Lord Hankey) during 1914–21 in his numerous roles as Secretary to the Committee of Imperial Defence, the War Cabinet and the Cabinet. Sylvester is an example of a civil servant who falls so much under the spell of his master that he is unable to return to normal departmental duties. In 1923 he left the Civil Service to be Lloyd George's personal secretary and remained with him until 1945.

In addition to and quite distinct from the three traditional private secretaries, Lloyd George created a Prime Minister's secretariat, sometimes called the 'garden suburb' from its location in specially erected buildings in the garden of No. 10 Downing Street. It comprised five people of varied training and experience on whom Lloyd George could depend. The secretariat wrote short memoranda to the Prime Minister about Cabinet items and departmental proposals he was most likely to be interested in and were able to circumvent massive paperwork by snatching short talks with him to put comments. It was an embryo of a Prime Minister's department, and performed functions once carried out by the traditional private secretaries. Formed in 1916, the group was initially headed by the Oxford Professor of Public Administration, W. G. S. Adams, who was responsible for Irish and agricultural affairs, and Treasury and machinery of government matters; Philip Kerr (Lord Lothian) dealt with foreign and colonial policies, W. W. Astor, MP (Lord Astor), with health and, together with David Davies, MP (Lord Davies), and later Cecil Harmsworth, kept the Prime Minister informed of the views of peers and MPs. Astor was the owner of *The Observer* and David Davies was a Welsh industrialist, both millionaires. The other member of the group was (Sir) Joseph Davies, a Welsh businessman and commercial statistician, who specialised in mines, railways and shipping questions. They were supported by about eight clerks. During the war they provided economic, political and diplomatic advice for the Prime Minister. Afterwards they were mainly used in his conduct of peace negotiations and post-war diplomacy, especially Kerr who was a source of information and advice quite separate from the Foreign Office. From Kerr's departure in 1921 and his replacement by Edward Grigg (Lord Altrincham) the 'garden suburb' declined, until it was abolished on Lloyd George's fall in 1922.

Lloyd George also created in 1916 what seemed at the time to be another institution that expanded his powers: the Cabinet Secretariat. Its secretaries, notably Sir Maurice Hankey and Tom Jones, his deputy, were confidential advisers to the Prime Minister, and seemed in this function to be little different from either the traditional private secretaries or the inhabitants of the 'garden suburb'. Informal practices blurred the distinctions of formal organisations. But the creation of the Cabinet Secretariat ultimately weakened the power of the Prime Minister and enabled the Cabinet to reassert itself later as the supreme collective decision-making body of British government. In its functions the Cabinet Secretariat removed a number of activities from the private secretaries: calling the Cabinet, preparing its agenda, circulating cabinet decisions and checking up on their implementation. Perhaps most important of all, it methodically recorded the minutes and conclusions of cabinet meetings and distributed them amongst the ministers. Previously the only record kept was a personal letter written by the Prime Minister, copied by his principal private secretary, and delivered only to the King.

The creation of the Cabinet Secretariat and of the 'garden suburb' reduced the influence of the traditional private secretaries. Their work became largely personal, arranging or averting interviews, organising the Prime Minister's daily timetable, dealing with patronage, honours and appointments, and generally being available with advice or expediting some mission. Some of the tedious routine of earlier private secretaries was eliminated since on Lloyd George's accession there was an increase in the clerical staff of the secretariat, as well as greater use of typewriters and telephones.

1922–30: THE REACTION TO LLOYD GEORGE AND THE RISE OF THE CIVIL SERVICE

Lloyd George's premiership seemed to many very close to a personal dictatorship, and after his fall there was a reaction against his style. The 'garden suburb' was abolished and the Cabinet Secretariat was considerably reduced in size. The private secretariat, however, was maintained. Bonar Law made great use of unpaid, informal advisers, like J. C. C. Davidson (Lord Davidson), who had been his private secretary from 1915 to 1920, and served as his parliamentary private secretary when elected to the Commons in 1920 and again in 1922–1923. Richard Law (Lord Coleraine), Bonar Law's son, acted in many ways as a private secretary, as did (Sir) Geoffrey Fry, a barrister and a former civil servant, who had been taken out of the Treasury by Bonar Law in 1919 to be his unpaid private secretary and remained to serve Baldwin in the same capacity.

On taking office Law cleared out the Lloyd George private secretaries, although A. J. Sylvester seems to have stayed on in the background for a few months until he joined Lloyd George's personal staff. Law appointed as his principal private secretary (Sir) Ronald Waterhouse, a figure of immense significance in the development of the private office. He was the last of the old style personal and political appointees and the first of the new style civil servants. His career began in the army where he saw much active service. He rose to be a staff officer in the Intelligence Department of the War Office. In 1918 he was appointed private secretary to the Chief of the Air Staff, Sir Mark Sykes, who was married to Law's daughter. In 1920 and 1921 he was a colleague of J. C. C. Davidson as private secretary to Bonar Law, then Lord Privy Seal and Leader of the House of Commons, and later to Austen Chamberlain in the same offices. In 1921 he served as private secretary to the Duke of York before being selected by Bonar Law to be his principal private secretary at No. 10 Downing Street. He remained there for Law's successor, Stanley Baldwin, in 1923–4, and more significantly for Ramsay MacDonald in 1924. MacDonald had been urged by people in the Labour movement to appoint one of their supporters for such a confidential position, but he kept on Waterhouse, who stayed to help Baldwin again in 1924–8: the first principal private secretary to continue under Prime Ministers of different parties and, since the 1830s, to serve more than two Prime Ministers.* He might have stayed longer but for his involvement in an extra-marital entanglement which necessitated his retirement from public life at the age of fifty.

Bonar Law was also served by a traditional Treasury official, (Sir) Patrick Gower. He had been Law's private secretary as Chancellor of the Exchequer in 1917–19, and later for Austen Chamberlain as Chancellor and Lord Privy Seal in 1919–22. He went to No. 10 in 1922 and like Waterhouse remained for both Baldwin and MacDonald. However, he did not stay in the Civil Service afterwards, but was enticed by Davidson to become the Chief Publicity Officer of the Conservative Central Office, where he remained until 1939. Waterhouse was the personal and political appointee who became a civil servant and Gower was a civil servant who became a party official. Also in the private office was Miss Edith Watson. She had been Law's private secretary from 1916 when he had first met her at the Colonial Office. She served him in all his subsequent offices and remained at No. 10 for Baldwin, MacDonald, Chamberlain and

* The record is held by Edward Drummond who served Canning (1827), Goderich (1827–8), Wellington (1828–30), and Peel (1834 and 1841–3). He was murdered in mistake for Peel by a madman.

Churchill, retiring at the end of the Second World War. During her career she was the permanent mainstay of the Prime Minister's private office, handling Parliamentary Questions and correspondence with the public.

Baldwin inherited Law's network of private secretaries, Waterhouse, Gower, Miss Watson, and Fry, and brought in his private secretary from the Board of Trade, (Sir) Patrick Duff, a civil servant who had been private secretary to Presidents of the Board of Trade since 1919. He remained in the Prime Minister's private office to serve MacDonald, becoming the latter's principal private secretary (1930–3). He later became the Permanent Secretary at the Ministry of Works, High Commissioner in New Zealand, and Chairman of the National Parks Commission. Baldwin also relied heavily on Davidson, who was very much like Corry and Sandars, although he was an MP and a minister. MacDonald took over the private secretaries of Baldwin in 1924, except for the clearly political figures of Fry and Davidson. But they returned on Baldwin's resumption of office in 1924, and were joined by another unpaid aide, Charles Baillie-Hamilton, then in his twenties, the son of the Earl of Haddington. In 1928 Baldwin lost both Waterhouse and Gower. The latter was replaced by (Sir) Graham Vincent, another Treasury official who had been private secretary to Treasury ministers. He remained in the private office until 1937 after becoming in 1934 the principal private secretary, serving both Baldwin and MacDonald. Waterhouse was replaced as principal private secretary by a civil servant, Robert Vansittart (Lord Vansittart), Assistant Under Secretary at the Foreign Office, who fulfilled Baldwin's need for a close senior adviser who was an expert in foreign affairs. He too, like Vincent, Duff and Miss Watson, remained when MacDonald again became Prime Minister in 1929. When Vansittart in 1930 became Permanent Under Secretary of the Foreign Office, Duff moved up to replace him as principal private secretary, and the new secretary from the Foreign Office was (Sir) Nevile Butler, later British Ambassador to Brazil and the Netherlands.

The 1920s were years of transition for the private office of the Prime Minister, and Ramsay MacDonald was the Prime Minister who had the greatest influence on its development. None of the private secretaries who served Liberal Prime Ministers from 1868 to 1921 ever served a Conservative Prime Minister, and none of the private secretaries who served Conservative Prime Ministers from 1868 to 1905 ever served a Liberal Prime Minister. Despite pressure from colleagues, MacDonald decided not to replace the private secretaries of his Conservative predecessors nor to put into the private office personal and political appointees. The Civil Service took over the private office. It had established itself as able to serve loyally Prime Ministers of any party. MacDonald, however, had need of assistants personally committed to himself. He used his children, notably Ishbel and Malcolm; his personal private secretary and typist, Miss Rose Rosenberg; and a personal private secretary, Herbert Usher, who had been a journalist and unsuccessful Labour candidate. He stayed with MacDonald until 1935 when, like some private secretaries of the nineteenth century, he became a full-time civil servant in the Treasury, rising to the rank of under secretary and eventually Deputy Secretary of the Central Land Board in 1948–57. In addition there were not one but two parliamentary private secretaries, a departure from custom not to be repeated until Harold Wilson appointed two for his Government of the 1960s.

During MacDonald's premierships a real distinction seemed to arise between the Prime Minister's private office, now wholly of civil service secretaries, and his personal and political assistants. The line between politics and administration seemed to be becoming clearer, at least in the personnel around the Prime Minister and possibly in their functions too. But the career of Usher indicates that the line was not a barrier. The political appointee could become a civil servant.

1930–75: THE CIVIL SERVICE DOMINANT

Since the appointment of Vansittart the private office has contained only civil servants. The one exception was John Wyndham (Lord Egremont), who was a personal appointee of Harold Macmillan in 1957–63. Wyndham was fully integrated into the private office and differed from his colleagues only in that he was not paid from public funds.

From the 1930s to the 1970s not only was the Prime Minister's private office dominated by the Civil Service, but it regularly drew its leading members from two departments, the Treasury and the Foreign Office. Between 1928 and 1945, however, of eight principal private secretaries only one was from the Treasury itself; the rest came from a range of different departments: the Board of Trade, Labour, the War Office, Health, the Admiralty and the Dominions Office. But from 1945 to 1975, of twelve principal private secretaries seven came from the Treasury, and each of the remaining five was somewhat unique. (Sir) J. R. Colville was a joint principal private secretary for Churchill during 1951–5. He had been one of Churchill's private secretaries during the war and had later been private secretary to Princess Elizabeth before returning to the Foreign Office. (Sir) F. A. Bishop, Eden's and Macmillan's principal private secretary in 1956–9, had served in a variety of departments before joining the Cabinet Office in 1953–5, to which he returned on leaving the Prime Minister's service. He was Permanent Secretary of the ill-fated Ministry of Land and Natural Resources from 1964 to 1965 when he retired from the Civil Service. Michael Halls had been Harold Wilson's private secretary at the Board of Trade from 1948 to 1950, where he must have so impressed Mr Wilson that in 1966 he was selected to be the Prime Minister's private secretary. He is the only principal private secretary of a Prime Minister to have died in office. A. R. Isserlis succeeded Halls in 1970 for a few months and was then replaced following the Conservative electoral victory of 1970. Isserlis had mostly served in the Housing Ministry and he had had a short spell in the Cabinet Office. Kenneth Stowe, appointed in 1975, came from Health and Social Security and the Cabinet Office.

There has never been a time since 1922 when there was no Treasury man in the private office. The other department most often represented has been the Foreign Office. In only four years since 1928 does it appear that there was no Foreign Office private secretary to the Prime Minister. And during 1956 and 1957 there were two Foreign Office officials as private secretaries, for both Sir Anthony Eden and Mr Macmillan. The Foreign Office private secretary is different from the others, since his responsibility covers only one department. He is regarded as its spokesman with the Prime Minister and *vice versa.* As closest adviser on foreign affairs he at times acts as the Prime Minister's agent on foreign missions. His loyalties may be divided between the department and the Prime Minister, and occasionally the Foreign Office has been uneasy about the advice being tendered to the Prime Minister by his private secretary. There is no pattern in the departmental origins of the other private secretaries: the range is wide.

It does appear that the Prime Minister can intervene decisively in the selection of his private secretaries. Some seem to have been appointed because they had served the Prime Minister well in a previous ministerial position. (Sir) Arthur N. Rucker, Chamberlain's principal private secretary in 1939–40, had been his private secretary when he was Minister of Health in the 1920s, and Churchill's first principal private secretary, (Sir) Eric Seal 1940–1, who replaced Rucker, had been Churchill's principal private secretary at the Admiralty. Joseph Burke, a private secretary of Attlee in 1945–6, had served him in that capacity as Lord President of the Council. Just as Prime Ministers can influence the choice of their private secretaries, they can also influence their removal, which possibly accounts for the brief term of A. R. Isserlis. Normally, however, an incoming Prime Minister accepts the principal private secretary, and other private secretaries, that he inherits from his predecessor of whatever party. If they are not really suited to the particular needs of a Prime Minister, they may leave after a short time. After serving the Prime Minister most have returned to their departments, although a few have left the public service. After the highly charged political atmosphere of No. 10 Downing Street a few found it difficult to readjust to life within the departments, especially after contacts had been made at No. 10 with influential people who made tempting offers.

Within the private office there has always been a hierarchy of secretaries, but their ranks were usually obscured until 1929 by simple alphabetical listings in the *Imperial Calendar*. After 1929 it listed the principal (Vansittart was the first to be designated principal in the *Imperial Calendar*), followed by the second secretary, until the 1960s when the *Calendar* began to list the main areas of responsibilities of the private secretaries: overseas affairs, parliamentary and home affairs, and home affairs and general. Since the late 1960s the categories have been: overseas affairs, home affairs (two secretaries), and parliamentary affairs. Within the office, therefore, there has been an increase in the formal specialisation of functions. Before the 1930s the tasks of the secretaries were very varied and were decided by the Prime Minister on no routine basis. The only exception was the handling of appointments, especially ecclesiastical, which by the 1900s had evolved as the responsibility of the Treasury clerk in the private office. In 1947 his duties were allocated to a special secretary for appointments. The first was (Sir) Anthony Bevir who had been in the private office from 1940 and remained until 1956. His successors also remained as private secretaries for a longer period than their colleagues: (Sir) David Stephens (1955–61) and (Sir) John Hewitt (1961–74). Each new secretary for appointments learns about his new responsibilities by taking office a few months before his predecessor leaves. Specialisation of functions within the private office could really only begin after the Civil Service took over the private office at the end of the 1920s and introduced bureaucratic methods.

1930–75: THE SEARCH FOR POLITICAL ASSISTANTS

The appropriation by the Civil Service of the Prime Minister's private office has meant that each Prime Minister has had to seek more strictly political advice from people not in the secretariat. Once, political advice had come from within the private office, but it became difficult for civil servants to be confidential advisers on highly political and personal matters. With Baldwin and MacDonald in the 1920s and 1930s there were political secretaries at No. 10, namely Fry and Usher. Chamberlain rejected this incursion of the political element into No. 10, and relied heavily on a civil servant, (Sir) Horace Wilson, the Government's chief industrial adviser, who was 'attached for service' with the Prime Minister as his personal assistant. Churchill was supported by two personal assistants, (Sir) Desmond Morton, his intelligence adviser, and Professor F. A. Lindemann (Lord Cherwell). The latter re-created a Prime Minister's secretariat along the lines of Lloyd George's 'garden suburb'. In 1939 Lindemann, an Oxford physicist, was asked by Churchill, then First Lord of the Admiralty, to form a branch to collect and collate statistics and to advise him generally. When Churchill became Prime Minister in May 1940 the unit was transformed into the Prime Minister's statistical section with a staff mainly of economists. It produced a flow of memoranda advising and informing the Prime Minister about the business of the Cabinet and its committees, and about departmental papers and ministerial minutes. In 1942 Cherwell was appointed Paymaster-General and his section became the office of the Paymaster-General.

After the war there was no revival of a Prime Minister's unit. Mr Attlee depended on his private office, but he did have in his first years two politically sympathetic advisers at No. 10 Downing Street: his adviser on public relations, the journalist Francis Williams (Lord Francis-Williams) 1945–9, and his personal assistant dealing with economic matters, Douglas Jay 1945–6, who commented on proposals coming before the Cabinet and its committees, thus enabling Mr Attlee to raise questions and delay for further consideration recommendations that might otherwise have been quickly adopted. With Mr Jay's departure on becoming an MP in 1946 there was no political capacity in No. 10 Downing Street to support the Prime Minister on a full-time basis, until Mr Macmillan introduced John Wyndham into the private office. The major increase in the political element at No. 10, however, came with Mr Wilson, first in his administration of 1964–70 and more significantly after March 1974.

In the first period he brought in as his personal and political secretary Mrs Marcia Williams (Lady Falkender), who ran his political office. An attempt by the principal private secretary, Derek Mitchell, to maintain a clear separation of functions between the private office and the political office produced tension between the two, which was not eased until Mr Mitchell had been replaced. Michael Halls, his successor, allowed a considerable overlap of responsibilities. He recognised that at the top politics and administration could not be kept distinct.

Another function once performed by the private secretaries was maintaining contact with the Press. This task has become more specialised and has been allocated to a distinct team at No. 10. The first press officer, 'to meet the need for a full-time public relations officer in the Prime Minister's Office', was appointed in 1931.[8] The same man continued until 1944. Since then a number of people have held this kind of post, and their supporting staff has grown, totalling seven in 1974. Their backgrounds have been varied: some have been journalists, sympathetic to the Prime Minister and his party, others have been civil servants specialising in information work. Some found it hard to keep a balance between the political and administrative aspects of their functions. Trevor Lloyd-Hughes, a former journalist, was a personal appointee of Harold Wilson in 1964, but he developed such a non-partisan attitude to his work that it was necessary to appoint more overtly political staff to put over a stronger party-oriented line.

When Mr Heath took office in 1970 he reduced the political element at No. 10. Instead of a political figure as his press officer, like Mr Wilson's Joseph Haines, he appointed as his press secretary a Foreign Office official, Donald Maitland, who was in 1973 succeeded by another Foreign Office official, Robin Haydon. But he brought in as political secretary a former Foreign Office man, Douglas Hurd, who had been his secretary in opposition and was in 1974 elected to parliament as a Conservative. Hurd, unlike Wyndham for Mr Macmillan, was not integrated into the private office but, like Mrs Williams for Mr Wilson, was kept apart from it.

When Mr Wilson returned as Prime Minister in February 1974 he increased the political element at No. 10 and organised it into more specialised sections. Mrs Williams and Mr Haines returned to their old responsibilities; but he appointed a former Labour MP, Albert Murray, to run the political office, Mrs Williams acting more as a personal secretary and confidential adviser. More significantly, Mr Wilson was the first peace-time Prime Minister to set up a secretariat like the 'garden suburb' or Cherwell's statistical unit. He appointed Bernard Donoughue, an LSE academic political scientist, to be his senior policy adviser and head of the Policy Unit, a team of about seven research staff which briefs the Prime Minister on a range of domestic policies in the medium and short terms. They try to ensure that the political values and policy priorities of the Labour Party are injected into proposals for government action. Its function, therefore, is like that of previous personal assistants, political appointees or special teams, to provide for the Prime Minister a source of advice and assistance different from that of the departments or his own private office of civil servants or the Cabinet Secretariat and the other units of the Cabinet Office.[9]

As chairman of the Cabinet the Prime Minister is particularly close to the Cabinet Office; he is in a sense the director of its work, but it is not his department since it serves the whole Cabinet. In the last twenty years the Cabinet Office has increased in size and in its range of responsibilities at the expense of the Prime Minister's private office. In contrast to the relative stability in the size of the private office, the staff of the Cabinet Office has soared: in 1951 it had 404, in 1963 379, and in 1973 599. The Secretariat continues to service the Cabinet in its traditional manner and acts as the general administrative co-ordinator of government. The Cabinet Office contains such specialised units as the Central Statistical Office, the Government's chief scientific adviser and his staff, the Central Policy Review Staff, and teams of officials particularly engaged in co-ordinating overseas and defence policy, relations with the European Economic Community, and proposals for devolution within the United Kingdom. The Prime Minister has always found in the staff of the Cabinet Office confidential aides, and he has at times located in the Cabinet Office personal appointees as his advisers. But they are not as close to him as his own assistants at No. 10 Downing Street.[10]

CONCLUSIONS

Since at the top politics and administration are inextricably entangled, the political appointees and the civil servants come into close contact and overlap in their functions. Relationships between the two, therefore, depend on tact and respect on both sides. Relationships between the various aides of the Prime Minister are fluid, despite the growing specialisation in their roles. They may have distinct titles, and apparently defined responsibilities on which they concentrate their attention, but they can be used by the Prime Minister for a variety of purposes depending on his need of the moment. The present system of small groups of civil service, political and personal advisers is flexible and easily adaptable to the changing requirements of a Prime Minister. If he had his own department, formal and structured, his personal power and influence might well be reduced. A department might, especially if large, develop a view and momentum of its own and even begin itself to rule. To control it the Prime Minister might have to acquire another set of private secretaries and political aides.

The political executive of Britain is not one man but a collective entity, the Cabinet. The plural nature of the executive means that its chairman, the Prime Minister, has no real need of a department of his own to control the work of government as a whole. The reason is that British government is more cohesive, less fragmented, than a system with a single executive. The Cabinet is a force for unity. It is supported by the Cabinet Office, which is the guardian and sustainer of the collective nature of British government. The creation of the Cabinet Office, its expansion and its increasing specialisation in recent years, have helped to pull the various departments of government together, and have avoided the need for any significant increase in the staff of the Prime Minister. Cohesion in British government is further encouraged because it is party government. The members of the Cabinet are colleagues of long standing within the party; party loyalties, as well as frequent and close personal contact, reinforce the bonds that link the members together in one government. Then on the administrative side, the Civil Service is far from fragmented. It is led by generalist administrators whose expertise lies in a broad view, in conducting interdepartmental negotiations and in forging consensus. Their careers are mobile; they have served in many departments, which gives them a wide perspective.

In Britain the Prime Minister has at his disposal a complex network of aides and assistants, including trusty members of the Cabinet and other ministers; leading civil servants, especially the official heads of the Treasury, the Civil Service Department and the Cabinet Office; together with officials from lower down in the Cabinet Office and members of such 'think-tanks' as the Central Policy Review Staff and the Policy Unit. He may also make use of military and intelligence advisers, influential Members of Parliament, prominent figures in his party organisation, political and personal secretaries, press and public relations aides, businessmen, academics, such personal helpers as his doctor or solicitor, and his family. Depending on his own style and perception of his requirements, he chooses whose advice and assistance he needs at each moment.[11] The combinations vary with each event, but at their heart is the private office of six secretaries. The essence of their activities has not really changed from that of the three secretaries a century ago.

NOTES

1 A list of private secretaries to the First Lords of the Treasury, 1743–1870, is given in J. C. Sainty, *Office-Holders in Modern Britain: I, Treasury Officials 1660–1870* (1972), pp. 74–6.
2 ibid., p. 74.
3 Information about the size of the private office is from *The British Imperial Calendar and Civil Service List*, now *The Civil Service Year Book*; the *Civil Estimates*; *H.M. Ministers and Senior Staff in Public Departments*; *Whitaker's Almanack*; and for 1868 to 1921 the Treasury Minutes T197 at the Public Record Office.
4 *H. C. Deb.*, vol. 692, cols. 33–6 (Written Answer), 23 March 1964; and information from the private office.
5 Information about the individual private secretaries is taken from *Who Was Who*; *Who's Who*; the *Dictionary of National Biography*; and *Burke's Peerage*. Their own memoirs, and books and articles about them, have also been consulted, together with studies of Prime Ministers and their colleagues.
6 A detailed analysis of the functions of the private secretaries will be the subject of a future article.
7 *H. C. Deb.*, vol. 293, col. 1565, 13 November 1884.
8 *H. C. Deb.*, vol. 416, cols. 548–9 (Written Answer), 21 November 1945.
9 The Policy Unit is examined in G. W. Jones, 'Harold Wilson's Policy-makers', *The Spectator*, 6 July 1974, pp. 12–13.
10 For a more detailed study of the Cabinet Office, see G. W. Jones, 'The Cabinet since 1950', in W. Thornhill (ed.), *British Government in 1975* (1975).
11 For an analysis of this system see G. W. Jones, 'The Prime Ministers' Advisers', *Political Studies*, September 1973, pp. 363–75.

2

Reflections on Democracy and Bureaucracy

CARL J. FRIEDRICH

When I wrote in 1941 on a 'new belief in the Common Man', I allowed myself to be misguided by my inborn optimism; for no such new belief has materialised. Quite on the contrary, the old belief has further disintegrated to the point where the future of democracy seems in serious doubt. Due to the exigencies of war and revolution, the word has been misused to such an extent that the cautious student of political matters is tempted to put the word into quotation marks. Soon after the establishment of the United Nations, an effort was made under the aegis of UNESCO to arrive at common ground, and more especially to iron out the contradictions between the Western tradition and the Soviet ideology.[1] The equivocal meaning of the term has been further complicated by the coming into being of many 'new states' based upon former colonies, now liberated through various processes, evolutionary and revolutionary, often quite violent. Following the precedent of Stalin's methods, some of the ensuing regimes became quite ruthless, yet continued to call themselves democratic. The confusion became more confounded by a quadripartite occupation regime over defeated Germany which has in the meantime given rise to two successor states, the German Federal Republic and the German Democratic Republic. Now both members of the United Nations, and both allegedly democratic, they incorporate the worldwide dialectic of democracy.[2] Both the popular democracy of the latter regime and the constitutional democracy of the first continually reject each other as undemocratic, and neither embodies what was originally understood by the term; for neither resembles what the early protagonists of the democratic belief, Rousseau, the Swiss, and the colonial Americans, strove to achieve when they sought to organise themselves as democracies. These matters are familiar enough, and the writings and controversies are well known.[3] Those who praised democracy, like Thomas Paine, and those who warned against it, like Alexander Hamilton, all thought of a regime roughly resembling the Athenian democracy which Plato and Aristotle had condemned. It was a small regime in which most of the citizenry could and did participate as voters, as jury men, and more particularly as soldiers—in short, a regime radically different from regimes such as that of a modern state of any size. Hence the arguments at the start of modern democracy were misleading because not really germane to it. The large size of the citizenry prevented participation of most citizens, even sporadically. In the course of the nineteenth century these former characteristics became more and more illusory. Democratisation, as it was called, acquired specific meanings; [4] for many, it meant the expansion of the electorate in several steps fought over by conservatives who argued against 'democracy' and progressives who promoted these measures. In recent years, democratisation came to mean an expansion of the participation of groups of people involved in a particular field of action: workers, students more especially, but also administrative personnel of every kind. Here is the centre of the conflict between democracy and bureaucracy.

It is undeniable and manifest in the extended pamphlet literature that these 'democratisation' efforts have in common a strong antibureaucratic bias. The 'radical elements' among trade unionists, traditionally supposed to be socialist in European countries of advanced industrial structure, proclaim a determination to recapture the true, i.e. ideologically fanatic, outlook of early socialism, and more especially of Marxism. The vogue of writers like Herbert Marcuse is largely due to such propensities. This is not to say that Marcuse is a true Marxist; the opposite is nearer the truth.[5] But Marcuse takes Marx seriously and the students who swear by him (or did so in the 'sixties) believed him to be deeply committed to what seemed to be Marx's call to revolution. Marx, too, was ardently antibureaucratic – a belief which animated the early revolutionaries in Soviet Russia. Lenin's and Trotski's accusation of Stalin as a bureaucrat was and is a slogan in the various democratic movements, and the same holds true about the outcry against trade union bureaucrats, and against academic administrators.

What, then, is bureaucracy? As essential to the modern state it creates special problems in and for a democracy because democracy requires the rulers to be responsible. As a young man I became fascinated by this problem of responsibility, for from Weber I had learned that the bureaucratic element was essential to the modern state,[6] and from prevailing views in America in the early 'twenties I took it that democracy and bureaucracy were incompatible, that is to say that no responsible conduct could be enforced by the incompetent people or its representatives. I argued against this widespread view in a little book entitled *Responsible Bureaucracy.*[7] It dealt with the Swiss Civil Service and undertook to show by empirical evidence that democracy was very well capable of extracting a measure of accountability from a bureaucracy. For Switzerland was a very admirable democracy, not only in name but in actual operation, and its bureaucracy was perhaps the best anywhere, as was demonstrated by the efficiency of the Swiss railways, operating under most adverse conditions (a very mountainous country with a very uneven distribution of population and economic activity). I mention the railways because a study of the governmental regulation of American railroads – my doctoral dissertation – had convinced me that the clue to their perplexing problems, and more especially government operations such as were attempted in the First World War, was the nonexistence of a large-scale bureaucracy in America at that time.

It is a well-known fact that all over the world the administrative service has grown very rapidly on all levels, and much faster than the population. There is a striking statistical table which Herman Finer [8] compiled which shows this quite dramatically. The asymptotic curve of the number of bureaucrats (civil servants, according to Finer) suggests that infinity is the limit at which the entire population have become bureaucrats. This phenomenon has given rise to much adverse comment. The best known, perhaps, is contained in Professor Parkinson's book *Parkinson's Law* in which he exaggerates to the point of absurdity the growth trend of bureaucracy.[9] This trend was already clearly discernible in the 'twenties and conjured up the vision of a society in which virtually everyone was engaged in some kind of governmental activity. This led me to say at the conclusion of *Responsible Bureaucracy*:

'When looking at the evolution of modern bureaucracies from this angle, one dimly perceives a federative commonwealth of mutual servants. Each great service would have its own internal controls, but these would be held together by an individual or a group or both, controlled in turn by the entire people. In short, we find that bureaucracy and democracy are not antithetical, but that they belong to each other as structural aspects of a fully organised living community.' [10]

This problem of democratisation is, as we said, very much involved in contemporary discussions of bureaucracy. In these and similar cases, democracy and democratisation are seen as a substitute for bureaucracy. The argument depends upon certain misunderstandings about legitimacy and authority. These in turn are the result of a mistaken view of power as necessarily to be understood in terms of command and obedience – a widespread view of power since Hobbes.[11]

The search for both legitimacy and authority has given ideological considerations a distinct appeal, especially in the developing countries. Well aware of this appeal, the Communist parties, during their Moscow conference in 1960, proclaimed a new formula for Communist strategy in ex-colonial underdeveloped countries: national democracy. This formula links the fight for national independence with the familiar 'lines' of Communist ideology, such as 'struggle against imperialism', and the themes of traditional democratic ideology, such as 'freedom of speech, of the press . . .' etc.[12] Unfortunately, all these formulas, once fought over in European history and filled with philosophical and political content, as well as designed for legal and strictly instrumental use, possess a certain anaemic quality within the thought context of the former European colonies.

When I say 'authority' here and elsewhere, my intention is to designate an aspect of power situations which has been obscured by authority being confused not only with legitimacy but with power. This confusion has had more serious consequences for the politics of developing countries, both in theory and in practice, than it had for highly developed ones. What has happened politically in these countries calls for a clear theoretical understanding of authority and power. To state the primary proposition at the outset: political authority is not some kind of political power, such as formal power or rightful power, as has been asserted repeatedly,[13] but is the capacity for communal reasoned elaboration on the communications issued by power handlers, whether they be commands, opinions, suggestions, explanations, or what have you. This capacity is a crucial aspect of power, leadership and rule; the ability to clothe power with authority is vital in rendering power consensual.

Many would concede the significance of authority of this kind, i.e. the capacity of reasoned elaboration, in technical fields such as medicine or engineering, where it is related to professional qualifications, but would question it in politics. The authority of him who wields power, it is claimed, must be seen in a context of 'blind' obedience to commands issued by him who has such authority, and the blinder the obedience the greater the authority. Yet, can it be seriously doubted that there are power situations which differ from others by the fact that the wielder of power has the capacity to elaborate what he prefers by reasoning which would make sense to those who follow him? What kind of reasoning is this kind of political argument? Is it not a kind of reasoning which builds upon the values and beliefs, as well as the interests, of the group within which the power is exercised? The much admired ability to coin slogans so characteristic of the great political leader, what else is it but the ability to sum up in a short sentence or phrase what is the core of his political programme? 'Workers of the world, unite: you have nothing to lose but your chains', or 'to make the world safe for democracy', or 'the four freedoms' – are not each of these and many other such phrases summaries of reasonings which might be elaborated? The power handler shares with his followers all or part of such values and beliefs, and therefore could, and at times will, explain to his following the reasons he acted in a certain way and more especially why he preferred them to act likewise.

Many of the more striking contrasts in the efficiency of political leadership become comprehensible by the dynamics of such authority. They also become researchable and assessable, if approached in this fashion. By contrast, such an intuitionist and romantic category as the most over-used 'charismatic leadership' leaves the relationship between leader and followers in a haze of incomprehensible psychologising.[14] Let me illustrate the value of an understanding of authority by reference to the contrast between Lenin and Stalin,[15] between Ho Chi Minh and Diem and/or Ky,[16] and between Muñoz Marin and Sanchez Villeja;[17] if a case from a developed country might be added for good measure, Adenauer and Erhard[18] might do. In all these cases, the first named of these leaders was far superior to the second in authority, though not in official power. He possessed to a very high degree the capacity of reasoned elaboration of his communications in terms of the values and beliefs of the community which he was addressing. This may be a matter of convincing interpretation of an ideology, as in the case of Lenin and Ho Chi Minh, or it may rather be the ability to speak in terms of the traditional beliefs of a national following: but in either case the reasoning was based upon communally cherished values and beliefs. It goes without saying, of course, that the effective community in the case of a movement leader is that of the movement, and not that of the nation within which it moves. Power – raw power, if you please – can be implemented and enlarged by the capacity for reasoned elaboration, communally reasoned elaboration: it *is not* power, but *generates* power. It is characteristic for such authority that it exists in particular power holders and handlers; he does not usually elaborate, let alone 'demonstrate'. Precisely speaking, authority is a quality of the communications as much as of the communicator. The process of ageing leadership in consensual power situations is typically one of disintegrating authority. The actions of the 'old one' no longer make any sense in terms of the altered beliefs; his capacity for reasoned elaboration is declining. In order to cope with the decline in his consensual power, such a leader tends to become increasingly coercive (Stalin).

Authority, then, is not a dialectic opposite of democracy, but it is a supplementary aspect of it. Since opinions, values and beliefs, as well as interests and needs, are continually changing in response to changes in the environment and to innovation in the political sphere proper (constitutional transformation, revolution, etc.), it is quite possible, and in fact recurrent, that political authority needs reconfirmation. Such reconfirmation may, in fact, be provided by elections which are preceded by a great deal of reasoned elaboration. But if, as in the case of General de Gaulle, a majority refuses to reconfirm, the authority is bound to be severely damaged, even though official power is retained. The activities of the French President can and indeed should be seen in this perspective as an effort to rebuild his authority; but his readiness to compromise on Europe, and his personal determination to reassert France's military autonomy within the Western alliance, were part of this effort. But while such electoral legitimisation is well established as a means of renewing authority (as well as official power), it is of doubtful value in many of the developing countries. Here an operational or functional legitimisation in terms of performance is much more likely to produce results, as may be the capacity to spell out the new developments in terms of a traditional belief system.

In Puerto Rico (US), Governor Muñoz Marin's behaviour provides a remarkable illustration of how a functional legitimacy in terms of performance and a traditional one in terms of cultural values and beliefs (Hispanidad) may be combined with superb inspirational leadership and effective use of official power to produce authority so overwhelming as to create the danger of universal acceptance and consequent political immaturity on the part of the electorate. Hence the determination of this remarkable man to step down and let others take over. Unfortunately considerable confusion has resulted and nearly anarchic conditions are threatening. The case of Puerto Rico is significant in indicating the limits of democracy, especially in situations in which no stable and responsible bureaucracy exists.[18]

There arises the problem of leadership and power. These have in recent years been increasingly troublesome. It is obvious that we cannot here get into this analysis. The instability of political leadership in such countries, noticeably Latin America, has been remarked upon repeatedly. Explanations in terms of geography and national character have been given but are not very satisfactory. Much of the political dynamics have remained obscure. Weak legitimacy claims and feeble authority are involved. What is power anyway? Many writers and theorists, from Hobbes to the present, have thought of it in terms of a possession, of something 'to have and to hold', and the term 'power holder' is common parlance. But while power often is such a possession, it is not always that; it is indeed not primarily that at all, but rather a relation. And if power is looked at in the dimension of time, it becomes clear that its relational aspect is the more manifest the longer the time span involved. For it is in the rise and decline of political power that the fact becomes evident that power is always related to other men. Indeed power is that relation among men which becomes observable in the behaviour of the following, to put it simply. Following means typically that a number of persons do what one of them wants. One might therefore say that when the behaviour of a group conforms to the wishes of one or several among them—and this surely is a recurrent phenomenon – the relation between them may be called the power relationship.[19]

In the emergent phase, this power exists only in the wielding of it, and he who wields it should therefore properly be called a power wielder or handler. Due to the institutionalisation of such relationships, transforming thereby power into rule, the power attached to a certain institution or office becomes a possession 'to have and to hold'. Therefore it is appropriate to say that power is to some extent a possession and to some extent a relation, or alternatively that power has dimensions or aspects, the possessive and the relational ones. It is the ratio of these two which is of primary importance to political science: where that ratio is greater than one, we are dealing with an institutionalised office; where it is smaller than one, we are confronted with, for example, the initiator of a movement. It is obvious that in developing countries, the relational aspect is apt to be pronounced, and hence power is frequently, if not predominantly, of the relational type. It is probably one of the major sources of error in political analysis that the highly institutionalised nature of power relationships in developed countries has misled observers into looking for that kind of power (a special point in such misjudgements is the notion of a power structure; structured power is power on the way to becoming institutionalised).

Since power, pragmatically considered, manifests itself in the conformity of the behaviour of the following, the question of 'signs' indicating the preference of the power handler is crucial. It has been a common error to restrict the analysis to those situations in which a man finds obedience for his *commands*. Related to this error is that which stresses the importance of sanctions. But much power is wielded without sanctions, and command and obedience is only one possible configuration of the power relationship. In situations of dynamic and highly fluid leadership especially, the power handler does not command, but he suggests or persuades; he may also mould the behaviour of the following through their anticipating his reactions (influence). Furthermore, there are the matched and balanced power situations in which negotiation and compromise are the manifest signs of the power involved. Here authority as described above frequently plays a vital role.

Clearly bureaucracy is primarily concerned with the possession of power. Hence in situations which are formed by the rebellion of subordinate elements, usually these elements while protesting against bureaucracy patently wish to acquire power and make it stable. In other words they seek to become themselves (part of) a bureaucracy.

Further consideration of the power relationship reveals that it is typically based upon values, interests and beliefs which either can only be secured by joint action of a group or which one person or group have, while others desire them. Thus protection against violence, both internal and external, is desired by most men, but only particular men or groups have been able to provide it. Traditional contractual theories have rationalised, justified and explained government by this value placed upon and this interest in protection. To some extent it is a matter of weapons technology whether such protection can also be secured through co-operation as in citizens' armies and the like. We see here that the power situation in which the relational aspect predominates is consensual and co-operative, but it must not be imagined that they can usually exist without an element of coercion entering in. Both consent and constraint are aspects of all power situations in varying degrees.[20] One of the primary problems in many of the emergent countries, as indeed after revolutions, is that the power of the leader has been predominantly consensual in the independence movement, but needs to be transformed into coercive power for a stable government. This is, of course, to some extent the problem of replacing power by rule.

Democratisation and bureaucracy go hand in hand. What appears to one group as democratisation of an existing power structure will appear to another as bureaucratisation of a new structure. There is nothing startling or surprising in this. It is the old problem abstractly stated by philosophers as that of being and becoming. The French writer Francis de Malherbe, in looking at the French revolution, said to coming generations: 'Que direz-vous, races futures, si quelquefois un vrai discours vous raconte les aventures de nos abominables jours? Lirez-vous, sans rougir de honte . . .'

Revolutionary situations are apt to cause such regrettable anarchies with their accompanying evils. Suffice it here to point out that existing political orders of every type and description contain both bureaucracy and democracy; hence the spread of the term, every emerging order needs to be both bureaucratised and democratised; that it needs both to be efficient and responsible – but never *is*, since each stands in inverse relation to the other.

W. Hennis has in a searching re-evaluation of the term democratisation attempted to state reasons for the popularity of the term. He has ventured in the course of his analysis to relate the appeal of democratisation to the equivocal attitude about youth, linking it to the Adam legend of the Old Testament. He argues that people wished they could be like Adam, unburdened by a long educational process and ready to change the world. It is a subtle argument and highly speculative.[21]

The widespread student rebellions in America, France and Germany usually were among other objectives directed against university bureaucracy, when they proclaimed 'democratisation'. The demands for student participation were understood as anti-bureaucratic. The German slogan about *Ordinarien-Universität* also carried the implication that aged and experienced 'full' professors – the American term – were bureaucratic, but not responsible in the democratic tradition. Their sense of responsibility was in terms of their function – teaching – and not towards the people or its representatives, let alone the students. A tenured professor (usually *Ordinarius*) who in the tradition of academic freedom was a lord, and hence a law unto himself, had in this view become a bureaucrat who used and abused his power much in the way of civil servants whose decisions could not be challenged by students, whether as individuals or as a group. His authority was final as to the requirements of courses and exams: he resembled an absolute ruler. To abolish such absolute rulership was and is seen as the task of democratisation. Hence groups cherishing a deviant political outlook, notably socialists and communists, not only sympathised with but supported the rebellious students. It is natural that such a position was bound to lead to the 'politicisation' of the universities. Hence the counter-attack was made in terms of opposing such politicisation.[22]

The rebellious attitude of students towards all authority has been puzzling to many who cherished a romantic feeling towards schools and universities. In each of the major Western nations such troubles have appeared, often misunderstood in terms of material and local causes which provided the causes for some of the rhetoric. Unloosened in the US by the deep national revolt against the involvement of America in Asia, officially defended and justified by the 'cold war' clash with the Soviet Russian Communists and communism in general, it especially provoked student anger by its direct threat to young men's life and limb.[23] Slogans like imperialism, colonialism, and even totalitarianism precipitated widespread internal conflict. Bureaucracy became the scapegoat of this widespread indignation. Unfortunately, the stuffy attitude of the officialdom involved in American foreign relations provided recurrent tinder for the flames. Feeling themselves guiltless defenders of the national interest, men like Rusk proved quite incapable of stemming the tide. Following the preceding era of McCarthyism which had aroused much suspicion against the bureaucracy involved in foreign policy, public reactions became more and more bitter: both the State Department and the defence ministries became the whipping boys of a more and more irresponsible press and other media.[24] Terms like 'the people's right to know' made their appearance, and the officials were increasingly suspected of secreting vital information and thereby rendering irresponsible a public service which had hitherto been proud of their 'democratic' obligations. (These impressionic statements could readily be supported by massive quantitative material, drawn from newspapers, congressional debates, etc.) Responsibility and the lack of it became familiar terms of mutual abuse in the argument between the public and the bureaucracy. In this rhetoric, the meaning of responsibility, democracy and efficiency became more and more obscure, and the question as to who ought to be responsible to whom became itself part of the universal discord and still is. As a result, the government service in its entirety became a victim of this disgust with the bureaucracy. Political science struggled in vain against this torrent of public misunderstanding.

Considered in broader perspective, American democracy has become more and more bureaucratised. Bureaucracy as a term has become more and more widely employed to designate the human beings – the personnel – engaged in administration. Coined in France in the nineteenth century [25] as a term of abuse, bureaucracy and bureaucratisation are now usually intended as pejorative terms protesting against the multiplication of such administrative personnel. Naturally anarchists have popularised this and so have orthodox Marxists. It is therefore not surprising that students have followed this usage. The modern state is a bureaucratic state, but the modern bureaucracy is or aims to be a meritocracy. Merit has acquired more and more of a technical sense. A mastery of fields of precise technical knowledge constitutes the merit which is demanded for entry as well as advancement. Robson has given a good deal of thought to these matters and his 'comparative studies on the Civil Service in Britain and France' are informed by this trend. He himself followed the approach first proposed by Max Weber.[26] In introducing the subject, Robson stated quite emphatically that bureaucracy is clearly indispensable to modern government. He rightly observed that 'the tone and temper of much of the literature of protest are not likely to add to our understanding of the problems associated with bureaucracy or to our solving them'. This is very true, but some of the protest points to very real difficulties and this is especially true of the student protest. There was much in traditional universities that needed change and it was not necessarily caused by bureaucracy. Many of these protests failed to state sound and workable alternatives and the anarchic formulations into which these protests were cast savoured of anarchism. Established bureaucracies in various countries and academic bureaucracy in particular have proved quite helpless in face of such anarchy.[27] The difficulty is in part due to a kinship between anarchy and democracy. In a sense anarchy is democracy without authority. What was said above on authority is relevant here. Hennis concluded his searching analysis with the observation that 'with the conception of democratisation hopes are awakened which are unrealisable'. In a sense these developments indicate the limit of democracy. In an interesting paper, based on and stimulated by observations in India, the Rudolphs have suggested reinterpreting Weber's concept, as have others. As a maker of reinterpretation, they are right, but a conceptual change does not suffice.

The very reality of democracy is at issue. A failure of modern administration implicit in the failure of rational bureaucracy suggests a failure of democracy itself. Recently, voices proclaiming such a future have multiplied. Many factors are involved. The long-drawn-out struggle over workers' participation in industrial management is symptomatic for many fields, including universities. Widespread bureaucratisation has interlocked these fields, and the failure of bureaucracy in one makes the failure of bureaucracy in another virtually a foregone conclusion.[28]

Indeed the modern bureaucratic state may have reached the limits of its potential growth. Formerly the assumption was often made that rationalisation could go forward indefinitely. To a point the old saying about the incapacity of trees to grow into the sky applies here also. In the case of rationalisation the chain of reactions is becoming fairly evident.

The student of history is, in the light of these developments, beginning to wonder whether we are back at a stage of political evolution closely resembling the time of the emergence of the modern state.[29] The anarchic conditions consequent upon the Reformation in sixteenth-century Europe provided the alibi for the replacement of medieval constitutionalism by centralised monarchical autocracy. The system which then emerged in France and Spain, as well as several regions of Germany and Italy, was to last two hundred years. Only in England was medieval constitutionalism in a steady evolution, interrupted only by the Great Revolution, transformed into modern constitutionalism. Most of us are loath to admit that only violence will cope effectively with such anarchism. Our reluctance is very natural, for the deployment of violence for the suppression of subversive activities constitutes a threat to the constitutional order we cherish. Reason of state may demand it if the state is seen as an abstract power system; but the reason of constitutional democracy is bound to be opposed. Perhaps the only promising road for a modern bureaucracy to cope with this challenge is that adopted by the British Parliament in the 'thirties when confronted with the challenge of the disorders of the fascists in England. In its Public Order Act, it undertook to identify specific acts of obnoxious behaviour and placed these acts under interdict. Opinions were exempted from such outlawry, but there always remains the problem of advocacy and the line between the expression of a radical opinion and the advocacy of a criminal act is very hard to draw. This the long and tortuous history of American legislation seeking to deal with subversive movements has amply shown.[30]

Alienation has been identified as one of the destructive forces of the social order. I wrote recently that 'the only effective political antidote to the crises and catastrophes is unbureaucratic inspirational leadership on a broad democratic base'. Such leadership may indeed arise, but in order to remain effective it would need bureaucratic support. In short, when faced with anarchistic breakdowns, rational bureaucracy needs strongly inspirational democratic leadership. What was said above on power and leadership applies here. It must be both responsible and efficient, and the bureaucracy which serves such leaders will in turn strive for responsibility as well as efficiency. The totalitarian systems of our time have repeatedly failed in this respect and for this very reason the last word has not been spoken about the future of such regimes.

NOTES

1 UNESCO, *Democracy in a World of Tensions: A Symposium* (University of Chicago Press, 1951), ed. Richard McKeon. The effort did not succeed. Cf. G. Sartovi's able review in the *International Encyclopaedia*, vol. IV (1968).

2 So great a philosopher as Karl Jaspers addressed himself to the problem in his controversial *Wohin treibt die Bundesrepublik* (1966), and his response to his critics: *Antwort* (1967). The closing chapter of Ralf Dahrendorf's decisive *Gesellschaft und Demokratie in Deutschland* (1965), pp. 464 ff., stressed the unresolved conflict as did the present mayor of West Berlin, W. W. Schuetz, in *Rethinking German Policy* (1967); for the divergent views of democracy are a main obstacle to German unification.

3 In my *Constitutional Government and Democracy* (1941 and later), as well as in *Man and His Government* (1962 and later), these views are placed in perspective and the literature is critically examined.

4 In a brilliant paper, Wilhelm Hennis has explored the problems of 'democratisation'; see his *Demokratisierung – Zur Problematik eines Begriffs* (1969). Interesting comparisons are provided by Harvey Wheeler's *Democracy in a Revolutionary Era* (1968). Heinz Villars in his *Demokratisierung* offers rich material, but does not transcend the inherent controversy and bases his discussion on the proposition that *democratisation* means 'Herstellung von Gleichheit und Freiheit in allen Lebensbereichen' ('establishment of equality and freedom in all spheres of life') and sums it up in the categorical assertion that democratisation and socialisation are the same (*ein und dasselbe*) – a

statement which clearly reveals this author's bias in his treatment throughout. The title for Deutsch is *Politics and Government* (1970), and has the subtitle *How people decide their fate* – an intended subtitle, I suppose.

5 Herbert Marcuse, *One-dimensional Man* (1964), p. 16 and elsewhere, contains explicit rejection of Marx's views, as does his *Eros and Civilisation* (1955); the attempt to combine Marx with Freud in his theory is foredoomed.

6 Max Weber, *Theory of Social and Economic Organization* (tr. A. M. Henderson & Talcott Parsons) (1947), pp. 329 ff. Cf. the critical evaluation in my essay in Robert K. Merton *et al.*, *Reader in Bureaucracy* (1952).

7 Carl J. Friedrich and Taylor Cole, *Responsible Bureaucracy – A Study of the Swiss Civil Service* (1932).

8 Herman Finer, *The Theory and Practice of Modern Government* (1932), vol. II, p. 1167.

9 C. Northcote Parkinson, *Parkinson's Law* (1957).

10 Friedrich, op. cit.

11 The large literature on 'power' need not be cited here; cf. the references in my *Man and His Government* (1963), Part II, and especially ch. 9; the relation of power to freedom is discussed in chs. 16–21. Two volumes of special value for my topic here are Karl Loewenstein, *Political Power and the Governmental Process* (1958), and Bertrand de Jouvenel, *Sovereignty: An Inquiry into the Political Good* (1957; French original 1955); a more recent restatement was offered by James S. Coleman, *Power and the Structure of Society* (1974), who stresses the role of corporate persons alongside natural persons in the political process and the exercise of power. See also K. Deutsch, *Politics and Government* (1970), ch. 2, pp. 23 ff.

12 Freedom of the Press has recently been criticised by many who object to the use made of such freedom as *power*; in the USA the bureaucracy has been in the forefront of such criticism.

13 E.g. by Harold Lasswell in his *Power and Society* (with Abraham Kaplan) (1950), especially ch. V, and paragraph 6, 5 at p. 133 ff. and my comments in *Man and His Government*, ch. 12.

14 The questions of typology are here involved; cf. for a discussion of these *Man and His Government* (1963), pp. 182 ff. A sound and discriminating discussion of charismatic power is given by Dorothy Emmett, *Function, Purpose and Powers* (1958), ch. VIII; she rightly brings out that 'inspirational' would be a better and more readily comprehensible term.

15 Adam Ulam, in his insightful *Stalin – The Man and His Era* (1973), offers many striking bits for a portrayal of this comparison, especially in chs. 6 and 7 where the transition is treated; cf. Leonard Schapiro's *The Communist Party of the Soviet Union* (1960) for comparative perspective on their leadership; see also Bertram D. Wolfe in his

Three Who Made a Revolution (1948), ch. XXVIII, whose documentation is dated.

16 The numerous writings on Vietnam fail to contrast these leaders except in ideological terms, a lacuna which badly needs filling.

17 The most trenchant characterisation of Muñoz's leadership has been given by Henry Wells in his *The Modernization of Puerto Rico* (1969), ch. 13; in the following chapter he also analyses the problem of the succession.

18 From the large literature on Adenauer, much of it grossly partisan, pro and con, the careful study by Arnulf Baring, *Aussenpolitik in Adenauer's Kanzlerdemokratie*, which contains a rich bibliography, might here be mentioned. The expression *Kanzlerdemokratie*, coined in Germany to deprecate Adenauer's forceful leadership, has fallen into disuse since; his successors failed to maintain this leadership – an evolution relevant to our argument.

19 Cf. my op. cit., n. 14, ch. 9.

20 See the work cited in preceding footnote.

21 W. Hennis, *Demokratisierung* – as cited above, n. 4 – offered a trenchant analysis of the abuse made of this term.

22 These developments were dispassionately analysed by Henry L. Mason, 'Reflections on the Politicised University: The Academic Crisis in the Federal Republic of Germany', article in the *Bulletin* of the AAUP, September 1974.

23 Cf. M. Lipset's informed analysis in Seymour Martin Lipset and Gerard M. Schaffander, *Passion and Politics: Student Activism in America* (1971). In his penetrating study of American universities, *The Academic Revolution* (1968), Riesman attributes little importance to this issue. In the special Winter 1975 issue of *Daedalus*, a number of contributions deal with it. The absence of this issue gives the student rebellions of Europe a basically different party-political flavour. Note e.g. the account by the rector of Heidelberg and two collaborators in *Scheitert die Hochschulreform? Heidelberg zum Exempel.* Democratisation is discussed pp. 218 ff. A broader comparative collection of materials is found in Fritz Vilmar, *Demokratisierung*, Band I: *Theorie der Praxis* (Darmstadt, 1973), Band II, *Modelle and Kaempfe der Praxis* (Darmstadt, 1973).

24 A fairly universal reaction against this misrepresentation by the media has now set in in the USA; it would be too long a discourse to review these writings. Cf. what I wrote in *Limited Government*, p. 80 f. concerning freedom of the Press and its abuse.

25 Cf. what is said in the article on bureaucracy in the *International Encyclopedia of the Social Sciences*, vol. II (1968), by R. Bendix.

26 See above, n. 25.

27 See my lecture 'Bureaucracy faces Anarchism', *The Clifford W. Clark Memorial Lectures* (1970), published in the *Canadian Journal of Public Administration*, and the references given there.

28 Comparative studies of democratisation in different fields, such as that by Vilmar, op. cit., give many illustrations, as does the literature on bureaucracy in general.
29 Roughly, that is, to the sixteenth and seventeenth centuries; it varies for different countries. A bibliography is found in my op. cit., n. 3.
30 My *Constitutional Reason of State* (1957), especially the concluding chapter, develops this theme more fully.

3

Participation and the Future of Government

BERNARD CRICK

Perhaps for the first time in recent British history, real doubts grow about the adequacy of our political system to adapt itself to social and economic change and to resolve new problems which are seemingly beyond its capacity of control.

For a traditional society the 1960s saw a surprising amount of institutional change. Civil service reform, parliamentary reform, local government reform, fiscal reform, law reform, considerable devolution of government – which is now likely to go further – and finally the joining of Europe. Even electoral reform may only be an election or two away. But there remains a feeling that all this is just scratching at the surface, perhaps the last gasp of a liberal preconception about government (that if the machinery is fair and rational, the right policies and results are bound to follow), rather than adequate responses to modern conditions. Such reforms may indeed be looked at by future historians more as symptoms of trouble than as parts of a cure.[1]

What are the troubles? It should be clear by now that inflation is not just a temporary accident, or a middle-term problem, it is a long-term condition of the kind of society that has arisen – arisen not by design, not to serve purposively the interest of any class, whether defined by wealth, status or office-holding, but as an unforeseen result of the mid-Victorian compromise between aristocratic government and popular democracy. Mr Enoch Powell has been damnably accurate in talking of 'the inflationary effects of democracy' – at least of the type of democracy we have got. Professor

Ernest Gellner has recently called it 'the Danegeld State',[2] which in an odd way is much the same concept as the fearful Tory's version of 'the Welfare State'. Marx predicted that government would get more and more autocratic and exploitative of the ever poorer people; Tocqueville more shrewdly saw autocracies of the future as dispensers of welfare – of a sort:

> . . . an immense and tutelary power, which takes upon itself alone to secure their gratifications and to watch over their fate. That power is absolute, minute, regular, provident, and mild. It would be like the authority of a parent if, like that authority, its object was to prepare men for manhood; but it seeks, on the contrary, to keep them in perpetual childhood: it is well content that the people should rejoice, provided they think of nothing but rejoicing. For their happiness such a government willingly labours, but it chooses to be the sole agent and the only arbiter of that happiness; it provides for their security, foresees and supplies their necessities, facilitates their pleasures, manages their principal concerns, directs their industry, regulates the descent of property, and subdivides their inheritances: what remains, but to spare them all the care of thinking and all the trouble of living? [3]

The English governing classes have been so sensible, clever and civilised in, first of all, accepting and assimilating the new business classes and the market economy, and then in buying off popular discontent, always in time but never in advance of need, both politically and economically.

However, a climate of expectations has been created – not just in Great Britain – in which it is seen as the primary business of government to expand continuously the standard of living. I am not doubting for a moment that 'welfare' is a necessary object of government, particularly in the modern world when we see the responsibilities and capabilities of government as going far beyond the provision of 'bread' – or whatever is the staple food – and defence. But I am doubting whether continuously expanding welfare is always possible, especially when it is seen as a gift or benevolence of government to people. For to expand productivity continuously, great adaptability and mobility and great effort are needed from producers. The political conditions for this must be right, and there is an even more ancient and fundamental function of government than dispensing welfare – that is dispensing justice. If the working inhabitants of a State refuse to adapt themselves to new conditions (for instance, if they demand the retention of jobs in failing industries), if they act politically about wages and yet refuse to institutionalise a genuine political economy (for example, national decisions about rewards, or a genuine and overall prices and incomes policy), or if they simply refuse to work hard (if the relationship between work and welfare seems arbitrary), then it is overwhelmingly likely that they regard basic factors in the system as unjust. There may not be one word of ideology motivating their behaviour, not even an implicit socialist critique of the capitalist system: simply a negative but real – and perfectly understandable – sense of injustice. The old social democrats said this, and so did Karl Mannheim in his infinitely over-complicated way.[4]

Look at it over a century and a half. The response of the ruling classes to the Industrial Revolution and hence the dependence of society on the skilled working man was a gradual broadening of the franchise and a grudging extension of political and legal rights. And this has brought with it, as some at the time feared and some hoped, a gradual politicisation of the economy: political pressures for welfare, of which the rise of the Labour Party together with the trade unions is the main example. But even the leaders of the Labour Party in power still see 'welfare' as a benevolence or gift of the State which they wish to give, when they can. They wish to give and are sad that there is now less to give; and the trade unions see it as their role to make sure that somebody asks firmly enough (a slightly less necessary role than in the past; and in any case their members now take the bit between their own teeth), so they keep out of direct responsibility for government, which their power would easily allow. But the gift relationship is inherently uneconomic, self-consuming, even degrading, unless the gross national product shows a steady increase. Ultimately purchased loyalty is fragile loyalty; people who are even vaguely conscious that they are being bought off turn all the nastier, experiencing guilt as well as deprivation of material self-interest, when the gifts cease to flow. I often think of an old Sheffield Labour alderman saying to me with tears in his eyes, after a very rough passage of abuse and insults at a crowded tenants' association meeting over rents, 'after all we've done for them' – waving his hand towards one of the largest (and most soulless) public housing blocks in the country – 'it makes me lose faith in human nature'. Of course, at the heart of the trouble is the plain fact that a utilitarian ethic has no place in it for an ethic either of loyalty or of sociability – as both conservatives and socialists should know. 'After all we've done for them', as many a colonial administrator used to say – it must then be very hard to let them do anything for themselves or imagine that they could do it better. One would even settle for leaders being more intelligent and inventive in means of finding out what people really want, and less arrogant in their assumption that their election is a divine sign that they 'know the people'.[5]

The old socialist argument will have to be revived out of the exigencies of economic survival. Democracy cannot stop short simply at the level of formal political institutions: it is likely that participation must extend into industry and firms of all kinds. If people are involved in making decisions and in seeing directly how their sector is affected by others, it is likely that the allocation of rewards in society will be more just. Basic to the origins of socialist theory, even before Marx, even before 'the great divide', are two things: not a demand for 'justice from government', but justice through self-government; and not a demand for fairer wages in the market, but for a replacement of the market as the means of determining wages.

The welfare state that has grown in this century has grown by demand working against government; but if it is not to break down, or become an intolerably oppressive instrument, then government will have to involve far more people. Our élites have kept their predominance by political skill not brute coercion; but they have kept their independence at the price of a growing impotence.

The modern world has been nowhere near as inventive in forms of government as it has been in forms of industrial and agricultural production, even of the conduct of war, certainly far less so – it is a platitude to say – than in science and technology. Even if we look at the component parts of political systems, what some might strictly call 'institutions', such as parliaments, parties, bureaucracies, and electoral systems, ways of controlling the police and military by government or courts, or ways of controlling populations by police and military, we find a paucity of invention. The only original ideas of government in the last hundred years have been totalitarianism as a system, the idea of a total control of society (which is now tending to lapse back into something more like old-fashioned bureaucracy); party, particularly one-party, as the monopolising device of government; and the commune.[6]

A reasonable stability of government could continue amid high rates of technological and social change, some still hope, not by need for new inventions, but simply by a wiser application for different purposes of already fairly well-known devices and principles – such as parliaments. Such devices and principles as elections, for instance, or informing the public why decisions are made (unlike in the secret government of old-fashioned autocracies), already vary widely in form and in independence, but could obviously be applied to many more institutions and types of decision. The arguments against referenda, for instance, are formidable in terms of the efficiency and convenience of carrying on government – I have used these arguments myself. The time comes, however, when one may need to consider the advantages of referenda as forms of political education and of popular participation – these might outweigh the other objections, they might even add to the real effectiveness of government if they demonstrated more public support behind it, as presumably the referendum on the Border in Northern Ireland in 1970 was meant to do.[7] Election is one thing where there is a real choice and quite another where there is no choice; we should think, however, not just of autocratic or totalitarian regimes but of some closer to home where the choice that is actually offered can be derisory; or when the whole business of choice has degenerated into a kind of auction between the parties for the provision of types of goods and welfare that they consider are politically viable, meaning convenient. In the past, like most in this country, I have regarded talk of statutory primary elections for parliamentary candidates as nonsense, but as membership of the main political parties continues to decline, the case for involving the public in selection of candidates may become overwhelming. And 'informing the public' can take the familiar form of a government being forced politically, as by Press and Parliament, to divulge information that it would not otherwise do; or it can take the form of government propaganda; or it can be seen as an enlightened step by governments to gain greater response from the people in areas where response is obviously needed – broadly speaking the whole field of wages and industrial relations and occupational mobility. Even the newer autocracies and remaining totalitarian regimes cannot ignore the masses, cannot thrive simply on passivity as did the old autocracies: they positively need loyal assemblies, enthusiastic demonstrations, elections with 99 per cent turn-out and constant propaganda, however false all these may be, precisely in order to mobilise the masses, precisely because every population in the world is restless for and believes in the possibility of an ever greater standard of living. No form of government or actual government can last that does not appear to guarantee this. We are no longer satisfied with believing, as mankind has believed through most of history, that the future should resemble the past and that we will be happiest when it does.

Everywhere the need is seen for the masses to be mobilised,

although everywhere, with brutal frankness in some regimes and with genteel evasion in our own, the ruling classes seek to do this without endangering their own essential privileges, that is to perpetuate themselves and their children in differential advantages. Even peasantries, as well as industrial workers, are under constant pressure to be more efficient, to produce more. In the 1930s there was a myth that the totalitarian regimes were economically more efficient, and that parliamentary regimes paid a high price for their liberty in terms of lower efficiency. The war dispelled this belief. That, in a grim sense, was our finest hour in that there was general agreement that Great Britain achieved a higher degree of mobilisation and effective control of manpower and resources than did certainly Nazi Germany, almost certainly even than Stalinist Russia which had been lamed by the purges of the mid-1930s. In the 1950s and 1960s there was a myth that the newly independent nations had evolved new forms of government including rational systems of one-party rule but with inter-party democracy. But by the 1970s it was clear that there was little substance in this claim. Most such regimes were fairly conventional autocracies and the claims of many of them even to be party states were true only in the narrowest, almost eighteenth-century sense of party as factions and followings of great men rather than as mass democratic movements. Only China, Cuba, Tanzania and Yugoslavia raised new hopes and problems.

Others doubt whether our existing institutions can adjust and change sufficiently to deal with the new problems. Few of the alternatives sound plausible, the soft and vague ones like government by coalition or by wise men, or even the more intellectual ones such as government by scientists or government by managerial élites – for none of these groups is likely to be any more effective than existing politicians and people in making political choices, in defining the conditions for political justice that will make government more acceptable and stronger to deal with new problems. Only some socialists pursued, albeit somewhat vaguely, some kind of new approach derived from a pre-Marxian tradition of socialist thought, though they usually call themselves Marxists, but an approach more symptomatic of modern problems than by itself likely to solve them. I refer to those who believe that government itself is so grossly oppressive and bureaucratic, in the sense of treating men as things and not as persons, that the people will either learn that they can do without it, or that when a few destroy it with 'creative violence', showing that its apparent vast strength is, in fact, but a brittle rigidity, there will be found no need to replace it: spontaneous co-operation will follow. Anarchism might have seemed a minor and discredited theory of the future of government, but for its sudden reinvention or rejuvenation by revolutionary socialists among students all over the non-Russian world in the late 1960s, and by a similar theory, though talking of a radical devolution of both government and industry into small and self-governed units, by some Liberals – not all of whom are 'young'. It may not be a specially plausible prediction, but it does furnish, in however strange a form, a good testimony to individual human freedom and a bad report on what contemporary society appears to do by way of fulfilling, in a just and stable manner, the perennial problem of government: the reconciliation of order with freedom.

These people are confused because of the traditionalist anarchist dogma that it is possible to dispense with central government. Far more likely that central government will remain, will probably express different objects and different ideologies in different circumstances, but will take the form more and more of a co-ordinating authority, than of an original ordering and creating authority, co-ordinating subsidiary groups into which the introduction of the devices of election typical of the narrow range of the political world of the moment will be novelties when introduced to reach into firm, factory and school. The idea of the 'commune' or the 'soviet' could become the very basis, that is the root and the energising condition, of effective government. The need for, and many of the main tasks of, central government are too obvious to need argument and cannot be dispensed with. Once allocative decisions are made, it is not difficult to imagine far, far more local autonomy in how to carry them out or in how to spend block grants or enabling grants. People could organise according to their social and industrial reality, as communes of producers and consumers, so that power would come from the roots of society, and the State, while not vanishing, as in anarchist theory, would be reduced to a co-ordinating role. One might call this view socialist pluralism, but it was also the vision of Lenin, for half a year in 1919 when he fell under the spell of the new and spontaneous Soviets and before he smashed them, and it was probably the main presupposition of many of the Czechoslovak reformers in 1969.[8] The idea that a commune can be a basic unit of government is the great ghost or heresy in Marxist theory, particularly because it was placed there by Marx himself in a misunderstanding of a somewhat more limited, albeit both splendid and terrible, event in Paris in 1870.

All that one can generally say about national forms of government is that it is always inherently unlikely that humanity will settle for any one solution. One wishes that one could go back to the universalist ideas of the Enlightenment and escape from many of the intolerances of the modern national, or rather nationalist, State. But it is extraordinarily unlikely that men will be ever able to choose which State to live in because they like it better than another constitution, framework of government or public spirit – as happened to a very limited extent in the world of the Greek city states, and was in some ways what the United States indeed represented to the poor and oppressed of Europe in the era of open immigration. It is unlikely that there will be world government, either by agreement or military domination, but equally unlikely, looking especially at Africa, Western Europe, Eastern Europe, South America, the Middle East and South East Asia, that such a multitude of small states will continue all claiming to be sovereign and yet in fact grimly dependent on great powers. Between the one and the other there are a large number of possible relationships of mutual dependence and clientage, as well as of particular forms of partial independence and voluntary co-operation, some of which are beginning to appear fairly clear but many more of which are likely to emerge. Certainly the national State is no longer sovereign: what may be called co-operative clientage may best express the relation of most states to each other, and often the Great Powers or grand patrons lack the full power to make the dogs wag their own tails.

One of the greatest problems of today and of the future is the concern with size and scale. There is at first sight a clear dichotomy between those who say that efficiency demands the largest units, the world of the super powers (even though here note how quickly it has changed from two, the USA and the USSR, to an emerging five, that is China, Japan, and Western Europe as well); and those who see liberty and justice as only secure in the small group, the anarchists, pluralists and syndicalists. But the most likely prophecy of common trends in the future is that things will get both bigger and smaller. It will not be the vanishing of central government that is likely, but the devolution to localities, unions, industries or professions and schools of more and more decisions – decisions subject to final central control, but whose initiative and form are local. Housing, town planning, education and welfare policies will become more and more devolved, with the State enforcing minimum standards, limiting maximum standards by financial control, but allowing more and more variation of practice. But at the same time, and this is equally important, some functions of government traditionally centred in the national State are now demanding larger units. Functions once left to the market, i.e. the determination of wages, will have to be taken up by government – so long as governments continue to do everything they can (including inflation) to avoid unemployment. Already in Western Europe we see a great concern with administrative devolution, at the same time as some key functions of government have passed beyond the control and competence of national governments. The situation is not entirely dissimilar in Eastern Europe. Foreign policy, defence, basic monetary, industrial and trading policy are supra-nationally controlled, but the practices and arguments for greater devolution and for greater autonomy of decision-making on the factory level grow stronger and stronger.

Perhaps it is not too rash to say that all the large countries in the modern world are trying to solve some of the same problems of the reconciliation of order with economic progress, that is of stability and innovation, in three ways. First, by allowing the growth and influence of more group representation within the State, that is groups outside the formal party, parliamentary and electoral systems. Secondly, the institutionalisation of these groups is recognised or encouraged, so that they begin, even in totalitarian regimes, to get some limited 'autonomy': they are devices for industrial mobilisation, certainly, but because they are more effective at this than the party or even parties, some freedom for them, some diversity, some political difficulties, have to be tolerated. Thirdly, that informal or formal processes of consultation between governments and these groups are beginning to emerge in all countries, have long existed in some, before major decisions can be taken. Leaders do like to know that they will be followed. For more and more it is recognised that the kind of economic and social policies needed in the modern State cannot be enforced, or will not prove successful, if the skilled working population and the managers are not convinced, and therefore drag their feet. If only George Brown had made some soundings as to whether the first and famous 'declaration of intent' to limit wages and prices was acceptable on the shop-floor not just to Westminster, Whitehall and the posh Press; and if only Harold Wilson had employed the under-employed Backbenchers of the Parliamentary Labour Party to try to change trade union opinion once it was found that it was not loyally following. Great industrial changes need positive response. And if much politics, even in liberal regimes, is, indeed, a matter of what people will put up with or accept rather than what they positively agree to, yet there are limits to what a skilled worker will put up with. Rebellion is no longer the ultimate or the realistic sanction against despotic government: rather, working slowly, badly, reluctantly, ineffectively – whether we are talking of the skilled worker or the university-trained manager.

Such pressures of the dependence of governments on technologists and experts are not likely to have democratic results in a conventional sense of more and more open political participation. But they may develop something quite as important, also a part of democracy, radical increases in the effectiveness of communications; and parliaments and elected assemblies still sit at the centre of such political communications networks.

It seems more likely that what basically restrains governments in advanced industrial societies and makes them serve popular purposes is first, the knowledge that their decisions become known (as it were, the eighteenth- and nineteenth-century battle against the inefficiency as well as the injustice of arbitrary autocracy); second, that the reasons for their decisions will become known (at least among a managerial élite whose intelligent and comprehending skills are needed); and third, that the consequences of their decisions will be evaluated critically, publicised and popularised intelligently, so that the skilled manual workers (on whom both capitalist and socialist civilisations depend) can be educated, mobilised and integrated to the ruling élites, all as part of one process. Such a process does not necessarily imply a competitive party system – as Western writers have been prone to argue: it plainly can or could work in societies as different as the Soviet Union, Yugoslavia and Tanzania; also in nominally multi-party States where in fact organised government for all practical purposes is all but identical with a single party or movement, as in India under the Congress Party or France under the Gaullists; and even, though more arguably, in cases like the United States where the policy differences between the parties are probably less than the policy difference within the governing parties of some one-party states.

There are severe practical limits to personal participation in decisions of central government in large industrial societies, and the case is no better if 'groups' are thought of instead of individuals. Participation does not always maximise communication.[9] Often party cadres or elected representatives in other countries find that their role is severely limited to mobilising support for their government; and even in the parliamentary democracies a person's hostility to secrecy may change abruptly according to what he conceives his new role to be, before and after election or nomination. Participation does not necessarily increase communication between rulers and ruled or in the intermediate range of groups whose democratic structure is vital. Perhaps it should, but plainly it does not always do so. And, on the other hand, it is possible in theory to imagine a government that is highly unrepresentative in a formal institutional sense, but is very honest or shrewd in the degree to which it both seeks for and provides accurate information and the habits it cultivates (which are as vital to political as to industrial technology or scientific invention and initiative) of publicly canvassing alternatives.

The growth of group representation as such is unlikely, in my opinion, to have radical effects on the formal machinery of central government which exists today, however much the style and purpose would be altered and devolution increased. But it does raise more acutely problems of communication: whether it is possible to increase the productivity of large and complex societies with only highly selective areas of free communication. It is likely that existing institutions will be forced, if they are not to prove economically stagnant or regressive, into a much greater openness and publicity. This will come about not out of demands from below on grounds of democratic principle, but on hard grounds of political theory: that States who can carry the voluntary enthusiasms of their populations with them are far stronger than autocracies based on passive obedience or regimes based purely on individual economic incentives. Problems of scale in modern societies have led more and more to the multiplication of accurate and true information in printed form on the technological – productive and the technological – educative fronts; it becomes increasingly unrealistic to think that this can be done and has to be done for economic institutions without being done for political institutions. But this does not by itself imply that the basic political institutions are likely to change, nor that ideologies will; it only implies that their mode of operation will have to become more open and participative if they are to fulfil what seem to be two basic conditions of all modern regimes: popularity in differing national senses, and the ability to increase the *per capita* income, not just the gross national product.

The suggested 'autonomy' of new groups and new institutions is likely to be less important than their 'openness', which will, of course, modify their 'autonomy', just as the 'autonomy' or sovereignty of the State itself will also be modified by 'openness' and publicity. In many ways the basic character of *planification* or public consultation, the new planning bodies of France and Britain and in some socialist States, is less to be seen as new versions of old interest groups, but as new devices for communication and mobilisation between government and the great variety of group and general interests which are, in practice, far too complex and interlocking to be, as some might suggest, 'institutionalised' as part of the constitutional structure. The difference is, I think, simply this – though it is easier to express than to explain briefly: we look at civil servants and know that, however they act, rightly or wrongly, they have authority for what they do – unless they are simply acting illegally; but we look at the leaders of group interests with suspicion as well as hope, for they should have to prove by the behaviour of their members that they are representative, for otherwise their advice may be dangerously misleading. A representative must have consulted those he represents if his representation is to be taken seriously. There seems to me to be the need for more public law controlling private jurisdictions in order to ensure both the rights of members and the authentication of so-called representatives who all too often simply pursue their own line.

All that I have argued assumes, of course, that States wish to carry on increasing productivity and living standards. The universal assumption that this must be done could be challenged; or it could be argued cynically that huge defence expenditures, particularly in the USA and the USSR, are very useful in preventing a sudden increase of individual real income which must then throw strains on to any kind of political system – releasing all these worrying and time-consuming demands for more participation and more information. In some ways the political strains of already advanced industrial societies who need to undergo great educational expansion to work modern systems of government, industry, and communications could be greater than those of newly industrialising States; the suffering in the latter is greater but the justification for censorship and the disjunction between participation and communication are far more obvious. Some States may simply decide not to run these risks – if risks are inevitable, results are not.

Napoleon once said that 'the politics of the future will be the art of moving the masses'. There is, indeed, a purely instrumental participation. But the masses have grown more educated; they see through this; and if there is no path of effective action, then they lapse into cynicism and are hard to mobilise. Where the stick has been abandoned, it cannot be picked up, and carrots seem lacking. As I have argued in this whole essay, politically there may be no alternative but to trust individuals; morally, the time may have come when we have to reckon with taking seriously platitudes and perceptions of individualism, but now in a social and collective context.

What this means in concrete terms is that participation cannot simply be a public relations job, nor can it simply be compulsory or involuntary involvement, mere consultation in some regimes, compulsory enthusiasm in others. Participation must mean effective influence by individuals, at whatever level of society, however small the group. However small the group in which these habits are learnt, the habits continue and are likely to prove contagious. Participation in local government is not simply being consulted, it is the ability to effect decisions, either in the maximal way of direct participation or the minimal way, but still novel and desperately underdeveloped, having to be asked before major decisions are made.[9]

If there were participation of this kind, it would, of course, challenge the existing party machines. The decline of membership in both the main parties has already destroyed not merely a great deal of their legitimacy but also their effectiveness both as devices for representation or for mobilisation. Somehow I cannot feel that the path of the future is simply a revival of active membership in the parties. Indeed, in many ways the party memberships seem to grow more extreme in their demands to determine decisions of government the less representative they have become of 'the people', whom they vaguely and solemnly regard as having deserted them – somewhat in the spirit of Berthold Brecht's famous quip about the East German Government during the workers' riots: 'The people have deserted us, let us elect another one.' The party is still highly important, but it counts for less. There is nothing to be regretted in the relative increase of pressure group strength as against party, only to ensure that pressure groups themselves are genuinely participative, representative and democratic. Parties will not vanish, they will simply count for less. And within the parties, as in the trade unions, there is still great scope for an extension of public law to protect the rights of members against the bureaucracies. And there is almost infinite scope and great need for firms, educational institutions and even newspapers, etc., to be treated in, to develop themselves in, the same way.

Nothing here of the most important theme perhaps, industrial democracy, only to reiterate as it is now becoming almost a platitude. The wisest big firms have already conceded certain rights, from the point of view of efficiency, of knowing how the firm is organised, rights of information and communication. It is now fairly clear that it is only the conservatism of big unions that is holding back the desires both of left wing and Liberal politicians to extend industrial democracy. The forms will vary and be many, but it is clearly a path of the future, not simply in terms of efficiency (it will probably aid that too) but also in terms of positively enhancing the conditions of life. More leisure better spent is not by itself the answer to the future welfare of humanity; it must concern increasing satisfaction with the basic working condition where necessarily much, even if no longer most, of life is spent.

This can only begin at the base, and the base is not a class base in this sense, but it is the basic communal experience beyond the family that everyone in common enjoys – and that is the educational system. One can stop a hundred miles short of 'the democratic school' or of Mr Illich's 'deschooling' and still say that the easy and affable assumption of autocracy in schools, not merely masters to pupils but the visible example of head teachers to other teachers, is a bad beginning in any education for participation and education for citizenship in all social and industrial groups. Pressures in the schools will increase, should increase, not to destroy learning in the name of equality and democratic participation, but to make far more voluntary participation and self-proposed and self-chosen project-work the path towards learning or vocational skills, or whatever else are clear objectives – education has no single objective, certainly not 'democracy' alone. Participation is not an end in itself, but at the moment the absence of it in so many schools is limiting what can effectively be done in society. The gap between rhetoric and reality is flagrant. And the example of deliberate non-participation will last so many of them the rest of the days of their lives. William Robson has always stressed the difference between a genuine political education and mere political training. But it may be that even political education is not something to be taught so much as to be learnt, and not learned passively, but actively by participation and action. Yes, informed and responsible participation, certainly; but the results will seldom be what those who would define 'informed' and 'responsible' at the beginning of a process would wish themselves to see.

One can find more and more in the first general theory of politics. Aristotle put forward two criteria for stability in the *polis* (or the kind of State that settled its affairs politically, not tyrannically). The first is famous: that men (or rather citizens) should *rule and be ruled in turn* – from this follows, in all but the smallest States, selection to office either by rota or lottery (which he regarded as the only fully democratic way) or by election (which he regarded as necessarily somewhat oligarchic – for either the best or the wealthiest got elected). But the second is less familiar: that the State should be no larger than the voice of the 'Stentor' (or herald) could be heard from boundary to boundary or, he put it another way but meaning the same thing, larger than that *citizens could know each other's characters* – he saw such knowledge as a necessary condition of justice. We might neglect his second set of criteria because they would seem, as many thought for long and some student radicals are thinking again, to doom democracy to small groups. But the limitation vanishes when suddenly the modern 'Stentor' is the Press, radio and television; then it is possible 'to know each other's characters' through them, even between States whose populations rarely if ever meet. Humanity has gone some way in exploring the inferences of Aristotle's first generalisation (though it could go further in seeing some of the advantages of lot and rota, or selection like juries, rather than election through, still worse nomination by, parties); but we have hardly begun to appreciate the second or to translate them into the conditions of mass societies and modern industrial States.

I make only a small apology for having written on such an abstract and generalised level. A *Festschrift* for the eightieth birthday of a man who has written so much and so well as William Robson, who has been of such incalculable influence in thinking about British government, is both the place for disciples and friends to carry on work in the same tradition as his, and for speculation about the fundamental nature and future probabilities of the things that still so actively interest him. At heart it is all a matter of what we conceive we are doing. Governments think that they are in difficulties because they cannot find ways of demanding enough from the population, though it may be that some of these difficulties of communication, of leadership and response, are precisely for the reason that the population is more educated and informed than it ever has been before, and that the politicians, with a few notable exceptions, are remarkably slow to recognise this fact. So much political illiteracy, yes, but as so much greater potential for intelligent participation. In any case, one of the main advantages both of greater participation and of greater communication is that they are educative. That is, educative not simply in the narrow sense of creating more information and knowledge, but in a broader moral sense of creating and stimulating more responsibility and, surely we must believe, of enhancing the personality of those involved. Perhaps many people are growing, quite simply, a bit fed up with having so much done for them and being given so few opportunities to do things, not for themselves in the old liberal individualistic sense, but to do things for themselves socially and collectively, in the plural, but also in a plurality of ways. It is not necessary for civil servants or inspectors to judge which of these ways are in some absolute sense the most efficient, for in their variety may be greater satisfaction, and variety in the conditions of work are as much a good as the product. The case for democratic Socialism, which informed the working life of William Robson, may need reformulating, the centralist tradition of the Fabians and the Webbs may only have been a necessary phase that either went too far or neglected the real grass-roots, but the case is still strong. Administration, Robson was always well aware, does not furnish its own goals.

NOTES

1 See Bernard Crick (ed.), *Essays on Reform 1967* (Oxford University Press, 1967), a symposium including an essay by W. A. Robson on 'Local Government Reform', and also essays by J. G. H. Griffith, Peter Self, and others. But somehow the whole symposium, if the editor and a contributor may ungratefully say, now seems a bit limited in political perspectives – reform for what? Very unclear all round. A recent somewhat similar volume, edited by Geraint Parry, *Participation in Politics* (Manchester University Press, 1972), necessarily raises questions more basic from more points of the political spectrum.
2 See Ernest Gellner, 'The Demise of the Danegeld State', *Political Quarterly*, April 1975.
3 Alexis de Tocqueville, *Democracy in America*, vol. 2, edited by Phillips Bradley (Alfred Knopf, 1948), p. 318.
4 See Karl Mannheim's *Freedom, Power and Democratic Planning* (Routledge and Kegan Paul, 1951), which is an important example of that 'real social democratic theory' which is always supposed not to have existed, either by Marxists, who do not wish to remember or who have isolated themselves in a purely self-satisfying sectarian literature, or by lazy social democratic publicists whose idea of theory is bounded by writings such as Tony Crosland's.
5 Perhaps this is what Lord Rothschild had in mind in his open letter of resignation to the Prime Minister from the Central Policy Review Staff, when he said that '. . . I wish we had had the time, the perseverance, or your instructions to set up a central but independent survey machine which, whatever anyone may say, does not exist, to help in finding out what the people really want Government policy to be on specific issues. (A survey machine is not, of course, referenda by another name.) Politicians often believe that their world is the real one: officials sometimes take a different view. Having been a member of this latter and lesser breed, it is, perhaps, inevitable that I should have become increasingly fearful about the effects of the growing political hostility between and among our people.' (*The Times*, 1 October 1974.)

6 See Ghiţa Ionescu's article, 'Lenin, The Commune and the State – 'Thoughts for a Centenary', *Government and Opposition*, vol. 5, no. 2.

7 The result of the referendum of June 1975 on Britain staying in the Common Market demonstrates several ways in which leaders can be very unrepresentative of their followers. The Tribune Group had no doubt that the people, if a referendum was forced, would reject Europe. Union leaders, Orangemen, Welsh and Scottish Nationalists all believed, in their different ways, that they could decide which way to go on the issue and that their followers would then follow. Both referenda and ordinary opinion polls can allow governments to appeal over the heads of group leaders to their followers, certainly on issues which the followers do not see as relevant to the other purposes for which they give trust and respect to their leaders.

8 Ionescu, op. cit.

9 One of the most suggestive writings on participation in local government is the first chapter of William Hampton's *Democracy and Community* (Oxford University Press, 1970). See also the interesting symposium (both for its strengths and its weaknesses) of 'Public Participation' in *The Journal of the Town Planning Institute*, April 1971. In retrospect, the famous *People and Planning* Report of the Committee on Public Participation in Planning (HMSO, 1969) is not merely a dog with good intentions but rubber teeth, but also purely a house-dog, a hound plainly fed off public relations, not a hunting dog meant to pursue new game. An important and neglected attempt to tie measures of participation to a radical participative theory was Geoffrey Green's 'The Skeffington Report', Social Science Research Council *Newsletter* no. 10 (November 1970), which makes important suggestions about possible measures of participation.

4

Rational Decentralisation

PETER SELF

INTRODUCTION

This essay is concerned with the geographic decentralisation of government powers. Most writers on public administration, as on management, are decentralists in principle, believing that many decisions ought to be taken at regional or local levels closer to the publics being served or controlled. Precisely the same attitudes are expressed as a rule by those politicians and officials who have considered the matter.

This favourable sentiment towards decentralisation in general seems often incapable of producing effective action. No doubt some of the protest against 'centralisation' illustrates an obvious and frequent conflict of values; one cannot get the technical gains of large-scale organisation or the egalitarian effects of administrative uniformity without substantial disadvantages, also 'remoteness', bureaucratic waste and duplication, etc. Cynics may also think that central government politicians and officials give only lip-service to the doctrine, and resist any actual attempt to diminish their powers. Certainly the post-1945 history of efforts to reduce central controls over local government in Britain seems to support this cynical hypothesis. So does the wide gap between Parisian discourse upon the vital importance of regionalism and the results to date.

Either an idealistic or a cynical view of decentralisation is much too simple. So is the view that the only barrier to effective decentralisation is the 'obsolete nature' of local government systems. This belief at least partly reflects the fact that a great deal more is known publicly about the 'inefficiencies' of local than of central government. In Britain, for example, a spotlight of continuous review and criticism has been turned upon local government since 1945, whereas the workings of central government have stayed obscure. One explanation is that local government has no strong political patrons or defenders, whereas central ministers, from a mixture of political interest and lack of time, have shielded their departments from all but the most perfunctory investigations. The Official Secrets Act, buttressed by Treasury conservatism, has deflected academic research from central government, whereas local government, much to its credit, has become a much more open field for such research.[1] There have been more high-level commissions or committees of inquiry into local than into central government and some of the best known have been headed by a prominent ex-civil servant.[2] In the USA, local government offers an easy target for reformers, although it also has sophisticated defenders.[3]

It is customary to draw a distinction between administrative and political forms of decentralisation, although the rationale of these two methods overlaps. Thus the delegation of administrative discretion to field officials is often aided by the participation of a local representative body, at least in an advisory capacity, while political devolution is sometimes in practice so closely circumscribed as to amount to little more than a form of administrative delegation. Both methods are subject to tests of functional performance. An administrative concept of functional efficiency should not stop with technical factors but includes a capacity for innovation and adaptation to local conditions and demands. Political devolution is concerned with the claims of territorial units to some measure of self-government, but needs also to ensure that these units are functionally effective. We will consider first an administrative and then a political approach to issues of decentralisation.

ADMINISTRATIVE DECENTRALISATION

Local Needs

A centralised decision model requires the issue of comprehensive rules and standards, and the upwards referral of all unusual cases. The values of this system are uniformity and consistency; maximum scope for the use of specialised techniques; and functional rationality over the distribution of resources. The defects of the system are slowness and inflexibility over particular cases and destructive effects upon the zest and initiative of field or local officials.

The context of this issue has been much changed by improvements in communications. It is no longer necessary to wait weeks for a local matter to be settled by headquarters, since a phone call should – in theory – settle the case immediately. An extreme example of the communications revolution was its effect upon colonial administration. Forty years ago a British official took over a month to reach his post in Rhodesia and was cut off from his superiors for months on end; today the journey could be accomplished in a day and field officers have far closer contact with headquarters. Because direct contacts were so slow and uncertain, traditional colonial administration represented a supreme and not unsuccessful case of 'co-ordination by ideas'. Before colonisation ended, however, it became practicable for the Colonial Office in London to control local decisions in considerable detail. It was this circumstance, as well as his bureaucratic laws of expansion, which explains C. Northcote Parkinson's paradox of the Colonial Office growing as the colonies diminished.

Quick communications have exploded much of the case for local flexibility, particularly in small countries such as Britain. This does not mean, of course, that problems of bureaucratic delay and rigidity have been solved, but these defects now derive from the characteristics of large-scale administrative organisation, not the specific factor of geographic distance. There can be as much delay around the corridors of Whitehall as in dealings between London and Penzance. Still, geographic distance, especially when coupled with cultural differences, seems to add to the victim's sense of grievance, and to render the ills of bureaucracy more visible. More to the point, effective geographic decentralisation is one important method, although only one, of unclogging the congestion of centralised controls and co-ordination.

Much classical defence of local government rests upon the distinction between national and local needs. For example, Sidney Webb, writing in 1901, defended local government as an instrument for satisfying the requirements of particular localities.[4] This type of argument fails to make clear the relationship between opinion and need. The provision of local services may vary according to the opinions of local councils, but it is arguable as to how far these variations reflect the needs or even the wishes of the local population. From another standpoint, the needs and even the demands for public services of such groups as old age pensioners, motorists, or children seem to vary very little according to their place of residence. Nor does there seem much argument of 'local need' for variations in the rules and enforcement methods of most regulatory functions, such as those concerned with road safety, fire dangers, food and drugs, or building construction. The growth of mass culture and easy communications, and the ascendancy of national over local politics, have brought about a recognition of *common* needs and demands, as well as providing the means for their satisfaction, in ways that could not occur when localities were relatively isolated and ignorant of each other.

It is true that 'the peculiarities of place' still has importance for some areas of administration. Thus the design and location of public buildings, or the redevelopment of central areas, are matters towards which local taste and tradition have something to contribute; but even here local taste is not the only factor, and local tradition may be better appreciated by outsiders, as in those cases when a central department attempts to persuade a local council not to ruin its architectural heritage. In some cases again a public development may be of interest only to a particular authority, as is a pier or marina to the council of a seaside resort. It is also true that the need for some types of service, and the best methods of provision, varies considerably with population density and degrees of urbanisation. However, this is a general geographic factor; the problems of conurbations are similar in many respects as are those of the remaining genuinely rural areas.

The traditional notion of 'local needs', which still casts its spell, was based historically upon the existence of a ratepayer's franchise. Local needs represented the services which local property-owners considered necessary and were willing to pay for, and which were largely of direct benefit to themselves. These included highways, paving, lighting, drainage, sewerage, water supply, fire-fighting, and police; and also the relief of poverty viewed as a duty of the local community. Quite logically, poor relief was the first local function in Britain to be subjected to a high degree of central management under the Poor Law Commissioners, to which public health was temporarily added during the period when local institutions were incompetent to prevent the spread of epidemics.

However, the problem of classifying services as either locally or nationally beneficial, which once engaged public inquiries into local taxation, has lost most of its interest in Britain although it still concerns countries like Canada where local finance carries a much heavier load. The ratepayers' franchise has been displaced by universal franchise. National finance now makes a larger contribution than local finance to local government services in many countries. Moreover national finance is extensively used in most Western States to reduce disparities of financial resources between local authorities. In Britain the remnants of earlier controversies still arise over the financing of those services, such as flood control, whose costs necessarily vary greatly according to geographic circumstances. Against the view that the prevention of natural disasters should be a national charge is pitted the equally reasonable view that persons who have chosen to reside in a particular area should bear at least some of the extra costs of that area's disadvantages. However, the latter opinion is now the weaker one.

The concept of local needs is no longer much adduced to justify variations of service, but it is freely employed to draw attention to the inferior services of certain areas. It has thus become a measure of deficiency of supply rather than diversity of demand. Even those parts of the United Kingdom which are most culturally differentiated do not so much demand different services as better ones. The existence of a separate Parliament in Ulster, with powers of internal legislation, did not lead to much variation in service or regulatory patterns from those of England. Public administration in Scotland is marked by some historical differences over matters such as education and law, but rather small differences over newer functions. The only special administrative feature of Wales is the highly controversial insistence of some local authorities upon use of the Welsh language and upon no drinking on Sundays. It would seem that variations of service levels provoke more resentment than satisfaction, and that uniformity is criticised much less than is diversity. These beliefs are perhaps stronger in Britain than anywhere, but they are a powerful force in all modern societies.

Social and political egalitarianism has been translated into administrative measures for the reduction of differences. The most obvious device is action by central departments to lay down minimum standards of service and to redistribute resources in such a way that these standards can be met. The forcefulness of such intervention varies considerably, according to the strength of political and professional demands for the creation of common standards. Thus the Department of Education and Science stipulates both basic standards and maximum permitted costs for school construction, in such a way that hardly any variations of quality are practicable. Some central departments remain content with more moderate standards and controls over priorities.[5]

The pursuit of egalitarian aims increases central controls in several ways. First, progress in areas of greater need may only be practicable, as in the case above, if projects of more affluent or simply more progressive authorities are held back. Secondly, the continuous pressure exercised by professional groups or zealous departments for the raising of national standards has a dampening effect upon local initiative. Thirdly, the incapacity of some local authorities to reach goals recommended by the central policy-makers produces arguments for placing an entire category of local government under tutelary control. Fourthly, inadequacies of local government areas is an obvious cause of intervention over the management of many services, such as police, fire, or town and country planning.

Local Experiment

Administrative progress depends upon cycles of innovation and experiment followed by consolidation and standardisation. This cycle applies equally to political, social, technical, and organisational forms of innovation. At any point of time, a large part of administrative practice is settled and codified, and innovation is occurring at the margin – either sluggishly or actively. However, this marginal innovation is of great importance, since it represents the frontiers of progress. Often mistakes will be made – but they are a necessary price of fruitful innovation.

Local experiments are a highly significant part of this process. It is not material whether the experiment is related to specifically localised requirements; the benefits flow from the fact that some new system is being tried out somewhere. Of course the scope for local experiment depends upon the nature of the function, as well as political and technical circumstances. For example, a national system of social security cannot be varied locally to try out the effects of new forms of benefits or contributions. If changes in these matters are to be made, they must be at once universalised. Local experiment in a service of this type is necessarily confined to minor organisational experiments with local offices; and even then care is needed to see that consequent variations of service, particularly for the worse, are not appreciable.

However, many services lend themselves to fruitful local experiment. In principle this is true of all administrative activities for which a 'one best way' has not been found. Fruitful innovation often depends upon a combination of technical or professional skills with social or political imagination. Thus there is much scope for local experiment over the design of public housing, the layout and management of old people's homes, or the creation of traffic-free precincts. In these cases and many others, a practical demonstration is more worthwhile than theoretical analysis of alternatives, and a bold experiment more fruitful than cautious adaptation of standardised methods.

The problem is: how to achieve fruitful experiments? The field officers of central departments are often in a position to exercise some administrative or professional discretion over individual cases, but they are ill placed to try out local variations of policies or methods. Field officers lack the status and prestige to introduce such innovations, and departmental ministers or senior officials fear political criticism if they treat localities differentially. Departments can and do sometimes carry out controlled experiments in localities over more technical functions such as traffic management, but usually they must introduce more controversial innovations everywhere simultaneously or not at all.

It is possible for experimentation to occur on a functional rather than geographic basis if several national agencies have parallel or overlapping powers. For example, two national housing agencies could be set up, offering different types of housing, or several agricultural agencies could offer similar services to farmers. This type of functional competition occurs frequently among American administrative agencies, but is rather rare in Britain or European countries. Such a method applies a more direct competitive spur to administrative innovation than does the more indirect emulation of localised agencies. However, emulation between localities is a more traditional and less wasteful approach to service experiments.

The elective basis of local government provides a vital political leverage for administrative innovation. It would be wrong, however, to assume that such innovation is usually or mainly rooted in local politics. In Britain, some forms of local experiment have derived from local party politics, a notable example being the introduction of comprehensive secondary schools by the Labour-controlled London County Council. However, this experiment also had a considerable impact upon the development of secondary systems by other local authorities, including those opposed to the idea of 'comprehensives'. The evolution of secondary education has followed the cycle of administrative activity noted above. The experiments in various localities were followed by national acceptance, on a modified basis, of the comprehensive principle which all education authorities were urged to adopt; but room still remains for variations in detail and further local experiment. In far more cases, the party political content of a local experiment is small, and innovation occurs through the personal or professional views of local councillors and local officials.

The contribution of local officials is considerable and sometimes decisive. For example, the British Town Development Act enables small or medium-sized towns to be expanded through an influx of population and industry from large, congested cities. A major factor over whether any town chooses to take advantage of this Act is certainly the personal energy and initiative of its chief official, the town clerk. Local government serves to legitimise the initiative of officials who, if they were servants of a central department, would have much less scope for such activity.[6]

Quite clearly these values of local government experiment only apply in appropriate circumstances. There must be the administrative and financial *capacity* to experiment, which varies widely among local governments and is also easier to satisfy in relation to social welfare than technological innovation; and also the *willingness* to experiment, which depends upon political conditions and administrative staffing, and certainly cannot be assumed since throughout history many local governments, especially rural ones, have been unenterprising. Often it is central government which is the innovator, but as noted above centralised innovation is usually restricted to matters which can speedily be generalised.

Delegation and Devolution

We can now redraw the distinction between purely administrative delegation and the requirements of devolution. In the former case, policies or goals are centrally determined and the local staff are trained to understand them; communications between centre and localty are frequent; local discretion is confined to individual cases within a framework of settled rules; and questions of change and adaptation are handled centrally although local staff may (and should) be encouraged to contribute their experience and suggestions.

This is a reasonable model for the operation of the field service of a central department. The exact degree of the local official's discretion is a product far more of his professional skills than of his geographic distance. Thus more discretion is given to a local architect than would be appropriate for a local clerical officer dispensing financial benefits. This model of limited discretionary delegation is applicable even to field services which must be carried out in remote and scattered places. The US Forestry Service, for example, complies with the model. It meets the problem of the physical remoteness of the foresters through a special emphasis upon training with as much mutual contact and career mobility as is practicable, and indoctrination, so that they understand the aims and methods of the organisation and the necessary limits upon their own discretion. The satisfaction of the foresters seems to depend upon their participation in a fairly centralised organisation rather than upon any idea of being rulers of their own little kingdoms.[7]

The concept of devolution,* on the other hand, assumes that policy-making itself should be divided to some extent between centre and locality. Under this situation, the first requirement of discretionary delegation – namely that central policies should be comprehensively and clearly stated – no longer applies. It is indeed the very existence of a policy uncertainty, or of problems of adaptation to rapid change, which creates the functional justication for devolution. This is the situation in which experiment and variety are intrinsically desirable.

The fact that central policies cannot be stated comprehensively does not mean that they should not be stated clearly. The administrative pathology of devolution is the tendency for central departments to make frequent *ad hoc* interventions instead of determining only general policies and standards. This situation is particularly likely to occur when the central staffs are politically sensitive and compliant, and must respond to frequent pressures for using the power of central government to remedy alleged deficiencies of local government. The political dominance of central over local government will then lead to a situation in which the power of controlling and supervising staffs is undesirably increased in relation to that of the operating agencies.

This is indeed the British situation. Some civil servants have reached the conclusion that the health of some departments, such as Transport, would be improved if they could 'cut their teeth' upon direct operating responsibilities, instead of just supervising the work of others.[8] The full logic of this approach would be the creation of integrated national services, and career systems, with goals centrally determined and full mobility of staff between central and local government. This would be replacing administrative devolution by delegation, which logically entails the resolution of policy uncertainties and the curtailment of local experiments save where these have a strong technical component. This concept of devolution implies a 'partnership' between central and local government, and its difficulties relate not to general principles, which have been indicated,

* The words 'decentralisation' and 'devolution' are loosely and often interchangeably used. 'Devolution' as used here represents a strong case of decentralisation, used here as a general term, as opposed to the weak case of 'delegation'. These distinctions refer to the extent of authority transferred from centre to locality, *not* to the political element in such transfers which is separately considered.

but to their detailed application. Thus any concept of 'policy sharing' has to wrestle with the erratic swings of national and local politics, especially the former. It is not necessarily wrong, as J. A. G. Griffith seems to suggest,[9] that the extent of central controls over local authorities should vary considerably between departments. It is right that the amount of central control should vary with the technical and professional conditions of each service, and with the extent to which uniformity of provision is demanded. What is mistaken is that local authorities should be given stones when they ask for bread. For example, instead of the clearer policy guidance which British local authorities would welcome over town and country planning, they have received delayed countermands over particular decisions. In the case of other services, such as education, policy control was for a time extended (although this is now relaxed) to the undesirable detail of departmental selection of school priorities, which destroyed the rationale of devolution for no appreciable gain. Remedies for these defects require much more specific attention by departments to the tasks of policy planning, and a reconstruction of government machinery so as to mirror the requirements of operating agencies.

The cycle of administrative devolution is extremely hard to work well. It requires subtle judgments about the line between 'major' and 'minor' policy decisions, the stage of development of different services, and the interactions between experiment and conformity. There can be no clear yardsticks for the measurement of the results of devolution, as with the financial tests of accountable management, and no exact science of its operations. The systems can only be judged ultimately in terms of the values which support it, and the extent to which these are actually realised.

POLITICAL DEVOLUTION

A political approach to governmental decentralisation reverses that of the last section, and deals with the intrinsic rights of local communities or regions to some measure of self-government. These claims are not logically or historically dependent upon functional performance, but have tended to become so. Just as an effective approach to decentralisation turns out to require some political basis, so localities claiming self-government need the ability to exercise functions effectively. The political rationale of local or regional self-government therefore needs analysis to discover what basis it provides for a rational framework of functional decentralisation.

This can be done by examining three basic arguments for political devolution and their relevance to modern administration.

1 *The Areal Division of Political Power*

The belief that strong provincial or local self-government is a desirable barrier to the encroachment of the centre, and a necessary safeguard of civic liberty, has lost much of its appeal. As an aspect of separation of powers, this belief provides a justification for federal forms of government; but federations are now more usually seen as the product of special geographic and historical circumstances, or as the necessary palliative for a sharp conflict of political allegiances. In all reasonably successful federations, the steady move towards centralisation of power often makes the constitutional framework somewhat obsolete. In unitary European States, the right of central government to exercise dominant authority is questioned only in those provinces where historical memories of political independence are still active, and elsewhere the contribution of local self-government towards preserving civil liberty is seen as only limited and qualified.[10]

Nonetheless the belief that local democracy has a concreteness and reality which are lacking in broader democratic structures continues to exist, particularly in countries with Anglo-Saxon traditions of government. As a theory of democratic participation and education, this concept still has validity (see below). As a theory of the proper exercise of political power, it is hard to sustain. All forms of representative government have their special advantages and drawbacks. Local government is relatively direct, but for this very reason is subject to the control of relatively small and often stable majorities. The petty interests which often establish an ascendancy over local government are no more objectionable in principle than the large interest groups which sometimes permeate the decisions of central government. There is, however, the difference that fluid majorities usually have greater impact at national than at local level, where the influence of interests or factions tends to be more durable, and where political power is more entrenched. These differences are illustrated by the fact that party politics at national level are frequently volatile, whereas the control of a local authority by the same party or oligarchic group is a very widespread phenomenon.

We need not agree with those European jurists who assert that national political will has a democratic purity and generality which are absent from localised assemblies, to concede that many local governments, especially small rural ones where democratic values are supposedly most palpable, are prone to strong factionalism and a stagnant conservatism. As James Fesler has pointed out, the myths of local democracy pay little regard to the record.[11] An aggravation of local democracy is that the citizens' attention has followed the seepage of power to central government, so that the theoretical values of local democracy are often vitiated from lack of popular interest. This is one reason why central legislatures or departments are often looked to for the correction of local vested interests, and for the overruling of narrowly based local majorities by broader based national ones. It is not the fault of local democracy that this should be so, but it is certainly its misfortune.

The revival of regional sentiments and aspirations in parts of unitary States provides a possible basis for modern political devolution. One difficulty with this revival is that it is extremely uneven, and occurs for the most part in those areas where a historical, cultural, or linguistic differentiation is sufficiently marked to provide a springboard for the expression of more generalised resentment against administrative centralisation. It is no accident that the areas in question are frequently geographically peripheral to the national society and relatively poor in economic wealth. Additionally, such units may form irrational structures for purposes of economic development or functional devolution. Despite these disabilities, the claims of such a region to a high degree of self-government may still be pressed and conceded on the grounds of the wishes of a majority of its inhabitants, assuming that this is indeed the case. Thus J. P. Mackintosh considers that Wales, despite its economic and functional disabilities as an administrative unit, and even the absence of a suitably located capital city, should nonetheless be conceded a separate parliament and a high degree of self-government.[12] Similar claims, of greater historical and functional weight, are often advanced for Scotland; and there are many regions in other States for which 'Welsh' or 'Scottish' types of claim are plausibly advanced.

It should be noted that political claims for regional self-government can be as much a barrier to the effective devolution of power as an aid to its achievement. For example, in the USA financial power has increasingly shifted from the states to Washington, because of the much more egalitarian and progressive character of national taxation. It would seem wholly in accord with the constitutional character of a federation, and also with rational concepts of the devolution of power, that a substantial portion of this national pool should be returned to the individual states in the form of an unconditional grant-in-aid. Such an arrangement has often been advocated, but so long as certain southern states are able to follow racially discriminatory policies which are unpalatable to a national majority, so long will administrative powers which might sensibly be devolved still be retained in Washington. The more conservative and emotional aspects of 'states' rights', and the political claims of a few states, prevent more devolution.

A strong political and emotional regionalism is an obstacle to the general devolution of powers, partly because of its confinement to certain areas, and partly because of the continuing conflicts of sovereignty which it occasions. There are two possible treatments of this type of regionalism. One is to hope that its extremism can be sufficiently abated for the region to share in a more functionally conceived plan of general devolution; the other is to concede the region a special status of semi-autonomy within the national framework or even to allow it political independence. There are no real principles for settling when secession is desirable, other than the possible test of an intelligible referendum, but the 'semi-autonomous' solution clearly will not work unless applied to rare and special cases. A State in which one-third or more of the population lived under such special arrangements while a unitary system applied to the remainder becomes as difficult to govern as the Austro-Hungarian Empire.

2 *The Claims of Local Community*

A second traditional basis for political devolution is the claim of localities to represent meaningful communities that have a high degree of social cohesion and interaction. This claim has been eroded by familiar causes. These include the physical spread and sprawl of cities, the great increase of geographical and occupational mobility, and the growth of community dependence through the provision of standardised welfare services.

It could once be reasonably argued that territorial communities had greater importance than occupational or other forms of association, because of the strength and durability of their social roots. The local territorial community was a 'microcosm of the State', a social and economic sub-system, in ways that could not be claimed for functional groupings. Today these claims seem much less plausible. Geographic propinquity is only one, and not necessarily the most important, of possible bases of social association.

Moreover such community attachments as still exist are diffused over vaguely conceived areas. The town or city has lost the observable frontiers which once helped to nourish civic sentiment. A modern citizen often moves within a concentric set of areas, which may comprise residential neighbourhood, local suburb, major city, and perhaps city region. Each unit may be meaningful to him for certain purposes, but all are vaguely apprehended and defined. Administrative areas are numerous and specialised, and bear only a loose relationship to experience of social and economic life.

Even so, it is possible to exaggerate the disappearance of localised community. Viewed particularly through American eyes, one can discern a society in which functional groupings have almost completely replaced territorial ones, producing Melvin Webber's state of 'community without propinquity' and the 'non-place urban realm'.[13] This picture does not square with the considerable revival of local neighbourhood and amenity societies, nor with sociological findings that the working and social lives of a majority still occur within fairly narrow bounds; often, for example, within the confines of one London borough. We have allowed the life-style of the man in the grey flannel suit to create an exaggerated picture of the mobile society.[14]

The decline of local community has created much searching for more meaningful geographic units, and the favourite product of these inquiries is the city region as created by modern transport. A pioneer of this thinking was H. G. Wells,[15] who based his advocacy of 'mammoth municipalities' upon the range of an hour's train ride. As Wells in fact foresaw, motorisation has increased the volume but not the ambit of daily travel, and a range of about fifty miles from the centre of a major city remains its usual limit, the bulk of journeys being much smaller.[15]

Numerous later concepts of the regional city or city region have been developed. One important distinction is that between the more or less continuously urbanised area, which corresponds to the UK census definition of 'conurbation', and the wider urban region defined by such criteria as overall population density, commuting zones, frequency of social and economic contacts, and the catchment areas of specialised services provided by a major centre. The first three of these criteria find a place in the US census definition of 'metropolitan area' and the fourth is the basis of Derek Senior's definition of city region, which provided the basis for his powerful memorandum of dissent to the proposals of the English Royal Commission on Local Government.[16]

The concept of a continuously urbanised area or conurbation has provided the basis for many schemes of local government reorganisation such as those for Greater London and Metropolitan Toronto. However, this concept does not adequately include the expanding but loosely structured zone of growth which surrounds all great cities or conurbations. In Britain, the adoption of protected green belts sometimes pushes this zone of growth still further afield. However there are many difficulties over the definition of city regions, whose boundaries depend upon which of many possible tests are applied. In addition smaller city regions can be descried within larger ones, and there is much overlapping between the service areas of rival centres. It seems unlikely that the urban hierarchy (in so far as it can be distinguished) will become more uniform and clearcut, since increasing mobility encourages the dispersal of activities among numerous places. Proposals for basing governmental units upon the concept of the city region encounter the greater difficulties in relation to the largest cities or conurbations. The resulting units would have to be enormous, amounting in the case of the London region (as H. G. Wells also recognised) to a sixth or more of the area of England.

Inhabitants of rural areas and smaller towns often resent the city region idea, viewing it as an imposition of the requirements of urban dwellers upon those of the surrounding hinterland. Traditionally the more rural areas were dependent upon urban wealth for the provision of services, so that a merging of areas carried advantages. This is still the situation in many countries. However, in Britain and the USA, and increasingly elsewhere, many rich ex-urbanites live beyond the cities, and increasingly it is the inner areas of large cities which have problems of poverty. Under these conditions there is little incentive for the surroundings areas to merge with a major city, and land use conflicts are endemic. The needs of a great city for water supplies, building land, recreational areas, and many other purposes can only be satisfied by 'invasions' of its hinterland, and commuters or ex-urbanites are usually the first people to resent others following in their footsteps or changing the 'character' of their favoured retreats.

For these various reasons, the city region offers rather a tenuous and slippery basis for the construction of new political communities. Its political visibility is rather low. Unlike the traditional town or village, its structure requires an imaginative effort to apprehend. The common interests of its inhabitants derive not from history, kinship, or culture, but from their apprehension of joint functional needs and problems. These functional needs are also differentiated and ideally require different areas for their performance. However, they share the common features that they cannot be well performed by traditional units of local government, and that some definition of city region offers a fairly satisfactory basis for their joint provision.

The most obvious problems shared by the inhabitants of a conurbation are those of traffic and transportation. One obvious danger of this situation is that a metropolitan or city regional authority, if such is created, may be unduly preoccupied with traffic and transport questions, since these form the one subject for which broad policies can be persuasively advanced. The demand for easier movement looks beguilingly simple. For example, in its first decade the Greater London Council concentrated primarily upon planning an elaborate network of urban motorways, subsequently much modified, because other goals which it was also established to promote – such as the protection of the urban environment and more equalisation of housing opportunities – were intrinsically much harder to promote.[17] Part of the problem is that functions such as housing, land use planning, water supplies, etc. need ideally to be organised upon a city regional rather than conurbation scale.

There are other types of geographic unit having common governmental problems. Examples are specialised economic regions, especially those dependent upon a narrow industrial or agricultural base. The problems of industrial decline and unemployment have forged a common political consciousness among the inhabitants of the north-east of England far greater than that possessed by the inhabitants of any city region; yet the claims of regional development depend upon national economic support and have limited relevance for the local management of public services.

There are also regions whose interlocking problems of natural resource development offer an administrative challenge equivalent to the quite different problems of the developed city region. The best-known example is the river valley basin which has related problems of flood control, navigation, irrigation, hydro-electricity, forestry, water supplies, agricultural conservation, recreation, tourism, and the construction of new communities. This complex of environmental functions also calls for co-ordinated administrative action, and for the political consciousness necessary to support it. It is a curious fact, however, that no elective governmental unit has as yet been based upon a river basin.

The conclusion to this section must be that natural units of geographic community, such as once existed, cannot easily be identified or re-created. However, we need not stop at this negative conclusion. Geographic areas can be identified which have important functional needs in common, and such common interests can provide the basis for a growth of political consciousness and activity. The most significant of such areas is the city region, despite the latter's problems of definition. However, the creation of a 'city region' authority entails such a broad area that political understanding or acceptance of its desirability is hard to achieve. Purely 'metropolitan' types of reorganisation require a large first step in government reorganisation.*

The concept of the city region could not provide an adequate basis for a general reorganisation in any case, because of the very variable size and fluidity of such units and their limited relevance to sparsely populated areas. However, the concept could make some contribution towards a more rational and politically acceptable framework of decentralisation. If, for example, a pattern of regional and local government were to be created, the larger city regions would form a good foundation for some of the regional units. Elsewhere the regional units would have to be based on other factors such as traditional provincial sentiments (where such exist), communication patterns, the structure of smaller city regions, and also distinctive rural zones as defined by the needs of agriculture, conservation, and recreation. Within these regions, local units could be based to some extent upon miniature city regions, e.g. a focal medium-sized town and its service area; or in populous areas upon urbanised sub-units such as the new London boroughs.†

3 *Participatory Values of Local Democracy*

A third basis for political devolution is offered by the participatory and educational values of a localised democracy. The number of local councillors is a vast multiple of the members of a central legislature, and small units increase the amount of participation. The values stressed by J. S. Mill are still relevant. Local government familiarises a large part of the public with the tasks and problems of government, and thereby alleviates discontents, strengthens political understanding and moderates abstract dogmas.

These values retain also their highly localised context. The most

* Description of urban units will escape the best attempts at definition. Metropolitan in this context is clearly a misnomer, yet it has become extensively used in a sense roughly equivalent to large city or conurbation; and again conurbation was rejected as a definition of Greater London by the Royal Commission on London Local Government on the ground that it does not comprise several towns run together but a vast single city – which was indeed a crucial basis of the Commission's argument for a unified government.

† A plan somewhat along these lines is contained in the 'second-best solution' put by Derek Senior to the Maud Commission. See the proposals on pages 83–92 of his Memorandum of Dissent, as revised on pages 143–6 (HMSO, Cmnd 4040 I, 1969).

functionless of English local government units, the parish council, emerged from the deliberations of the Redcliffe-Maud Commission as a much more significant focus of interest and activity than much larger and stronger bodies. A social survey done for the same Commission discovered that a majority of people identify local community with a town only if it has under 30,000 inhabitants, otherwise looking to a neighbourhood of local streets.[18] The highest polling in local elections used to occur in small urban district councils (now abolished), which were otherwise not very remarkable bodies. The strength of localism and parochialism in its literal sense is shown by the readiness, even eagerness, of councillors to belong to unimportant bodies.

These participatory values seem to have decreasing relevance to the management of public services. In England it seems to be the theme of reforming committees that two types of councillor are now needed. There will be a relatively small but important group of policy- and decision-makers, who necessarily will become half-time or full-time politicians; and a much larger group whose tasks will be criticism and advice, not policy-making or part-time administration.[19] Such statements may be admirable as expressions of the requirements of the system, but it is doubtful whether they correspond to either the wishes or capacities of those concerned.

There are several ways of trying to preserve the valuable traditions of local participation. One is to leave the present set of local councils in existence, with their established powers, and simply to supplement or gradually supersede their efforts through the creation of more functionally effective agencies. This corresponds to the American idea of 'substitute administration', but it leaves sedimentary layers of government whose existence is a source of financial waste and democratic confusion. Secondly, powers may be transferred to a higher level of government, but some discretionary authority handed back under schemes of delegation. This is a favourite British device, although it has not worked very well. Finally, one can accept the full logic of the growing split between functions and localism, and reduce existing local councils to a purely advisory role, transferring executive powers to a higher (also elected) level. This was the approach of the English Commission, somewhat modified in application by the provision that existing councils might retain very limited powers, if they had the wish and capacity.[20]

The assignment of an advisory role removes that experience of actual administration which has always been a special merit of local self-government. It places local councils on the side of all those protesting groups and societies which form a growing feature of modern government. Useful as such bodies might be, they cannot directly bridge the gap between administration and public, or reduce ambivalence and ignorance about modern government. If the local democrat's role is to be an advisory one, it might be better discharged through the creation of local advisory committees on a functional basis. This would give more specific recognition to the councillor's role as consumer's champion, but under circumstances in which he could invoke no legal authority to remedy grievances.

The rationale for a modern system of political devolution is inevitably a hybrid affair. W. J. M. Mackenzie states that 'English local government is justified because it is a traditional institution. It is justified because it is an effective and convenient way to provide certain services. It is justified because we like to think that our central government needs the kind of qualities which are best trained by local self-government.' [21] But none of these reasons is sufficient on its own. Tradition alone is inadequate. The second justification is contingent upon functional performance; and the third one is cautiously stated – after all, most Members of Parliament do not have experience of local government, and those that do have not shone especially – and in any case is affected by the changing role of local representatives. Yet Mackenzie may be right to suppose that belief in local government is axiomatic in England.

It seems more probable that local government is acceptable as a balancing factor in the total scheme of administration. It concedes a very limited influence to local opinion over the operation of public services; provides a basis for a limited amount of experimentation and variety; sets a certain distance between the tasks of policy-making and execution; and offsets the frequent reluctance of the Exchequer to finance further development with the demands of local clients for better services. The last point needs explanation. When local government is highly dependent upon local taxation, it is liable to be parsimonious about social services, but when financial partnership prevails, the local interest in service improvements is likely to exceed that in economy. However, this situation produces its own dysfunction. If local authorities have insufficient motive to act economically, they will be controlled more closely, particularly in societies where resources are perennially scarce and there is a heavy stress, rightly or wrongly, upon central economic management. This is the position in Britain and in France, although the USA remains rich or prodigal enough to dispense with pervasive forms of central economic control.

ROADS TO REFORM

Pressure is growing for the creation of larger units of local government. This is illustrated by the politics of metropolitan integration, which has become a live issue in many of the great urban complexes of the USA, Canada, and Britain. The structure of local government, as it has grown from ancient roots and under the influence of the local autonomy principle, presents a variegated and fragmented pattern. Pressure has built up for reorganisation plans which often founder upon the diverse interests and wishes of the existing local government representatives, and upon the inchoate state of public opinion. Nevertheless, the line of development seems to be (slowly) towards metropolitan reorganisation. The reasons for this can be seen by considering the operative values at stake.

Pro-Reform	*Anti-Reform*
Rationalisation (economies of metropolitan scale	*Competition* (spur of diverse administrative units)
Equality (concepts of common citizenship, common standards of service, pooled costs)	*Diversity* (value of local autonomy)

The first pair of values reproduces within the governmental sphere the familiar disputations of economic theory. The economics of scale which produce big business also push towards metropolitan integration, where such functions as water supply, main drainage and sewerage, main highways, recreational facilities, hospitals, higher education, etc., can be planned and organised to serve a vast urban population more effectively than is possible with a fragmented system. The counter-arguments for competition seem, under modern technological conditions, to be practically rather weak, although ideologically (as with economic thought) somewhat stronger.

In the USA the competition favoured can be either that between geographically contiguous local authorities, of which great numbers cluster in metropolitan areas, or between different vertical levels of government providing overlapping and hence partly competitive services. The second approach is the more politically persuasive, and could support an extension of state activities in metropolitan areas;

but both forms of functional competition produce formidable problems of policy co-ordination, and considerable obstacles to political understanding and effectiveness.

The second pair of values represents an equally familiar tension, with (again) the pro-reform value steadily gaining strength. The increased mobility of the population; the decline of local particularism and community feeling; the pressure for high common standards of education, health, etc.; resentment against idiosyncratic service and tax levels; all these factors point in the same direction. They operate with great power in a small, ethnically fairly homogeneous country like the UK, with lesser but still considerable power in the USA, where suburban municipalities have more privileges to protect and much more leverage for their defence.

The likely pace of development towards more integrated forms of metropolitan government can in fact be plotted according to three factors:

1 The rate at which the pro-reform values are gaining over the anti-reform values in terms of their generalized diffusion and appeal.
2 The specific institutional conditions which may block or divert reform movements.
3 The particular power balance existing in a metropolitan area.

I think it is likely that the first settles the general direction of change, the second settles its precise institutional character, while the third settles its precise timing.

Recent developments in Greater London and Metropolitan Toronto sustain this thesis. The device of independent investigating commissions is an institutional aid to local government reorganisation in both Britain and Canada. In the London case a particular political situation was probably decisive for the timing of change. The Conservative Government, which appointed the investigating Royal Commission and initiated legislation on the basis of its report, was certainly not unhappy to dispense with the existence of the Labour-dominated London County Council. It is true to say that only the Conservatives could have reorganised London government.*

* But I would certainly reject the thesis that the membership of the Royal Commission was deliberately packed to get a desired result. If nothing else, the 'rules of the game' prohibit this kind of act in Britain; also, if the reorganisation of London government was a party political move, it was singularly ill-generalled. The exclusion of certain fringe boroughs from the new Greater London Council, done under pressure from local Conservatives, helped to ensure that the GLC entered on its history with a firm Labour majority.

In Toronto a precipitating factor was the financial embarrassment of some suburban municipalities.

However, the basic significance of changes in cultural values is also evident. In the case of Toronto, there has been particular objection to the wide spread of school costs and standards, and criticisms of the ineffectiveness of the smaller suburban municipalities. Armed with this evidence of the local relevance of the general values listed in my scheme, it would not even have required knowledge of the local power structure to predict the proposals of the one-man Royal Commission which re-examined the structure of Metropolitan Toronto. In fact the Commissioner's proposals included (1) virtual unification of the school system and (2) amalgamation of thirteen municipalities into five.[22]

In the USA plans for metropolitan reorganisation are often blocked by special institutional barriers. Chief among these is the position of the states, which are generally small enough to regard their metropolitan areas (particularly if consolidated) as powerful rivals, while effective consolidation would also involve a substantial realignment of state boundaries. Very possibly, the 'metropolitan state' would today represent a more rational organising principle than the historic state, but it will not easily be considered in that light. Further the traditional behaviour of state legislatures has led to home-rule charters and other devices for safeguarding local government autonomy which act as barriers to change. In addition, the 'anti-reform' values of competition and diversity still have more appeal in the USA than in Britain or in Canada. Yet it is possible that the complex structure of metropolitan government acts as a protective shield enabling these values to be drawn on for the benefit of particular interests to a much greater extent than they are really held.

The political and social effects of metropolitan integration also need consideration. It is contended by some American political scientists that such schemes are undesirable, not simply because they lessen functional variety and competition, but also because they reduce the political protection available to ethnic minorities. The political machines of big cities were built upon the special favours which they performed to ethnic minorities, and it is claimed that such groups suffer from 'Anglo-Saxon' ideas of municipal reform, which put their emphasis upon impersonal service and technical efficiency, not the special favours and welfare services which the poor need. In a big metropolitan authority the blacks and the poor would be heavily outnumbered, and governed in ways that are said to be less to their taste and advantage than the practices of the city machines.[23]

The practices of the one-time London County Council were poles apart from those of an American city machine, yet some of the objections to this authority's abolition followed similar lines. The LCC contained a high proportion of relatively poor people, and its welfare services were of a very high order. The substitution of the much larger GLC brought in a large majority of middle-class suburbanites, more concerned with roads and traffic management than with welfare services.

These arguments are too particularist to be wholly convincing. The existence of a welfare-minded authority like the LCC seems to be the result of special circumstances and traditions, rather than of any general form of local government organisation. It was natural for Labour stalwarts to deplore its passing, but there can be no guarantee that a system based, for example, upon the separation of rich and poor, or of inner and outer areas, would produce the desired effects. In the USA, the city political machines are in any case losing some of their grip and shedding their traditions. The numerical and cultural ascendancy of middle-class suburbanites over the urban poor may be a growing problem of modern society, and some types of local government system may help to alleviate it, but which ones is less certain. An effective two-tier system has advantages from this standpoint. Many of the new London boroughs are carrying on the welfare traditions of the LCC.

Stronger units of local government certainly favour the devolution of power. There is less need or pretext for the supervision of 'weak' authorities; less need to supplement local staff with specialised or technical resources; and more scope for effective local or regional experimentation. These gains will be further consolidated if the system of decentralised government is more uniform as well as stronger. However, the scope for uniformity is qualified by the different requirements of densely and sparsely populated areas.

The administrative and political balance should also change. The scope for methods of integrated management and long-term financial planning which are open to large authorities require corresponding changes in the methods of central departments. Instead of detailed 'vertical' control by departments over functional allocations of expenditure, it is preferable to let a local authority establish its own 'horizontal' priorities between various services and projects. One implication is that central government approval of local financial outlays should be concentrated in one department, and confined to general review of the authority's total requirements, based on long-term 'rolling' estimates. Departments will still be able to insist upon the achievement of appropriate minimum standards of service, but they will have to desist from financial control of particular projects. Large local authorities also require senior officials and staff of a very high calibre. It is clear that such staff cannot be attracted, and will not function effectively, unless there is reasonable local freedom to plan service developments.

It is difficult to predict the political strength of large local authorities. Apart from the obvious political pull of size, the answer seems to turn upon patterns of political recruitment. Theoretically a system of elected regional councils might either become stepping-stones for ambitious politicians en route for central legislature, or else the focal points for a distinctive regional politics of protest against the centre. Except in very differentiated or disaffected regions, the former development would seem much more likely in all countries where national political parties are strong. However, it seems quite likely that some specialisation of metropolitan or regional politics will usually occur, helped along by the continuation of quasi-amateur traditions of political life in countries such as Britain. The persons who already serve on such bodies as regional economic planning councils, regional hospital boards, and the Greater London Council are indications of the possible scope of political recruitment to large authorities. While the element of party ambition is not absent, many of these people are primarily interested in regional and local government, and still seem ready and able to put in largely unpaid public service.

However, there are also limits to the reduction of central controls which could result from a more rational system of decentralisation. Nothing can remove the ascendancy of national finance, service standards, and general policies, where there is the wish to exercise it. A reasonable devolution of powers requires political and administrative restraint at the centre, based on recognition of the costs and frustrations of detailed interventions.

A reform of local government finance is often regarded as the key to more effective devolution. This viewpoint tends to overlook the great superiority of national over local taxation in respect of progressiveness and flexibility. It is extremely hard to find any satisfactory major source of local or even regional taxation other than the much maligned rates or property tax. The fact that rates are somewhat regressive is not a basic objection so long as they form but one element of a generally progressive system of taxation; yet it is essential to make local property tax as equitable as possible if it is to provide the essential basis for a degree of local autonomy.

Whatever financial reforms are achieved, it seems inevitable that local or regional authorities should depend upon the central Exchequer for a high proportion of their resources. This conclusion is reinforced by the fact that no enlargement of local areas will of itself equalise resources; very substantial differences will remain: even large regions differ substantially in wealth and the poorer ones could not manage without substantial national or (in Europe) international aid. The best prospects for reform, therefore, are that central financial aid should be given in the form of a single financial grant, allocated according to general criteria of needs and resources; that central financial control should be exercised (as already suggested) through the consolidated approval of current and capital budgets; and that departmental requirements about service standards or policy advice should be laid down quite independently of financial control.

This essay has questioned some frequent beliefs about the rationale of local self-government. It has not accepted that the maximisation of consumers' preferences is an adequate argument for maximum local autonomy, because small units are liable to be even more neglectful of their minorities than are large units (and no system can be constructed to prevent minorities). Moreover local service variations express not so much the variability of local 'needs' or service demands as they do variations in available resources, political party strength, and administrative talent. The popular pressures for removing service inequalities that are due to local poverty or to political cum administrative inertia are everywhere much more powerful and apparent than is the existence of a demand for genuine diversity of local service provision. Once the political and cultural barriers of 'localism' are down, the case for such diversity requires a sophisticated understanding of the policy process.

On the other hand there is an important *administrative* case to be made for local self-government which has two prongs: the decentralisation of overloaded government machines, and the conditions of innovation and experiment. Some services may be best managed in a uniform way and could be wholly centralised, but many services require a mixture of minimum standards and central guidance together with local innovation. Innovation necessitates not only professional skills but a local political base which can provide both political impetus and legitimacy. Hence it is best done through partly autonomous elective authorities.

The specifically *political* case for such bodies depends upon the traditional values of widespread participation in the work of government, coupled with recognition of territorial forms of community.

Unfortunately these two values tend to be maximised at an organisational level that is too low for modern functional purposes, while appropriate geographic units (such as the city region) often lack political appeal. The reform of local government is about the reconciliation of these conflicting considerations and offers many complex alternatives.

A large devolution of power is improbable in modern States, save perhaps to particular regions which successfully assert their right to self-government. Nor is it desirable. High common standards of service are reasonably expected and demanded, and some aspects of economic and physical development should be centrally planned. The role of regional or local units of government is to execute public services effectively, to allow for experiment and flexibility, and to achieve a 'horizontal' co-ordination of functions and resources as balance to the much too dominant vertical lines. This type of devolution is needed as much for functional as for political reasons, although both are important. Rational decentralisation requires a partnership between centre and locality, and a blending of administrative and political considerations. This circumstance constitutes both its difficulty and its challenge.

NOTES

1 According to one survey, university research projects (1972) included: Local and regional government 46, Central government of the UK 0! Admittedly this is for various reasons a slightly misleading impression. Richard A. Chapman, *Teaching Public Administration* (Joint University Council for Social and Public Administration, London, undated).
2 Lord Redcliffe-Maud, an ex-civil servant, was chairman of both the Royal Commission on Local Government in England (reported 1969) and the Committee on the Management of Local Government (reported 1967).
3 For a defence of local government complexity, see Edward C. Banfield and James E. Wilson, *City Politics* (Cambridge, Mass., 1963).
4 Sidney Webb, *The Evolution of Local Government* (1899, reprinted London Municipal Journal, 1951).
5 J. A. G. Griffith, *Central Departments and Local Authorities* (London, 1966).
6 Peter Self, *Cities in Flood* (London, 2nd edn, 1961), chs. 3 and 4.
7 Herbert Kaufman, *The Forest Ranger* (Baltimore, 1967).
8 This point of view is particularly expressed in relation to education and to highways.
9 Griffith, op. cit., ch. 8.

10 Arthur Maass, *Area and Power: a Theory of Local Government* (Glencoe, Ill., 1959).
11 James W. Fesler, 'Approaches to the Understanding of Decentralization', paper given to sixth world congress of the International Political science Association (1964).
12 John P. Mackintosh, *The Devolution of Power* (London, 1968).
13 Melvin M. Webber, 'Community Without Propinquity' in Lowdon Wingo Jr. (ed.), *Cities and Space* (Baltimore, 1963).
14 See for example, Graham Lomas, 'Labour and Life in London' in D. Donnison and D. Eversley (eds.), *London; Urban Patterns, Problems, and Policies* (London, 1973).
15 H. G. Wells, *Anticipations of the Reaction of Mechanical and Scientific Progress upon Human Life and Thought* (London, 1914). See also D. Senior (ed.), *The Regional City* (London, 1966).
16 Royal Commission on Local Government in England, Report, vol. 2: Memorandum of dissent by Mr D. Senior (London, 1969).
17 Peter Self, *Metropolitan Planning* (Greater London Papers, no. 14, London School of Economics, 1971).
18 Royal Commission on Local Government in England, Report, vol. 3: Research Study no. 9, Community Attitudes Survey.
19 Report of the Committee on the Management of Local Government ('Maud' Committee, London, 1967); The New Local Authorities: Management and Structure ('Bains' report, London, 1972). See also A. Eddison, *Local Government: Management and Corporate Planning* (London, 1973).
20 Royal Commission on Local Government in England, Report, vol. 1, ch. 9.
21 W. J. M. Mackenzie, *Theories of Local Government* (Greater London Papers no. 2, London School of Economics, 1961).
22 Royal Commission on *Metropolitan Toronto* (Goldenberg Report) (Government of Ontario, Toronto, 1965).
23 Banfield and Wilson, op. cit., and E. C. Banfield, *Political Influence* (New York, 1961).

5

The Problems of Devolution – the Scottish Case

JOHN P. MACKINTOSH

In 1931 Professor Robson wrote *The Development of Local Government* which was a handbook for all students of the subject. In 1947, he reissued his book with a new Prologue which set out his philosophy and fears in detail. In 1966, he reprinted the Prologue as a separate book, *Local Government in Crisis,* and in all of these he sounded a genuine note of alarm. Professor Robson argued that if local government was to have any vitality, it must be given a reasonable degree of independence from central government and sufficient scope and resources to have a separate and vital existence.

Considering the conditions necessary to exercise these powers and to have the requisite vitality, Professor Robson came to the conclusion that the top tier would have to be larger and cover what were, in effect, regions of the UK. For many of his students these ideas were an inspiration and I went on from the Prologue to look at the situation in Scotland. There, local authorities were weaker than in England, services were performed unevenly by a staff with fewer professional qualifications and it was hard to persuade people of adequate ability to stand for election. In time, more and more control passed into the hands of the regional department of the Civil Service, St Andrew's House.

I recall being inspired by Professor Robson's work to look afresh at Scottish government, not from a nationalist point of view but from his standpoint as one who wanted a more democratic and vital form of local self-determination. The result was a series of articles published in *The Scotsman* in 1957 in which I urged that Scotland be treated as a single region of the UK and a two-tier system of local government established. The top tier was to be an all-Scottish elected authority which would take over the powers of St Andrew's House and of all the *ad hoc* administrative boards that had been established. Beneath this Scottish authority, there would be a second tier of local districts with minor functions.

No one took any notice of these proposals. They were easily defeated at successive Labour Party Conferences. (The Scottish National Party – SNP – was then a group of cranks suffering from an inferiority complex or from Anglophobia, to quote Hugh McDiarmid's hobby from *Who's Who*.) Only in Northern Ireland, in the *McCrory Report* of 1970, was such a two-tier system of a single regional government and a series of subordinate district councils recommended, and by then the Northern Irish situation had deteriorated too far. In the late 1960s, however, royal commissions were appointed to report on local government reform in England and in Scotland.

The Scottish Commission under Lord Wheatley began by declaring the all-Scottish Assembly or Parliament outside its terms of reference as it involved 'constitutional questions'. It proceeded to advocate a regional two-tier system with seven regions and a number of districts, but one of the regions, Strathclyde, was to include 2½ million people – half the population of Scotland. These regions, according to Wheatley, should have more powers and independence than the old county councils in the hope of attracting better councillors and of giving local government some real policy-making scope.

Meanwhile, the SNP suddenly began its rapid climb to significance. Starting with 62,000 votes (2·5 per cent of those cast) in 1964, it shot up to 839,000 votes or 30 per cent of the total in the election of October 1974. All this happened while the leadership of the Scottish (and British) Labour Party was declaring that nothing needed to be done and that the demand for more self-government would disappear in a day or two.

In pursuance of this policy, in 1969, the Labour Government sought to tide over the forthcoming general election by appointing a royal commission under Lord Crowther and later Lord Kilbrandon, called The Commission on the Constitution. While it sat, SNP support grew and the party captured its second seat at a by-election in Govan. The recommendations of the Wheatley Commission were looking more and more out of date. The SNP was fuelled by the successive failures of British parties and British governments to meet the legitimate aspirations, in economic terms, of the electorate.

While most Scots had had a dual nationality, part Scottish and part British, events ranging from loss of Empire to relative economic failure led them to devalue the British aspect and to lay more emphasis on their Scottish features. Meanwhile, and in consequence, SNP strength grew. At the general election of February 1974, the Nationalists shot up to 23 per cent of the poll and won seven seats.

The major parties, till then inactive over the Report of the Commission on the Constitution, decided to take action. The National Executive of the Labour Party twisted the arm of the Scottish Executive until a specially convened Scottish conference of the Party reversed its anti-devolutionist stand. The Scottish Labour Party adopted a proposal for a directly elected Scottish Assembly in August 1974. But the proposal included two riders: the post of Secretary of State and the full existing number of Scottish MPs (71) must be preserved.

On this ticket, the Labour Party went in to do battle in the second general election of 1974 and though the Conservatives lost a further four seats to the SNP, Labour just held off the challenge, though the SNP rose to second place in Scotland with 30 per cent of the poll. Many Scottish Labour MPs attributed their survival to their advocacy of an Assembly and, directly the election was over, they pressed the Labour Government for action. The Prime Minister responded by appointing a 'Devolution Unit' in the Cabinet Office to prepare the necessary Bills. The timetable was a Bill in late 1975 to be enacted in the 1975–6 session with elections to the new Scottish Assembly or Parliament to be held in May 1977.

If, by the end of the decade, an effective and respected Scottish Parliament is an established part of our institutional framework, then 1975 will be seen, in this perspective, as one of the formative years. But the events of 1974, the decision taken by the Scottish Labour Party that August to create an Assembly, the Labour victory (with the SNP coming second) at the General Election in October and the subsequent creation of a devolution unit in the Cabinet Office to frame a Bill, will probably only be regarded as preliminary steps in a long and arduous journey.

While the rise of the SNP and the worries of the major British parties have been enough to start the process, it is not evident that there is sufficient political pressure to overcome the very difficult obstacles that remain. The devolution unit is headed by two English ministers (Mr Short and Mr Fowler) and though both realise that a half-hearted measure would be worse than nothing at all, they are also conscious of the need to reassure English MPs, many of whom have serious doubts.

The Scottish and Welsh Under-Secretaries in the unit are both genuine devolvers and the former has committed himself to a thorough-going measure since he took office, but it is not clear that his views are accepted throughout the Government.

Part of the difficulty that those preparing the Bill face is that the Government's commitments include contradictions and the resulting confusion helps to conceal very serious political problems.

The first difficult commitment is that the office of Secretary of State is to be retained. But it is quite impossible to devolve political decisions on any reasonable scale to a Scottish Parliament while leaving the Secretary of State with his present authority. Two different authorities cannot take the same decisions.

A Secretary of State could be kept merely to deal with the annual argument about the allocation of any extra funds to Scotland, but this would scarcely be enough work to occupy a Cabinet Minister and the situation would lead to constant embarrassment as the Secretary of State had repeatedly to explain that he was no longer responsible for Scottish health, housing, education and so on. On the other hand, if the Secretary of State is to remain responsible for overall policy in these fields, this would mean that the Scottish Parliament operating through its executive could be allocated only trivial powers.

Besides being politically unacceptable, to divide authority in this way would build in a constant source of conflict between a Minister supposedly still 'Mr Scotland' and a Scottish executive backed by a directly elected Parliament wanting to pursue distinctive policies.

An alternative, now apparently favoured by the Scottish Labour Party Executive, is to transfer all the St Andrew's House powers to the Parliament but keep what are called 'the economic powers' and control of the new Scottish Development Authority for a Secretary of State who would remain a member of the UK Cabinet. Thus there would be someone to put 'Scotland's case' to the Prime Minister and the rest of the Cabinet when there was a British policy decision which affected Scotland; for example if the British Steel Corporation wanted to close its plants north of the Border or if the Admiralty was preparing to close naval dockyards, including Rosyth.

While it may be true that a Secretary of State inside the UK Cabinet can exert strong pressure and that Mr Ross has got more for Scotland than Mr Brian Faulkner, as Northern Ireland's Prime Minister could get by inter-governmental negotiations, part of the reason is that Scotland has 71 MPs and Northern Ireland only 12. Also, could a Conservative Secretary of State deciding which areas and industries should be encouraged live with a Scottish Labour Prime Minister and Parliament who had to build the roads, provide the houses, the water and the drainage?

It seems to be a recipe for conflict. The more logical division would be to leave all the national powers to control overall economic policy to London but to transfer the application of aid within Scotland and questions of location of new industries to the Scottish Parliament. Also it is doubtful whether any Parliament which had nothing to do with jobs or employment or the distribution of industry would be acceptable in the current climate of Scottish opinion.

The second Labour Party commitment which is causing great difficulty is the insistence that the present number of Scottish (and Welsh) MPs at Westminster be maintained. Yet both these countries are now over-represented and while it may be possible to make a case for extra MPs for peripheral areas in a highly centralised state, it is hard to do so once a considerable area of domestic policy-making has been transferred to Parliaments sitting in Edinburgh and Cardiff.

Moreover there was ample evidence in recent debates on devolution that English MPs of all parties would not tolerate over 100 Scottish and Welsh MPs casting the deciding votes on English health, housing and education, while they were prevented from having reciprocal powers over Scottish and Welsh affairs. But there is the grave complication that to reduce the Scottish and Welsh representation at Westminster to the same proportion to population as obtains in England would, in effect, cut out more Labour than Conservative seats and, had this been done since 1945, there would have been no Labour Governments in 1964 and 1974.

Even if it was politically feasible to reduce the number of Scottish and Welsh MPs to the same proportion to population as in England (cutting seven Welsh and fourteen Scottish seats), this would not completely solve the problem. There would still be English resentment that the Scots and Welsh were having their political cake and eating it. Also, the effect might be to make Scots and Welsh MPs at Westminster into second-class citizens.

They would be frowned on in debates on English domestic questions and would be largely restricted to broader UK questions, on which many of them have shown little interest in the past. And when Scottish and Welsh affairs arose, perhaps the London Government would prefer to deal directly with those who would claim to be the authentic spokesmen of these countries, their elected leaders in Edinburgh and Cardiff. It is worth recalling that it was on this problem of the status and powers of Irish MPs at Westminster that Gladstone's Second Home Rule Bill foundered.

In addition to these contradictions in the commitments accepted by the Labour Government, other more straightforward problems still present acute difficulties. There is the key question of the functions to be developed. On this, on the quality of those elected and on the capacity of the Parliament to make some evident impact on the people of Scotland, rests the political viability of the entire exercise.

Bound up with this is the further question of the financial resources available to the Parliament, the methods by which it is elected and the overall British political milieu in which the newly established Parliament will have to operate. Now, when the Bill is being framed, is the time to discuss these subjects so that the public can form its opinions and exercise a helpful influence.

If the question of the appropriate powers is taken first, there are two clear-cut positions – the minimalist and the maximalist – each based on a fairly coherent philosophy. The minimalist fears that every concession to the case for devolution is likely to produce demands for more.

Those taking this view accept that a gesture must be made to meet immediate pressures but only enough to give Labour (or Conservative) candidates some ammunition while they wait for the British economy, the country's self-confidence and its prestige at home and abroad to revive. This school of thought also fears that any elected authority will consist of party hacks who have not been able to obtain selection for parliamentary or regional constituencies and so its scope to do damage, both in terms of making the nationalists' case and of general incompetence, must be severely limited.

This approach wants to emphasise that the elected authority is merely an assembly; the less like a parliament it is, the better. Thus, it favours the committee system rather than the ministerial system (the latter would produce that dangerous exemplar, a Scottish Prime Minister).

The minimalists also want to keep the main lines of policy in the hands of the Westminster Government. Education would be devolved but not the fixing of the school-leaving age or teachers' pay and conditions. Agriculture would be assigned to the Assembly but not the fixing of those prices which were outside Brussels regulations and so on. At the same time, the local government regional and district councils would be preserved so that the Assembly would be left a narrow slice of subordinate policy-making sandwiched between a Secretary of State and St Andrew's House which settled the broad principles of policy and the regions and districts which actually supplied the services.

The maximalist view considers that to grant such limited powers would be to get the worst of all worlds. The result would satisfy neither the devolvers nor those still opposed to any decentralisation, while it would present the SNP with an open target for attack.

The maximalists would want to give the widest possible powers to a body to be called a Parliament with a Prime Minister and a Cabinet and all the normal parliamentary procedure. (On a small point; it should sit in Parliament House and not in a disused school or church hall.) The objective would be to create a body with such scope that able Scots who had not hitherto contemplated a political career would be enticed into standing. Also, once elected, the members, whether nationalist or not, would be absorbed by the task they encountered and not inclined merely to complain about limitations on their powers.

In time, their inclination might well be to ask Westminster to resume certain functions because these were better run on a uniform basis for the whole of the UK or because they were too great a burden on the finances of the Scottish government. Thus the objective of this approach is to find a viable level of devolution which would last and, far from being a stage on the slippery slope to total independence, would concentrate the Scots' minds on what was best settled in Edinburgh and what ought to be left to London (or Brussels). This would remove any sense of grievance about remote control and, as a result, would confirm the unity of the UK.

In the post-war history of federations, there is no doubt that the maximalist view has some validity. Relations between central and state governments in the various federations have varied but, in all countries where there has been a genuine degree of local autonomy, there has also been a tendency for some powers to drift back to the federal government.

This has happened in the United States, Canada, Australia, India and West Germany. On the other hand, where, as in France, there has been only a limited concession of purely administrative powers to the departments, public discontent has remained and there has been continued pressure for a more genuine form of regional self-government.

The one example there has been in the UK of a local parliament also supports the maximalist case. The Stormont Parliament created in 1920 was an administrative success (the communal political problem was not the product of this institution), it lasted for 50 years and it established a distinctive local role while voluntarily handing back a number of important powers to Westminster. The minimalists will say 'quite so, but why not accept this and arrange by law for the Scottish and Welsh Parliaments to receive only those powers that Stormont ultimately decided to retain?'

The answer is that in psychological and political terms, there is a world of difference between subordinate parliaments deciding, as the German State Governments have done, that it would be preferable for higher education, originally allocated to them, to be shifted to the central government and an open assertion by the centre that the local parliaments are not fit to handle higher education. Also, such an attempt to divide each function between the central and the regional parliaments involves too much rigidity and neglects changes in fashion and in the cost of certain services.

So there is the strongest case that the Devolution Bill should be drafted on maximalist lines and that the Scottish Parliament should be given all the functions of the Secretary of State, including the Scottish end of regional development powers, the location of industry and the Scottish aspect of the Ministries of Energy and of Transport. With such extensive powers, a Scottish Parliament could have real scope and, therefore, a real chance of being a success.

What are the chances of the proposed Scottish Parliament having the extensive powers which would, in this view, be essential if it is to establish itself as a vital and effective governmental institution; as a stopping point short of independence which really satisfies Scottish aspirations for greater self-government?

One must be frank. At the moment, the chances appear slight. The most telling weakness is that no senior or significant Cabinet Minister is publicly committed to this policy. The Secretaries of State for Scotland and Wales are the key figures. Both in the past opposed devolution and though now both are prepared to accept the need for some move in this direction, there is no evidence as to whether they are prepared to do battle for the maximalist solution.

On the other hand, a number of English Ministers regard the whole exercise not merely as a concession to nationalism, but as an unfortunate tendency where any real changes are likely to have dangerous consequences and must be kept to a minimum. No UK departmental Minister will want to lose the Scottish end of his operations and those ministries which are already purely English will want to reduce the risk of a Scottish Government engaged on the same tasks embarking on embarrassing experiments or alternatives of priority.

With no Minister strongly committed to the policy, much will depend on the Civil Service and it seems likely that the only coherent proposals around which the arguments will take place will be those contained in the papers put up by Whitehall and by St Andrew's House. For a while, Lord Crowther-Hunt was in charge of thinking on this issue but, though he is still playing a part in the preparation of the Bill, his chief responsibility is now in the Ministry of Education.

Furthermore, his Minority Report to the Kilbrandon Commission shows that he is a minimalist. He wants the main lines of policy on all issues to be reserved for Westminster and Whitehall. He considers that a Scottish Assembly (as he would call it) ought to operate through committees rather than through a cabinet system and that the Assembly should look more like a large county council than like a subordinate parliament. Judging by recent debates, this would appear to be acceptable to Welsh Ministers and most Welsh MPs but it is certainly not enough to satisfy Scottish devolvers in or out of the Labour Party.

With this broad division of opinion in the parties and, one suspects, within the Government itself, will there be any pressure for a more thorough-going solution from the Civil Service? It is to be feared that, though many in St Andrew's House are Scottish bred and educated, they may shy away from recommending a maximalist approach.

The reason is clear enough. These very able and dedicated men are not diverted by party loyalties or by any idea that they are part of a UK governing élite. They have only one loyalty and that is to the task in hand. They want to see Scotland well governed.

When I put my fears about the attitudes of Scottish civil servants at a seminar in Edinburgh University, a senior official rose to correct me. He said neither he nor his colleagues objected to working for a Scottish Cabinet, provided they were satisfied that it could do the job.

And are they so satisfied? There are many reasons why they may well have doubts. First, they may fear that the calibre of those elected will be inadequate. One of the basic ideas of the recent reform of local government was that given greater powers and more freedom from central government control, new, more capable and more representative people would be attracted into local government.

But, in the event, the Civil Service refused to diminish its power to guide and control the new regional and district councils and, looking at the composition of these councils, they may well feel that their caution has been justified. They may fear that the Assembly will be composed of Glasgow Corporation and Strathclyde Regional Council rejects, a few landed gents and a large number of SNP members who would have a vested interest in the experiment failing.

The other source of Civil Service advice is the Whitehall departments. Recently, at a social occasion in London, I found myself among a group of senior civil servants. Before any introductions could be made I asked one of them what he did. 'Oh,' said he with a grimace, 'I am on the devolution caper.'

'Do I take it, you would define the word "caper" as an essentially silly and meaningless performance conducted simply for the effect it has on those watching?' 'That sums it up perfectly,' he replied.

While the advice of St Andrew's House officials is of paramount importance when the transfer of Scottish Office functions to the Assembly and its leaders is being settled, Whitehall's views will be taken into account when those powers currently exercised in Scotland by the Departments of Trade and Industry, of Employment, of Energy and of Transport are being considered. Above all, the two Whitehall departments that will matter are the Civil Service department which will be commenting on the impact of the proposals on the structure of government and on the Civil Service itself, and the Treasury which will be concerned about the amount of money a Scottish Government will have at its disposal and its capacity to act in a manner which might not fit in with the economic policy in vogue at any particular time in London.

On the first point, if all the powers of St Andrew's House are transferred to a Scottish Parliament and Executive, then does Scotland have a separate Civil Service with its own recruitment? Will this end the practice, from time to time, of transferring senior officials from Whitehall to Edinburgh and vice versa? But if an attempt is made to leave some overall policy powers in agriculture, education, health and housing with the Secretary of State and the London Cabinet, which civil servants will work for him and which for the Parliament's Ministers? And can UK-recruited civil servants looking to eventual promotion to top jobs advising the Secretary of State or other UK Ministers be loyal to a different set of Ministers at an earlier stage in their careers?

It seems essential to make a split between the officials responsible to different political masters but such a horizontal cut across the functions and personnel of St Andrew's House would create enormous difficulties.

Then there is the question of the financial and economic powers of the Parliament or Assembly. From the recent White Paper on

Public Expenditure, it is clear that the Treasury would not concede powers to tax or to spend money which would in any way diminish the Treasury's capacity, real or imagined, to control aggregate demand. The question is whether the Treasury would still want powers to authorise or to refuse particular items of expenditure so that certain uniform standards could be enforced and to ensure that its concept of value for money was accepted.

The problem is that the monies available to a Scottish Parliament would probably only be enough to maintain existing services. To do something new or different would involve either raising more by taxation or cutting existing services or getting a bigger grant from the Treasury. It is hard to see that department granting much scope in any of these three directions.

The Scottish Parliament would be reluctant to levy higher petrol duties, car licence fees or income tax than the rest of the UK while Whitehall would certainly be unhappy at special Scottish policies designed to save money (such as a reduction in the school-leaving age). And if the Assembly asked for a bigger grant, there would inevitably be a demand for close supervision of how the extra was spent.

Besides the St Andrew's House and Whitehall civil servants, many others will have doubts about the merit of a thorough-going policy of devolution. The new regional councils will just have started and they will put up a struggle to prevent the Scottish Parliament having powers to alter the framework of local government. But if the present regional system remains, this reduces the scope of the Parliament very seriously. One would expect a Parliament with a desire to be really effective would end the regional councils (it could keep them as administrative units with their staff) and have only one subordinate level of government, the district councils.

In addition, the universities will fear what some of them will regard as 'local government control' and they will struggle to remain part of the UK University Grants Committee system. The doctors, likewise, having fought off control of the area health boards by the regional councils, will certainly fight against direct control by elected representatives in a Scottish Assembly. Scottish industry has shown some fear that such a body would be Left-wing dominated and might press for a reduced level of economic powers.

Facing all these real problems in creating an effective Scottish Government, together with the opposition of so many articulate and influential pressure groups, it is not clear that there are any senior Ministers determined to see that the policy is carried through for its own sake. No one, at that level in the Government, would have wanted to push through a Devolution Bill had there been no SNP challenge at the last two elections.

Both Mr Short and Mr Fowler recognise that if the Scottish Parliament or Assembly is to achieve its political objectives, then it is pointless to produce such a weak body that no one is impressed or satisfied. The only virtue of a concession to pressure is if the force behind the pressure is diminished. About 66 per cent of Scottish voters in successive polls say they want 'more self-government' but not total independence. The effort of overcoming the very complex problems involved in devolving adequate powers will only be worth while if this section of the populace do feel they have got what they wanted.

If, despite all the difficulties, a Scottish Parliament is established with the full powers at present deployed by St Andrew's House, with some of the functions of the United Kingdom economic departments and adequate financial resources, is the institution likely to last? Is the position of 'more self-government without total independence' a stable one which can attract public support and retain reasonable stability over a period of time?

The evidence from the various federations in the Western world, where the position of the subordinate assemblies or parliaments is often buttressed by special constitutional provisions enforced by a supreme court, is that there tends to be a drift of power in favour of the central government.

The regions find certain functions too expensive for them and accept loans or grants in return for implementing uniform, nationwide schemes (for services such as health or the provision of unemployment benefits). In addition, it is not always clear that the regions or states produce an adequate standard of political life, though national leaders have come from the states in the United States, Canada and Germany.

But is a new Scottish Parliament, created not so much for its own intrinsic virtues as to ward off nationalist pressure, likely to attract the kind of people it needs and will it be able to avoid having its powers sucked back by Whitehall and Westminster?

On the quality of people available, at present there is no group or coterie in Scotland with experience of governing at that level – for obvious reasons. Many in other walks of life have shown an interest in the idea of a Scottish Parliament, but it must be remembered that the candidates who are likely to win the elections will have to come through the political parties.

The elections are likely, at least at first, to be actively contested. Electors will be mobilised by the party machines on the basis of traditional loyalties and it is hard to see many Independents being successful. So the question is how many of those who have an interest in standing are prepared to go through the humdrum work of party meetings and accept the limitations imposed by membership of a party in order to be able to play a part in the Scottish Parliament?

Then there is the problem of which system of election should be adopted. The Labour Party have declared themselves in favour of the present single-member constituency as it is familiar and would, they think, give them a large majority equivalent to their majority among Westminster MPs (forty-one out of seventy-one).

But the single-member system only just managed to produce this result last October with the Labour Party getting 36 per cent and the SNP collecting 30 per cent of the votes cast. According to the present timetable, the elections for the Scottish Parliament should take place in the spring of 1977. If, as seems probable, the two years between now and the elections are difficult with living standards not rising (or falling), serious inflation and unemployment, it is only necessary for the SNP to pick up 3 per cent and the Labour Party to drop 3 per cent for the single-member system to produce a nationalist majority in the Scottish Parliament.

It may seem cynical to evaluate electoral systems on the likely results, but when the main object of creating a Scottish Parliament is to establish a satisfactory political situation short of independence, it would be foolish to proceed in a manner which produced the opposite result; a Parliament whose majority did not seek to satisfy the desire for more self-government but to arouse and stimulate a more extreme passion for total separation.

Even if the Labour Party won a majority in 1977, with the SNP clearly the main Opposition party, in time there would probably be a reaction against the majority and this would then give the SNP control.

Also, part of the object of setting up a Scottish Parliament would be to involve the SNP in the practical task of governing the country. The value would be that the Nationalists would then become immersed in housing, education, Highland development and so on; so that a combination of arguing about these issues and of visiting London and Brussels to co-ordinate policies and compare plans might convince them that the days when small countries can maintain the fiction of total national sovereignty and political self-sufficiency are over.

For all these reasons, a system of proportional representation would seem to be best. It would mean that the SNP would be likely to be included in the new Scottish Government, but they would have to share office with one of the parties which was keen to make the Scottish Parliament work and become established as a viable institution.

At the same time, the kind of proportional representation which leaves the party machines in complete control of the list of candidates should be avoided. A system of largish constituencies with several members elected on a preference vote or a combination of single-member seats plus a national list allocated on a proportional basis (as in Germany) would seem to be best.

It would also be important to ensure that Westminster MPs could stand for the Scottish Parliament. Some in the minority parties and some in the major parties whose chief interest in Scottish domestic affairs would want to double up (as Gerry Fitt did when Stormont was in existence).

If, among those elected, there were some Westminster MPs, some regional councillors of the calibre of Geoff Shaw or Peter Wilson and some of the prominent figures in other occupations who have political affiliations but have not yet stood for office, then the new Parliament would get off to a good start.

The question that remains is whether a Scottish Parliament led by the Prime Minister and Cabinet it selected could do enough or have sufficient impact to build up public confidence and become an accepted and valuable feature of Scottish life.

It must be appreciated that such a Parliament would not have a markedly greater share of UK resources to devote to Scottish affairs. The Kilbrandon Commission pointed out that if UK expenditure per head on the kind of functions that could, in a maximalist solution, be devoted to a Scottish authority was taken as 100, then Scotland got the most of any part of the UK at 129 per head. For political reasons, it might be sensible to earmark part of the revenues of North Sea oil for the Scottish equalisation grant, but whatever the source, so long as this island remained a United Kingdom, no one area is likely to be more than 29 per cent per head better off than the average.

If there were therefore no extra resources available so that Scottish school teachers could not be paid more than their English counterparts or more motorways built than had been planned or a sudden leap forward made in the provision of health centres, what could a Scottish Parliament do that was new or distinctive? The answer can only be in terms of its capacity to handle matters better than the present system.

Take, for example, the management of Scottish education. Just now, it is hard to say who takes the decisions or provides the leadership. One thing is clear. The Scottish politicians can contribute little. They have, perhaps, one 2½-hour debate a year on the subject plus some questions. Cooped up in Westminster during the week and running from one constituency engagement to the next at weekends, they cannot be in touch with all the aspects of the educational scene at home.

As a result, Scottish educational policy muddles through as the consequence of English decisions, and with Scottish local variants proposed by the inspectorate and by the St Andrew's House civil servants with some ideas coming from the universities, the colleges of education and certain influential teachers. But it is a confused process without any central point or focus and with no one responsible for imposing any pattern or coherence.

A Scottish Parliament with a full-time Minister of Education and, it would be hoped, a Select Committee on Education, could provide a centre and a stimulus for thought on Scottish educational questions. Then the unrest which largely escaped public notice and erupted in the recent industrial action over pay might have been understood and the blunders over teachers' pay avoided.

In any case, Scotland would have had its own version of the Houghton Committee with the profession and local political leaders fully represented, so that Scottish needs and deadlines would have been the first priority.

Such examples could be multiplied. The health service in Scotland is run by a complex mass of cross consultation between the various professions, the area boards and the St Andrew's House department. Because there is no centre of political authority which can listen to the various arguments and then take decisions, most moves can take place only on a basis of total consensus. So everything is slowed down; the ability to impose a veto is more important than the capacity to give positive leadership.

To cite only one example, to change half a dozen empty and closed maternity beds in Peebles Cottage Hospital to geriatric beds (where there is a queue of patients waiting) takes 18 months of consultations.

But while it could do many things so much better by having the time and the capacity, a Scottish Parliament could not regenerate the Scottish economy if the UK was in a depression.

Existing aids to industry could be used to greater effect. The

Regional Employment Premium at present is given to all industrial firms so that this lavish subsidy is doled out to the oil companies in the North-east who do not need a penny of it while less is available for struggling firms in remote areas far from the oil boom. Nevertheless, though existing monies could be better used, Scottish wages, investment and employment rates would still be dependent on the conditions prevalent in the UK economy.

And this is, in fact, the central point. Most of the drive behind the SNP has come not from a desire for a Scottish Parliament but from disappointment over the performance of the UK economy. If there was a continuous boom, then the problem in political terms would probably disappear whatever instituional reforms were introduced.

Yet it is a pity not to make the best of even the most depressing national problems. If it is accepted that greater self-government in the various parts of the UK (including the English regions) is desirable, then it is a mistake to quibble about the particular conditions that make the necessary changes politically acceptable.

But it must be appreciated that there are also considerable dangers. This policy of devolution could have been carried out easily in the early 1960s.

After the Hamilton by-election of 1967, it became harder as the policy appeared to be a concession to SNP pressure. Now, after the two 1974 elections, it is even more dangerous, since to create an emasculated Assembly that pleased no one would not meet the basic objectives of more local self-government and would also strengthen the Nationalists.

It is to be hoped that there is enough political push and realism to get the problem solved and an effective, powerful Scottish Parliament established now, as a further failure leading to a renewed attempt to find an adequate answer after a debacle at the next General Election may be too late.

6

Instrumental Participation and Urban Government

L. J. SHARPE

I

Recently, a publisher's advertisement made the claim that 'participation has become one of the most popular words in the language of politics'. If we allow a little commercial licence (the remark was made in relation to a book on participation which the publisher was promoting), this claim does not seem to be far from the truth, for, in so far as it is possible to talk of common trends, participation does seem to dominate a great deal of current theorising about politics; moreover, it has also come to dominate a great deal of political activity too. Participation, in short, is in vogue in both thought and action. I would like to deal very briefly with the thought first.

It is impossible to mark the precise beginning of the vogue since such movements of opinion seldom have a precisely identifiable beginning, but evolve via the confluence of diverse trains of thought and practice and once established often develop a capacity for self-sustaining growth independently of causes by a process of repetition and emulation. Bearing this cautionary thought in mind, the essay by Duncan and Lukes, published in 1963, is as good a starting point as any.[1] In it the authors are mainly concerned with attacking two interlocking and dominant schools of thought about democracy on both sides of the Atlantic during the 1950s. The first was exemplified by, among others, the writings of Talmon, Lipset and Morris-Jones.[2] To cut a long story short, this school argued in the name of personal liberty that participation had no special relationship to democracy. The non-participation or apathy of the electorate was an important attribute of Western democracy: the right to be apathetic was both a reflection of the avoidance of ideological conflict and of the freedom from constraint enjoyed by the individual in liberal democracies – the 'liberal' prefix was usually *de rigueur* in this literature. This situation was to be contrasted, so the argument ran, with the position of the individual in totalitarian States where participation was demanded from above, the better to oppress the individual in the name of some version of the general will.

The second and more numerous group which Duncan and Lukes attacked was the 'value free' empirical research school exemplified by Berelson, Burdick, and Milne and Mackenzie [3] which, on the basis of survey findings, found that most people did not participate much in politics beyond the act of voting. The empirical school therefore concluded, following Schumpeter,[4] that democracy ought to be redefined around the notion of competing élites for whom the mass were able to express their approval or disapproval from time to time at the polls. Like the personal liberty school, public apathy was seen as a positive good since like the existence of groups it tempered the inherent tendency in mass democracy to irrationality, authoritarianism and class conflict, all of which could threaten the stability of the democratic State. The competing élites model was not only closer to reality, it was what ought to be in any case. At this point the two schools joined hands since both seem to have been dogged by the cold war and in consequence gave the highest priority to the maintenance of stability in existing democracies in the face of what was seen as the totalitarian threat from the eastern bloc. Precisely what the link was between instability and totalitarianism was rarely specified and much of the argument seems to have been designed not so much to reveal the conditions for totalitarianism as to find excuses for defending the *status quo* in Western democracies however much it might have departed from the democratic ideal. At the heart of the matter for both schools was the claim that democracy was merely a method of government and implied no ultimate ends.

Duncan and Lukes's case for participation as a necessary condition for democracy against both schools rested on two claims. The first, mainly directed at the personal liberty school, was that the classical democratic theorists advocated participation precisely to avoid the oppression of the individual: as they emphasise, only the individual himself can adequately judge and safeguard his own interests, and they add a quote from J. S. Mill in support of this contention: 'in the absence of its natural defenders the interest of the excluded is always in danger of being overlooked'.[5] Duncan and

Lukes saw no reason to believe that active participation of this kind in defence of individual interests necessarily led to coercion and the libertarian school was merely a more up-to-date version of the anti-democratic fear of mob rule. The fatal weakness of the personal liberty school, they conclude, is that 'no middle way is conceded between the concentration camp and a cautious conservatism'.[6]

The second prong of the Duncan and Lukes case for the restoration of public participation as an integral feature of democracy is mainly directed against the empirical school. The founding fathers of modern democracy, they point out, 'never claimed to be simply describing existing reality, for they were asserting, at least in part, a set of ideals'.[7] The ideal that participation served was the realisation of the moral autonomy of the individual. Such realisation would not be easy nor swift, but it was an essential aim of democracy. It therefore followed that classical democracy was not rendered unrealistic or Utopian because it had not been realised in practice. It followed, too, claimed Duncan and Lukes, that the Schumpeterian competing élites theory could not be an adequate substitute either.

There can be little doubt that Duncan and Lukes make out a very convincing case and the influence of their refutation of what was then the current orthodoxy can be traced through much of the literature that emerged subsequently which attempted in a more elaborate way to restore participation to its original central place in democratic theory.[8]

Boiled down to its barest essentials, the case for popular participation that this new school has promoted is first, that it is necessary for self-protection, and second, that it elevates those who undertake it.[9] These two functions are what Parry has termed the *instrumental* and the *developmental* roles of participation and Verba and Nie have called *instrumental* and *consummative*.[10] Together they form the cornerstone of classical democratic doctrine reaching back to Aristotle.[11]

II

So much for theoretical preliminaries. In the realm of practice, considerable impetus was given to the emerging theoretical debate on participation that the Duncan and Lukes article reflected by two developments. First, there was the direct action movement that sprang up in this country during the latter half of the 1950s as a wing of the much wider Campaign for Nuclear Disarmament (CND) which sought to abolish British nuclear weapons.[12] This was eventually called the Committee of 100. Briefly, the objective of the direct action wing of CND was to achieve the aims of CND not by the conventional techniques of cause groups – even those of fairly activist ones like CND – but to take physical action to disrupt the operation of military installations by occupation or to disrupt the normal processes of urban life by mass 'sit downs'. The aim was not so much directly to affect government defence policy but to gain publicity and win converts to the nuclear disarmament cause.[13] Now it should be emphasised at this point that direct action participation did not begin with the Committee of 100 for it has been a traditional feature of British politics whether undertaken by trade unionists, suffragettes, or squatters. In the main it has been pursued by those who wish to promote changes in public policy that none of the major parties are willing to support and who are not prepared to wait in the hope that one of the parties will change its mind. All that is being claimed by citing the direct action wing of CND as a progenitive movement is, first, that it appeared after a long lull in direct action politics. Leaving aside the short-lived squatters movement of 1946–1947, there has been a gap of some twenty years since the direct action politics of the 1930s. Secondly, the new movement seen in retrospect does appear to mark the advent of a new *Zeitgeist* that has influenced a wide range of new political movements on both sides of the Atlantic. Indeed it directly influenced [14] the second development in the practical expression of the new participation to which we must now turn.

This development has its main roots embedded in the spate of federal legislation in the United States during the early 1960s that was designed initially to combat juvenile delinquency and then later the whole 'culture of poverty' in the inner city.[15] That this legislation should have generated a whole new dimension in the developing debate on participation and provided the means whereby these theories could be given practical expression was to some extent fortuitous since the primary purposes of the enactments were conventionally redistributory and ameliorative. The catalyst was the somewhat vague requirement that the implementation of the Economic Opportunity Act of 1964 should entail the creation of 'community action organisations', which meant bodies which were 'developed and conducted with the maximum feasible participation' of the residents of the areas that were involved. The requirement had been inserted almost as an afterthought into the Act.[16] Afterthought or not, it gave a new, powerful and officially blessed impetus to the direct action movement that had already been established some years before in the southern states and found expression in consumer boycotts, voter registration and school desegregation drives on behalf of the blacks. It was this direct action element that was gradually absorbed into the wider community action movement, but in its early stages had been influenced by the example of the Committee of 100.

The essence of the community action movement was 'self-help': the formal political institutions had failed to help the poor, so the solution lay in bypassing them, creating a new system of 'counter-government competing against the established government',[17] centered in the locality and run if possible by the poor themselves through a technique of more or less permanent mobilisation of those affected.[18]

Although most of these federal programmes have since been wound up or very severely curtailed, the participatory self-help doctrines they inspired have made a considerable impact on local politics in other countries. In Britain this influence has taken a number of forms and has affected not only the theoretical debate,[19] but also has precipitated a whole new style of what has been called 'micro-politics' at the local level[20] and influenced a number of official reports.[21] It may also be discerned, suitably moderated in the British fashion, in the various positive discrimination policies pursued by central government since the late 1960s, particularly the Education Priority Area Programme, which aims at improving the educational opportunities of school children mainly in inner city areas and includes the stimulation of parental participation in the programme.[22] It also underlies the community development projects of the Urban Programme which covers a wide range of public services and is aimed at combating the multiple deprivation of inner city dwellers by pumping in extra public resources and creating new community organisations.

Community action provides a useful title for this type of radical participation since, in a more secular age, it is a more acceptable appellation than moral elevation. However, it does in fact embrace both aspects of the central aims of classical democratic theory noted by Duncan and Lukes in the sense that it is both instrumental and developmental in intent. It is also worth noting that this participatory movement, because it embraces both aspects, is also internally consistent with classical theory, since the two forms are interconnected and self-sustaining. Only by exercising power can the man in the street acquire the ability to defend his own interests. As Duncan and Lukes pointed out, 'through the possession of legal rights men become capable of properly exercising them, and thus they approach that moral autonomy which is the true end of life'.[23]

III

The rediscovery of participation as a central feature of democracy in the early 1960s which we have just explored has, of course, had many other offshoots in addition to these, including a much more rigorous examination of the way in which conventional representative democratic processes may exclude certain policy options by reifying the interest of dominant groups into the institutional arrangements of government, or by restricting the spectrum of acceptable policy choices.[24] The rediscovery of participation has also led to a renewed interest in workers' control and the democratisation of the authoritarian procedures of industrial organisation.[25]

Similarly, it has sparked off a new interest in the decentralisation of urban government to very localised institutional forms and purposes. This we may call the neighbourhood government movement.[26] In one sense the neighbourhood government movement epitomises the whole of the new participation, for one of the strongest common threads running throughout its literature and practice is the demand for citizen involvement and control at the point of execution of public policy: at the front line or retail outlet of government. In short, decentralisation of political power and the new participation have been inseparable partners. For this reason it is at first blush somewhat surprising that the new participation has not led to renewed interest in the role of conventional local government as an instrument for improving the quality of democracy. Yet despite the central importance given to it explicitly by the founding fathers of modern democratic theory who always figure predominantly in the new participation literature (Tocqueville and J. S. Mill, and implicitly by Rousseau), there is hardly any interest in local government *per se*. An exception to this is Dahl who as something of a convert to the new participation sees the city as 'the optimum unit of democracy in the 21st century'.[27] But even he has somewhat modified this view in a later work.[28] Local government is one of the institutions – arguably the most important – in modern representative democracies that provides, if only for reasons of scale, an avenue for popular participation in the primordial sense that it is more accessible than national government to the recipients of many public services and in this respect meets the requirements of instrumental participation better. Above all, it provides the opportunity for ordinary men and women to pursue developmental participation to an extent that is impossible for central government.[29]

The reason why local government has been shunned is not hard to find since the community action movement, and to a lesser extent the direct action movement, had their origin in the deficiencies not of central but of local government and community action has been directed against the deficiencies of local rather than central government. Even if this were not so, a strong hostility to formal government in whatever form is to be expected given that there is a strong anarcho-syndicalist element in the tenets of community action and an equally strong populist element as well. The first is derived from the direct action wing, for although there are strong Gandhian elements in the theory of direct action as April Carter has concluded, 'The major influences on the current conception of direct action have been anarcho-syndicalism'.[30]

The populist element in community action seems to be derived from its American origins in the sense that the American democratic tradition tends to view government almost exclusively in terms of the popular will. Most of the formal institutions of government are thus objects of suspicion since they can become autonomous of the popular will and therefore potentially oppressive. Weak government, or even no government at all, is almost always to be seen as being democratically superior to strong government.[31] So, although the instrumental aims of community action are fairly clear-cut, in the sense that they are essentially collectivist because they seek to obtain a shift in power and resources in favour of the poor, the institutional arrangements for effecting such a shift are much less clear-cut and tend often to dissolve into hazy nostrums involving the permanent mobilisation of the poor and the avoidance of any kind of permanent institutions above the level of the neighbourhood group on the grounds that all formal organisations have an inherent tendency to bureaucratisation and to the abuse of power. As one, by no means unsympathetic, observer has put it, some community activists are 'apt to mistake noise for action, forgetting that it is easier to hold up the traffic and get on to television screens than to create administrative structures and professional procedures with the staying power to bring about a continuing improvement in the living conditions and life chances of poor people'.[32] If Parry's claim that one of the fundamental weaknesses of the classical theory's emphasis on participation is that 'the modes of participation were insufficiently specified',[33] then it would seem to be *the* fundamental weakness of the community action school. All the benefits of the collective control of collective action are demanded without any of the costs. Given such a world view, it is hardly surprising that the party-dominated, highly professionalised, cumbersome and necessarily somewhat remote character of present-day urban government is not seen as a suitable instrument for community action.

IV

So much for the community action wing of the new participation. I would now like to turn to another of its main features so far unmentioned. This is a more purely instrumental form of public participation that is much more difficult to trace to any theoretical origins and seems likely to have emerged irrespective of the growth of direct action politics or of community development legislation in the United States. This form of participation, although it does adopt direct action tactics on occasion, is not necessarily concerned with redistributive public policy, or with teaching the inarticulate and under-privileged how to defend their interests, still less with any notion of enhancing the moral autonomy of the individual in pursuit of a truly democratic society. It is essentially a much more prosaic demand of those affected by public policy to have a say in the determination of that policy as such and has no particular connection with combating poverty or multiple deprivation. The rest of this essay will be devoted to a discussion of this form of participation as it has affected British urban government, especially land use planning. But before doing so, it is important to emphasise that this participatory form seems to have arisen at about the same time as community action and also appears to share some common origins with it that have not been discussed so far.

Both forms, for example, seem to reflect the general crumbling of authority; to form part of the so-called 'crisis of authority' that seems to be occurring at all levels of society in Western democracies, whether in government at both the central or local level, the school or the university, the national industrial bargaining table or the shop floor, or in the attitude of the media to those in authority. Put in its crudest terms, the general public seems to be much less willing than it was in the past to give those in authority the benefit of the doubt when interests are in conflict. Precisely what the origins of such a fundamental and pervasive change in public attitudes are attributable to must necessarily remain in the realm of conjecture, but arguably one factor is the disappearance of the cohesion-inducing effect of an external threat to the State. Europe at least has experienced no major conflict for nearly thirty years, nor is one in prospect. It is at least plausible to assume that such a long period of peace has weakened those bonds uniting nations which we like to think have more laudable origins but which were probably more closely associated with war or threat of it.

A second sense in which community development shares a common origin with instrumental participation is the more obvious fact that the increasing scope of modern government and its increasing centralisation has meant an increasing disparity between the promise of democracy and its actual performance. At the risk of over-simplifying what is a notoriously unresolved problem, it is reasonable to suppose that if democracy is to mean anything it is that the individual elector has some direct say in the way the society in which he lives is governed. But, given the scale of most democracies, this is impossible to achieve except for a tiny handful of the electorate. The individual elector's participation in his own government is limited to very little beyond the act of voting. He may in addition seek to persuade governments to a certain course of action, either as an individual or through an organised group, but beyond this his ability to participate has effectively passed to a representative.

Given the scope of government and its complexity, however, the role of the representative is necessarily limited and he too has to relinquish a direct hand in government to an executive – a cabinet or a president. The emergence of the mass political party has modified even further the elected representative's link with government and the massive growth in state activities, entailing as it does the creation of a swarm of quasi-independent public agencies that lie outside the formal processes of public accountability and control, has intensified this remoteness. Both the executive and the public agencies have in turn to rely on a vast army of full-time technical specialists and bureaucrats for the actual execution of government business. The success of this long chain of control depends on a shared sense of public trust in government. This is an aspect of representative government we will return to in a moment. Meanwhile, it must be emphasised that if the representative's participation in the process of decision-making is now remote, then by definition the individual elector's is even more remote. In other words, in attempting to reconcile the modern nation state with the democratic ideal, the participatory role of the electorate has to be largely nullified. The growth in public pressure for participation of whatever kind doubtless reflects public frustration thus engendered.

These would seem to be the limits of the more important share origins of the two participatory movements. Where they clearly differ, as we have noted, is that the instrumental wing does not necessarily have an egalitarian intent, nor any concern with the fundamental basis of democratic government. It is usually solely concerned with power relationships, and as such may be positively inegalitarian in effect. One of its principal characteristics is that it seems to be part of a wider growth in consumerism in advanced industrial societies. I shall return to the link between instrumental participation and the consumer movement and some of its other origins later; at this stage it needs to be emphasised that, broadly interpreted, instrumental participation precisely because it is instrumental has had a pervasive influence that may be discerned in most of the more recent developments in British politics from the increasing volatility of party allegiance and the growth of cultural nationalism to the rapid growth of local conservation societies. I would now like to look at its impact at the local level where it has wrought important changes throughout local government and has been particularly important in land use planning.

V

The promotion of instrumental participation is one of the ostensible objectives of the new land use planning process inaugurated by the 1968 Town and Country Planning Act. The fact that land use planning was the first major local service to adapt its procedures in recognition of the public demand for instrumental participation is hardly surprising since land use planning raises problems of public acceptability in a peculiarly sharp form. Unlike other major services such as education or housing, it may have few tangible or visible outputs and operates on a lengthy time cycle. Whatever their cost, the public can appreciate the products of the education service because it can see them in the form of new schools or more 'O' level passes within a fairly short time interval and without necessarily impinging on private property rights. Planning outputs, by contrast, almost always interfere with private property rights in often dramatic and sometimes poignant ways for reasons that are not immediately comprehensible to the general public and evoke considerable hostility towards the planning process: the aged widow dispossessed of her home to make way for a road widening; the small family shopkeeper driven out of the city centre to make way for a new shopping precinct at rents that will be far too high to allow him to return. The claimed benefits that are to accrue from these changes – better traffic flows, or a more congenial shopping environment – are problematic or too abstract to have a wide public appeal. Sometimes they may be too technical and therefore incomprehensible, or so delayed in their ultimate fruition as to be to all intents and purposes unrealised.

The new system, by requiring that the structure plan consists of a statement of the plan objectives and the reasoning behind them (instead of the detailed land use map that was the 'plan' under the old system), is intended as an important gain for public participation at the public inquiry on the plan or to give it the new name, 'examination in public'. But the advantages gained by objectors from being given a clearer target to shoot at may almost certainly be outweighed by the fact that the general public are normally interested not in abstract objectives, but in precise land use changes preferably set out in visual terms on a map so that the effect of change can be more easily judged.

In practice then, the new participatory arrangements will mainly benefit those of the public who have the expertise to argue their case, or who can command such expertise, but it will not necessarily benefit the ordinary citizen. Indeed, the ordinary citizen will have no automatic right to appear at the examination as he did under the old system. His automatic right to participate will be confined to the local plan inquiries and there will be no appeal from the local plan inquiry to the minister as there used to be under the system that operated prior to 1968.

The second participatory gain that the new system seeks to achieve is public consultation in the early, formative stages of the plan-making process when some of the key decisions which predetermine the ultimate character of the plan are inevitably made. Under the old system, practice varied considerably up and down the country, but generally speaking the planning process was for most of the public a closed one. Even when the plan was in its final form prior to ministerial approval, it was difficult to evoke public interest and many planning authorities made little attempt to change the situation.

The broad proposals for enhancing public participation contained in the 1968 Act have been translated into operational processes by the Skeffington Committee.[34] As a result of their proposals, consultation with the general public can now take place at various stages of the planning process for both structure and local plans. Of particular importance in this context is the requirement that the planning authority put forward alternative proposals at the initial stage of the plan-making process.

The precise reasons for these changes are difficult to unravel but it has been alleged that given the pressures created by instrumental participation one motive was a desire by the planning profession to bypass the elected councillors and generate a direct quasi-political relationship between the professional planner and the electorate. Whatever the truth of this interpretation, it is certain that these changes have the broad support of the professional land use planners. Half of the members of the Planning Advisory Group,[35] from whose report the 1968 Act stems, were professional planners working in local government. To some extent the profession's support for the new public participation procedures is hardly surprising since those of the procedures governing the preparation of the new structure plans prior to central approval, as we have noted, offer *less* opportunity for detailed criticism by the public. Greater participation at other stages of the planning process is seen as compensation for this loss.

It is also likely that the new participation procedures were seen by the profession as a gift-offering to win back the waning support of the general public and so safeguard the future of planning as a public service. Whether they will succeed in doing so must be a matter of conjecture. What cannot be denied is that these new opportunities for public participation have coincided with a sharp increase in public dissatisfaction with all aspects of environmental planning both for land use and for transportation. This is what we have called instrumental participation and this is as good a point as any to examine its implications for a public service like planning, for they cut deep to the very basis of the service, to what may be called the operating ideology of planning.

In a representative democracy where, as we have noted, the bulk of decision-making has to be made at three removes from the electorate by full-time, non-elected professional specialists, the system can only work if there is implicit public trust of government. That is to say, however disagreeable particular policies pursued by government may be, there is agreement that collective action is necessary and agreement on the broad techniques and modes of operation employed. Thus, to take the example of public education, there may be political conflict about the location, type and size of a school, but everyone – elector, representative and technocrat – is broadly agreed that there ought to be an institution called a school manned by people called teachers who take over the role of parents within its precincts and that children within specified age groups should be compelled by law to attend them.

It is this agreement on the modes of operation of a public service that may be called its operating ideology. It is impossible for representative democracy to work if there is no accepted operating ideology because without it discussion on all policy issues other than the very minor ones has to go back to first principles. In this respect the relationship between the elector and the elected, on the one hand, and the full-time professional on the other, is no different from that between the client and his lawyer or plumber. It is essentially a principal and agent relationship and for it to work there must be a firm foundation of agreed modes of operation if the agent is to be able to carry out his task, and this implies a sense of mutual trust running from electorate through the elected members to the technocrat. When this public trust collapses public suspicion of the elected representative and the professional expert replaces it; government becomes in the eyes of the public a predator and the operation of the service is subject to continuous debate because nothing proposed can be taken on trust. All major decisions have therefore to return to first principles and the role of the technocrat is severely curtailed. In effect everyone if he so chooses becomes his own expert. Policy is no longer the result of the interplay of expertise, values and particular circumstances and becomes instead the outcome of purely political forces bearing upon the particular issue. In short, the primacy of the electorate, which in normal circumstances in a representative democracy is merely suspended (because the majority are broadly agreed on the operating ideology) but never revoked, reasserts itself and the interplay of interests generated by instrumental participation becomes the normal mode for reaching policy decisions.

In both land use planning and in transportation planning in Britain something like this situation seems to be developing and major planning decisions have ceased to be accepted as they were in the past simply as the consequence of the planning committees' (or at the national level the minister's) appraisal of a necessarily limited range of options and therefore as being largely inevitable. Planning, together with transportation, has in consequence come to dominate local politics in many towns in recent years, often relegating the traditionally important housing and education issues into second place.

This is especially so in relation to urban road development where the Buchanan Report,[36] published in 1963, seemed to be regarded as the basis for the operating ideology for the emergent service of transportation planning. Judging, however, by the stiff public resistance that has emerged in many cities to plans for building new urban roads to relieve inner city traffic congestion, of which the halting of the London motorway box is perhaps the most spectacular example, there must be considerable doubt about this. These relief roads derived their rationale from one of the Buchanan redevelopment strategies which aimed at accommodating traffic in urban areas by a limited building programme of new roads that would be segregated from residential quarters, thereby striking a 'balance' between the needs of cars and pedestrians. But it is clear that public opinion has swung towards a new *modus vivendi* that seeks severe restraint on the use of cars in central urban areas and the development of more flexible forms of public transport rather than providing more road space to accommodate them.

VI

The clearest expression of the growth of instrumental participation is the rapid growth of local group politics over and above those producer groups that normally involve themselves in local politics such as chambers of commerce, teachers' associations, trades councils, and so forth. Over the past decade there has been a remarkable flowering of voluntary group activity at the local level whose purpose is to complement, or improve, the quality of public services by representing the interests and opinions of those who consume the service, or are affected by it.[37] This growth forms part of a much wider change in British politics – the so-called consumer movement referred to earlier – but it is likely that it also has its origins in developments more specific to the local level. Among these is probably public dissatisfaction with the inevitable rigidity of the two-party system in urban areas, and the increasing professionalisation of the middle class. This latter change has meant that the middle class, which supplies the bulk of political leadership, has become more critical of public services than in the past.

First, because they carry over the professional norms they employ in their jobs into the public sector. In some cases, it is not just norms but precise skills, so that the embarrassing situation can arise that the group is able to command greater expertise than the public authority. Second, the expansion of government responsibility in a wide range of services that previously were bought by the middle class in the private sector has brought them into the local political arena. Another reason for the expansion of group politics at the local level is the growth of formal education among the public generally. All surveys show that it is the extent of full-time education that appears to have the closest link with the propensity to take an interest in, and to participate in, local politics both public and voluntary.[38]

If these are some of the non-planning reasons for the growth in instrumental participation and the collapse of public faith in the operating ideologies governing the planning of the environment locally, there remain others that are more directly linked to the planning process itself. It is difficult to disentangle all of them, but clearly one factor is sheer disenchantment with the results of the planning process that have emerged over the post-war period. In short, performance does not seem to have matched expectations. Whether it ever could is very doubtful since some of the apparent inability of the planning process to produce environments commensurate with the controls exercised is almost certainly due to the sheer financial costs, given that the planning authority has had to operate for most of the period in a free market for land. But above all, despite what appears to the public as draconic controls over the most unconsequential forms of development, the planning authority has in reality determinant control over only a fraction of the underlying processes by which environments are changed.

There seems to be the least public enthusiasm for one of the most visible products of the planning process, namely, the comprehensive redevelopment scheme, either for central area shopping and offices or for housing. At their worst, central area schemes sweep away the seedy but unselfconscious variety of form and spontaneity of the old centres only to replace them with a barrack-like and windswept symbolic environment that lacks any human scale, or any link with the local vernacular architecture. In some of the older towns the wholesale redevelopment of their irreplaceable medieval cores has become something of a national scandal.

The comprehensive redevelopment of housing has evoked even greater public disquiet since it has often involved the wholesale clearance of areas that were not by any measure slums, areas that also possessed a strong sense of local identity. The former inhabitants have often been shipped out to peripheral sites bereft of shops, pubs and jobs to live in ill-built point blocks that may also be barrack-like and windswept and oppressively impersonal as well.[39]

All these changes to an urban fabric that has been familiar and evoked a sense of community to generations of inhabitants is bound to induce unease and insecurity, especially in a society that dislikes rapid change of any kind. Moreover, such alterations in land use widen the frontier of potential dissatisfaction precisely because every change afflicts someone and, as we have already noted, it is precisely the affliction of the individual – the widow, the small shopkeeper, the marginal owner-occupier – that evokes the greatest public concern.

Finally, to these tendencies must be added what is perhaps one of the most decisive sources of the growth in instrumental participation in planning, and this is the steadily rising proportion of the population who are owner-occupiers. This is now over 50 per cent and it means a growing public sensitivity to physical change, precisely because of the link between house values and alterations in the immediate environment in which the house stands.

VII

It is worth developing the implications of the operating ideology model of decision-making a little further since it may provide firmer ground not only for analysing the origins of the new participation, but also for examining wider questions concerning the locus of power in the chain of control that is an essential feature of a representative system.

One advantage of the operating ideology concept is that it helps us to understand a crucial and much discussed link in the chain of control, namely that between politician and technocrat. Discussion in the academic literature of this link usually boils down to some attempt to answer the question, 'who controls whom?' And the answer usually given is that one or other of the partners dominates and it is usually the technocrat.[40] It would be unfair to assume that this conclusion is solely due to the fact that academic investigators tend to get on better with technocrats, who usually have a keener appreciation of what the academic is about, or because the most rudimentary analysis may be given a superficial gloss of reality by refuting the conventional view that in a democracy the people's representatives must be the masters. No, the deficiency of the technocratic dominance thesis, as with its twin the political dominance thesis, is that both get off on the wrong foot in the sense that they assume two sets of people coming together for the first time rather like delegates at a diplomatic conference. In reality, the politician and technocrat are much more likely to have known each other over a long period and they will certainly know the context in which each operates. Each side can therefore make calculations which strike a balance between what they want and what they know each is willing and able to accept. The technocrat is not offering disembodied advice but framing his recommendations in the knowledge of prevailing conditions, and prominent among these conditions are the preferences and predilections of the committee chairman, the committee itself, and the majority of the council. Here we enter the world of anticipated reactions and in that sense get a little nearer to the reality of the relationship between politician and technocrat since the concept of anticipated reactions recognises that the technocrat relates his advice to the prevailing political constraints; that in other words the relationship has to be viewed over time. However, it is incapable of yielding much more since we can never know what the technocrat would have recommended had he been given a free hand.

The concept of the operating ideology, while it doesn't answer this conundrum, does have the advantage of broadening the scope of the relationship between technocrat and politician, not just over time but out into the wider world beyond the confines of the committee room so that we may assess it in the context of the accretion of law and custom that determine the prevailing operating modes of the policy in question. This is the operating ideology, and depending on the extent to which it retains public acceptance, both the politician *and the technocrat* are its prisoners. Viewed in this way, no one is necessarily 'controlling' anyone else: the technocrat is the full-time expert in the operating ideology and the politician a part-time one. Within the chain of control in a representative system the locus of power shifts over time. At the early stages in the evolution of a new operating ideology, or where the old one is getting seriously out of step with majority wishes, the electorate gets as near being sovereign as it is ever likely to be. At a later stage when a new operating ideology has been forged, when, that is, all the elements in the representative chain are broadly agreed, then we may discern the technocrat in command. Although this may be the usual situation and despite the fact that bureaucracies once established have a remarkable staying power, unless bureaucracy adapts when public opinion shifts then it is eventually doomed. The capacity of technocrats and politicians to adapt must never be confused with their power to resist broad changes in majority opinion. Likewise, nor should the glacial rate at which such change often occurs.

The electorate, then, may not be the passive, alienated, powerless mass beyond the gates, but rather, the ultimate arbiters of the operating ideology; slow moving, cumbersome, inchoate, yes, but ultimate arbiters in the sense that no operating ideology can survive, nor a new one take its place, without the support of majority opinion.

This brings us to a second possible advantage of the operating ideology concept which has special relevance to the main concern of this essay, for it provides a firmer basis on which to assess instrumental participation, that is to say, to see it as the assertion of the electorate's ultimate controlling power over the representative chain. When the public withdraws its support the operating ideology begins to crumble and the power of the politician and technocrat begins to crumble too. Viewed in this light, we may at least question the vast weight of literature that in its various ways discounts the role of the electorate in representative democracy in favour of some version of the inevitability of élite predominance derived from Schumpeter, or alternatively or in unison, the inevitability of bureaucratic autonomy.

It would be absurd to deny that the élite theory, either in its pure Schumpeterian form or in the bureaucratic dominance variant, doesn't have a lot to be said for it as a descriptive account of how representative democracy works. In any organisation beyond a fairly modest scale there will be leaders and followers and the former are likely to have more power than the latter; though whether calling those leaders élites helps us to understand the relationship between followers and leaders is doubtful, but that is another matter. Equally, the scope and complexity of government that the public demands must mean the employment of larger and larger complements of technocrats who will demand that autonomy, broadly speaking, commensurate with the skills they provide. Above all, government in a democracy must possess the capacity to govern; that is to say, it must have that functional effectiveness that makes a reality the choice between alternative policies that democracy claims to offer the electorate.[41]

All this must be conceded to the élite model. What cannot be conceded is that this necessary concentration of power in the modern democratic polity tells us the whole story about power distribution within it, for the élite model tends to assume that because the executive predominates it must also control the possibility of change; that since no one relinquishes power voluntarily executive dominance is an end state where movement can be only towards greater centralisation of power. The élite model mistakes public dependence on strong government for its domination by government and is, in consequence, incapable of explaining the crumbling of authority that is upon us, or its various manifestations whether they take the form of developmental or instrumental participation. Those who like Duncan and Lukes resisted the Schumpeter model when it dominated democratic theory during the 1950s have been largely vindicated both in prescriptive and descriptive terms.

VIII

If the élite model has difficulty in explaining the new participation there is one explanation for the upsurge in instrumental participation that seriously undermines the operating ideology explanation. This argues that instrumental participation is merely a new, more aggressive, expression of the social and economic inequality in industrial society, inequality that outweighs the equality of the ballot box. Far from reflecting the reassertion of the popular will, instrumental participation merely distorts its impact even further by strengthening those who are already strong against those who are already weak – the upper end of the social scale against the lower, the middle class against the working class.

In planning, so this argument runs, instrumental participation seeks merely to immobilise the planning process sufficiently to ensure that its diffuse and imprecise benefits (as described earlier) are made rather more specifically in favour of middle-class interests.

There may be a great deal in this claim; certainly there is ample evidence that the middle class are more active, more participative and more demanding in relation to government, especially local government.[42] But before accepting it a number of questions need to be answered. First, if the 'haves' are in fact in the saddle we must not only abandon the operating ideology assumption but the élite assumption as well, for by definition the élite are not dominating everyone. Moreover, if government is merely the handmaiden of the richer and the more powerful, how do we explain the existence of a planning system that they disapprove of and one that is patently not always working in their interests? Take, for example, the construction of new urban access roads to city centres which is something of a test case of whether or not the planning system is dominated by middle-class interests. Given that almost all British urban centres have chosen to redevelop their central areas instead of building out-of-town shopping centres on green field sites, the need to provide new road space to accommodate a rapidly increasing car-borne population became an essential feature of the development plan. Since it is in the city centre that the bulk of middle-class shopping and services tend to congregate and where predominantly middle-class tertiary employment is also concentrated, the building of these new access roads may be identified as a strong middle-class interest. All the more so if we take into account the fact that the car is overwhelmingly the most popular form of middle-class transport. Yet, as we noted earlier, very few of such roads have been built and most towns have now abandoned new urban road building for central area access in favour of traffic restraint policies and subsidies to public transport.

Before accepting that instrumental participation in planning is merely a middle-class activity, we must also ask why it is that community action groups are also engaged in attacking the planning system. Sometimes they have found common cause with more conventional instrumental activists such that at least one observer has identified the alliance between the two as being one of the major threats to the planning system.[43] Moreover, one of the most thorough assessments of who has gained and who has lost as a result of the planning system has concluded that although the very poorest have faired worst the beneficiaries have not been wholly middle class.[44]

Further speculation as to the adequacy of the class explanation for the new participation in planning need not detain us further. Sufficient doubt has been cast on it for this role to suggest that at the very least it cannot be the sole explanation. There remains one other possible advantage that the operating ideology concept may have for understanding representative democracy. This is derived from the fact that it relates the distribution of power to particular functions and thus makes it possible to distinguish different power relationships in different services or policy fields. Leaving aside the more general crumbling of authority that, as we have suggested, affects the whole range of government activities, it may help us to explain why it is that in this country there appear to be very wide disparities in the capacity of government to act. On one view we are the great lovers of strong government. We are one of the few countries where public trust of government is deeply embedded and the epitome of stable democracy. On another view, British government is incapable of sustaining a consistent policy for more than very brief periods, it is the slave of the short run and paralysed by the uncompromising truculence of selfish groups it is fast approaching being 'ungovernable'. It is perhaps typical of that self-indulgent pessimism that seems to be the dominant mood of so much academic writing on British government and on British planning in particular, that both conditions are deeply regretted with all the gloom and foreboding that only academic commentators can muster, the first on the grounds that it merely confirms the élite thesis and the consequent inadequacy of traditional democratic theory. The second is regretted because stability, order and efficiency are seen as unquestionably desirable ends that are independent of whether or not the system fulfils the requirements of traditional democratic theory. Although it has not addressed itself directly to either of these somewhat contradictory conclusions, it should be emphasised that it has been the overriding intention of this essay to strike a more optimistic note about the current state of health of democracy in this country.

NOTES

1 G. Duncan and S. Lukes, 'The New Democracy', *Political Studies*, vol. XI (1963).
2 J. L. Talmon, *The Origins of Totalitarian Democracy* (London, Mercury Books, 1961); S. M. Lipset, *Political Man* (London, Mercury Books, 1963); and W. H. Morris-Jones, 'In Defence of Apathy', *Political Studies*, vol. II (1954).
3 B. Berelson *et al.*, *Voting* (Chicago, University of Chicago Press, 1954); B. Berelson, 'Democratic Theory and Public Opinion', in H. Eulau *et al.*, *Political Behaviour, a Reader in Theory and Research* (Glencoe, Free Press, 1956); E. Burdick, 'Political Theory and Voting Studies' in E. Burdick and J. Brodbeck (eds.), *American Voting Behaviour* (Glencoe, Free Press, 1960); R. S. Milne and H. C. Mackenzie, *Marginal Seat: 1955* (London, Hansard Society, 1958).
4 J. A. Schumpeter, *Capitalism, Socialism and Democracy* (London, George Allen & Unwin, 1950).
5 Duncan and Lukes, op. cit., p. 159.
6 ibid., p. 177.
7 ibid., p. 161.
8 See, for example, J. Walker, 'A Critique of the Elitist Theory of Democracy', *American Political Science Review*, vol. 60 (1966); P. Bachrach, *The Theory of Democratic Elitism* (Boston, Little, Brown, 1967); A. MacFarland, *Power and Leadership in Pluralist Systems* (Stanford, Stanford University Press, 1969); C. Pateman, *Participation and Democratic Theory* (London, Cambridge University Press, 1970); D. F. Thompson, *The Democratic Citizen* (London, Cambridge University Press, 1970); G. Parry (ed.), *Participation in Politics* (Manchester, Manchester University Press, 1972); S. Verba and N. H. Nie, *Participation in America: Political Democracy and Social Equality* (New York, Harper Row, 1972).
9 Duncan and Lukes, op. cit., p. 159.
10 Verba and Nie, op. cit., p. 5.
11 G. Parry, 'The Idea of Political Participation', in Parry, op. cit.
12 See April Carter, *Direct Action And Liberal Democracy* (London, Routledge, 1973) for an account of the direct action movements during the post-war period and for a discussion of the theoretical relationship of direct action to conventional participatory modes in democratic countries.
13 ibid., p. 62. For accounts of the CND movement see F. Parkin, *Middle Class Radicalism* (Manchester, Manchester University Press, 1968), and C. Driver, *The Disarmers* (London, Hodder and Stoughton, 1964).
14 'Introduction' by M. Harrington in J. Newfield, '*A Prophetic Minority*' (London, Blond, 1966), p. 14.
15 P. Marris and M. Rein, *Dilemmas of Social Reform* (London, Routledge, 1967).

16 D. Moynihan, *Maximum Feasible Misunderstanding* (New York, Free Press, 1969), p. xvi.
17 G. Parry, 'The Idea of Political Participation', in Parry, op. cit., p. 15.
18 See P. Jacobs and S. Landau, *The New Radicals* (London, Penguin Books, 1967) for a more detailed exposition of the radical participatory philosophy. See also F. M. Cox *et al.*, *Strategies of Community Organization* (Illinois, Peacock, 1970), especially part VI.
19 See, for example, Anne Lapping (ed.), *Community Action*, Fabian Tract no. 400, June 1970.
20 D. Donnison, 'Micro-politics of the City', in D. Donnison and D. Eversley (eds.), *London: Urban Patterns, Problems and Policies* (London, Heinemann, 1973).
21 See, for example, *Report of the Committee on Local Authority and Allied Personal Social Services* (Seebohm), Cmnd. 3703 (HMSO, 1969); and *Report of the Committee on Public Participation in Planning: People and Planning* (Skeffington) (HMSO, 1969).
22 See *Educational Priority: E. P. A. Policies and Problems*, Dept of Education and Science, HMSO, 1972; and E. Midwinter, *Projections: an Education Priority Area at work* (London, Ward Lock, 1972).
23 Duncan and Lukes, op. cit., p. 160.
24 See E. E. Schattschneider, *The Semi-Sovereign People* (New York, Reinhart Winston, 1960) and more especially the delineation of the 'non-decision' by P. Bachrach and M. Baratz in 'The two Faces of Power', *American Political Science Review*, vol. 56 (1962); 'Decisions and Non-Decisions: An Analytic Framework', *American Political Science Review*, vol. 57 (1963); and *Power and Poverty* (London, Oxford University Press, 1970).
25 Both Bachrach (*The Theory of Democratic Elitism*) and Pateman (*Participation and Democratic Theory*) place most emphasis on workers' participation in the work place as the principal mode for fulfilling the objective of classical democratic theory.
26 Advocates of neighbourhood government include M. Kotler, *Neighboorhood Government* (Indianapolis, Bobbs-Merrill, 1969), W. Farr *et al.*, *Decentralizing City Government* (New York, Praeger, 1972) and J. Baker and M. Young, *The Hornsey Plan* (Halstead, The Association for Neighbourhood Councils, 1971). For a general appraisal of the movement see A. Altshuler, *Community Control* (New York, Pegasus, 1970) and D. Yates, *Neighbourhood Democracy* (Lexington, D. C. Heath, 1973). The latter also includes case studies of various experiments in decentralised urban government.
27 R. A. Dahl, 'The City in the Future of Democracy', *American Political Science Review*, vol. 61 (1969).
28 R. A. Dahl and E. R. Tufte, *Size and Democracy* (Stanford, Stanford University Press, 1973), especially ch. 7.
29 See L. J. Sharpe, 'Theories and Values of Local Government',

Political Studies, vol. XVIII (June 1970), for a further discussion of the function of local government in mitigating the participatory deficiencies of national government. For a much more sceptical view, but one which does nonetheless concede this role of local government as having a scintilla of validity, see J. G. Bulpitt, 'Participation and Local Government: Territorial Democracy', in Parry, op. cit.

30 Carter, op. cit., p. 3.

31 See L. J. Sharpe, 'American Democracy Reconsidered: Parts I & II', *British Journal of Political Science*, vol. 3 (April and June 1973), for a discussion of this aspect of the American democratic tradition.

32 Donnison, op. cit., p. 395.

33 G. Parry, 'The Idea of Political Participation', in Parry, op. cit., p. 33.

34 *People and Planning*, op. cit.

35 *The Future of Development Plans*, The Report of the Planning Advisory Group (PAG) (HMSO, 1965).

36 *Report of the Committee on Traffic: Traffic in Towns* (Buchanan) (HMSO, 1963).

37 See M. Broady, *Planning for People* (London, Bedford Square Press, 1968), for a discussion of the growth of local group politics. Also Donnison, op. cit., and D. Hill, *Participating in Local Affairs* (London, Penguin Books, 1970). For the most comprehensive discussion of the role of groups in local government, see K. Newton, *Second City Politics* (London, Oxford University Press, 1975), chs. 3 and 4.

38 See Appendix I of *Report of the Royal Commission of Local Government in England* (Redcliffe-Maud) vol. III, Cmnd. 4040 (HMSO, 1969), which summarises the results of the various surveys that have examined the personal characteristics of local activists. For a similar survey of American data see L. Milbrath, *Political Participation* (Chicago, Rand McNally, 1965), chs. 3 and 5.

39 See N. Dennis, *People and Planning* (London, Faber, 1970) and *Public Participation and Planners Blight* (London, Faber, 1972) for critical accounts of this kind of comprehensive development in Sunderland. See also J. Gower-Davies, *The Evangelistic Bureaucrat* (London, Tavistock, 1972), for a similar critique of comprehensive housing development in Newcastle.

40 See, for example, J. M. Lee, *Social Leaders and Public Persons* (Oxford, Clarendon Press, 1963), part III; J. A. G. Griffith, *Central Departments and Local Authorities* (London, George Allen & Unwin, 1966), p. 534; and R. J. Buxton, *Local Government* (London, Penguin Books, 1970), ch. 2.

41 For a more detailed elaboration of the link between the functional effectiveness of government and democracy, see part II, op. cit., Sharpe.

42 Verba and Nie, op. cit., part II, and Redcliffe-Maud *Report*, op. cit., vol. III, appendix 7.

43 D. Eversley, *The Planner in Society* (London, Faber, 1973), part 3.
44 P. Hall *et al.; The Containment of Urban England* (London, George Allen & Unwin, 1973), vol. 2, ch. 12.

7

The Public Corporation: Allocative Efficiency and X-Efficiency

C. D. FOSTER

Economists have devoted considerable effort to discussion of pricing criteria and financial targets for the nationalised industries. The pricing criteria usually advocated are based on marginal cost pricing. The nationalised industries have often been criticised by economists because they have failed to adopt marginal cost pricing.

But more recently some economists have argued that this concentration by economists on pricing criteria has been misplaced. Even if the nationalised industries were to adopt marginal cost pricing, it would make a trivial difference to their efficiency and the allocative efficiency of the economy. It is far more important, they argue, for the nationalised industries to measure their technical efficiency, and in particular, what they call X-efficiency. Within reason the relation of price to marginal cost, and the extent to which public corporations meet their financial targets, does not matter.

In Section I, some earlier arguments, put forward by the Webbs and by Professor Robson, on the need to measure changes in nationalised industries' efficiency, are examined. Section II describes Richard Pryke's work on nationalised industry efficiency, which in Section III is contrasted with arguments about allocative efficiency as developed in relation to nationalised industries. In Section IV arguments are considered which set out to demonstrate the triviality of allocative efficiency and therefore the paramount importance of X-efficiency. Various reasons are given in Section V why this extreme position is fallacious. In Section VI some further arguments of Pryke's on the unimportance of allocative efficiency in relation to public enterprise are criticised. The conclusion is the unremarkable one that both allocative and technical efficiency, or X-efficiency, are important in public enterprise, and we do not have the information to know which is the more important.

I

MEASURING THE EFFICIENCY OF PUBLIC ENTERPRISE

As long ago as 1920 in their blueprint *A Constitution for the Socialist Commonwealth of Great Britain*, the Webbs [1] had argued that state enterprise would require organs of report and criticism. True to their Fabian tradition, information of interest to consumers, managers and employees should be published and analysed.

'In place of the jealous secrecy in which the 1,400 separate colliery companies at present enshroud their operations, and the bureaucratic concealment which today marks alike the Post Office and the railways we visualise the administration of each national industry and service, no longer concerned for magnifying the private gains of particular capitalist groups, or enhancing the net revenue of the Exchequer, but merely for increasing the net efficiency to the service of the public, in the glare of a whole series of searchlights, impinging at different angles upon what is essentially the same problem – namely how to obtain for the community as a whole the greatest possible efficiency in relation to the efforts and sacrifices involved.' [2]

Thus they believed that state enterprises should be required to disclose far more information about their workings than private enterprise; and that as evidenced by these data their performance would be criticised and appraised – preferably by experts who were neither involved with the employees, management or politics – 'the disinterested professional expert who invents, discovers, inspects, audits, costs, tests or measures . . .' [3]

In his first book on *Public Enterprise* [4] Professor Robson argued that for this purpose the annual reports that even then all public enterprises were required to produce, were insufficient. They were too narrow in scope. Moreover, they put the onus for disclosure of

[1] S. and B. Webb (1920).
[2] ibid., p. 186.
[3] ibid., p. 356.
[4] Robson (1937).

information and self-criticism on the enterprise itself. 'It is asking too much,' he wrote, 'to expect the responsible board of a great undertaking to draw attention to its weak points; they may even be unaware of them. If we are to develop effective organs of public criticism, permanent organs of scrutiny and investigation will have to be developed.' [5] Robson suggested an audit commission whose function it would be to hold periodic efficiency audits on each nationalised industry. 'The ideal body would consist, first, of a number of eminent specialists in such fields as applied economics, finance, industrial psychology, statistics, business organisation, public relations, engineering and so forth, giving their whole time to the work; second of a number of persons engaged in outside occupations of varied kinds accustomed to master the broad outline of an administrative situation at short notice . . .' [6] And he saw its remit as very broad: 'Such a body would consider the character, quantity and quality of service rendered; price policy and efficiency of administration; personnel questions, including pay, recruitment and methods of promotion, relations between the board and the consumer; capital expenditure and the methods of financing it; in short all the most important problems involved in a socialised undertaking.' [7]

In 1920 nationalisation seemed a not unlikely, even imminent, possibility because of the finding of the Sankey Commission on the coal industry (of which Sidney Webb was a member).[8] One of the purposes of Professor Robson's 1937 collection of essays [9] was to demonstrate by then how much public enterprise existed in Britain: the Port of London Authority, the BBC, the Central Electricity Board, the London Passenger Transport Board, the Forestry Commission, and others.[10] Yet this nationalisation had been pragmatic and undertaken by Conservative or Liberal governments. It is not particularly surprising that such governments did not consider the Webbs' or Professor Robson's ideas on machinery to monitor the efficiency of public enterprise.

More might have been expected of the post-war Labour Government, but there was little effective progress to report when Professor Robson returned to the problem in a book written just before the

[5] ibid., p. 380. [6] ibid., pp. 380–1. [7] ibid., p. 380.

[8] *Report and Minutes of Evidence on the First Stage of the Industry.* Coal Industry Commission, Cmd 359 (1919).

[9] Robson, op. cit.

[10] One author reminded readers that even then more than 300 ports operated as some form of public enterprise.

Labour Government's fall in 1951.[11] More data had been disclosed by the National Coal Board and the British Transport Commission than by the private undertakings they had replaced; but Robson pointed out that informed debate in Parliament and elsewhere on the performance of nationalised industries required more information than this. A select committee on the nationalised industries had been proposed. To be effective, Professor Robson argued, it would require a specialist staff of the kind he had recommended in 1937 for his audit commission. Indeed a select committee backed by such a staff could perform the function of such an audit commission. But the Labour Government turned down the idea of a select committee, both with and without a substantial staff, using time-honoured arguments against all organs of scrutiny and criticism, repeatedly successful in Britain: 'the commission would be regarded by the public corporations as hostile to them and would therefore be resisted; that the corporations would tend to withhold information from it whenever possible; and that for an outside body to have the right to investigate and criticise would tend to have a paralysing influence on the vigour and enterprise of the public corporations.' [12] The implication was that it was for the nationalised industries to decide what expert advice and criticism they should receive. This, Professor Robson argued, was utterly unacceptable.

He also regretted that despite prolonged search he had been unable to find a statistician prepared to contribute to the volume an essay on the 'physical measurement of efficiency' in the nationalised industries. It would seem that he had run into the objections (1) that there was no unique measure of efficiency – neither the Webbs nor he had ever maintained there was – and (2) that once a criterion of efficiency was agreed, its measurement was necessarily so complex that nothing simpler was worth attempting. Those approached had answered that their researches were not enough advanced for this to be worthwhile. Understandably Professor Robson held that 'this lack of statistical knowledge is a matter of serious consequence to the public . . . we must . . . try to evolve statistical yardsticks which will express the performance of an undertaking in terms of the service or commodity which it provides, in such a way as to serve as criteria of efficiency in nationalised industries.' [13]

When Professor Robson came to consider the question for a third time in 1960, the matter had become if anything more serious. As Robson realised, the nationalised industries were operating in the

[11] Robson (1952). [12] ibid., pp. 320–5. [13] ibid., pp. 6, 7.

limelight whether they wanted it or not. The denigration of public enterprise had been such that public opinion generally believed the worst. They were popularly held to be inefficient, conservative, tradition-bound and uninnovating. Therefore it was all the more necessary to have independent checks on their efficiency – to defend them where public opinion was wrong and to goad them to do better where it was right.

Yet in spite of this, there was almost no progress to report. After he left office, Herbert Morrison, who had been responsible for policy on nationalised industries in the 1945–51 Labour Government, said he had tried to urge the nationalised industries themselves to set up a 'common efficiency unit' as their own collective efficiency audit.[14] One cannot be surprised that boards were reluctant to create their own critics. What was surely more surprising was that Morrison felt that they rather than Government should take the initiative. More hopefully, the idea of a Select Committee on Nationalised Industries, rejected by the Labour Government, had been taken up by a Conservative Government and in 1957 began its series of detailed reports on nationalised industries. But there was no question of it having a substantial staff. The Committee devoted an entire report in 1959 to its own belief that it required an accountant and an economist. As Professor Robson observed, 'it seems to an outside observer somewhat remarkable that the Select Committee should have had to meet seven times, hear evidence from the highest officers of the House of Commons, the Leader of the House and the Leader of the Opposition, high Treasury officials and eminent representatives of the Institute of Chartered Accountants, and to issue a report of nine pages and about fifty pages of evidence in order to obtain the services of an accountant and an economist.'[15] His own view, as one might have expected, was that two experts was too few for the necessary audit function. Although the Committee has since received permission to have one part-time expert assessor working on a report, it is difficult to fault Professor Robson's prediction that 'without technical, economic, statistical and administrative advice of high calibre, the committee will remain a group of well-intentioned laymen whose opinions carry great weight. The committee are better than nothing for they provide *inter alia* an opportunity to clear up misunderstandings and mistakes; but they would be immeasurably strengthened if they were supplied with the reports of an Efficiency Audit Commis-

[14] Evidence to the Select Committee on Nationalised Industries, HMSO, HC 235/1952/3; H. Morrison (1954), p. 294; see Robson (1960), pp. 204, 205.

[15] Robson (1960), p. 201.

sion or the advice of a highly qualified staff.' [16] Some of the Committee's reports have been excellent and influential; but Professor Robson was right to predict they would be at their best when clearing up confusions over criteria. When it came to questioning actual decisions – for example, on major investment – or appraising the performance of nationalised industries, the Committee was unable to press its inquiries far enough to come to a firm opinion one way or the other. Because it had to rely on the data given it by the nationalised industries and by government departments, it was not able to be as incisive as it would have been if it had had its own staff and had been better informed.

Neither has there been any other real progress in this direction since 1960. The second (1967) White Paper on the financial and economic objectives of the nationalised industries [17] had a section on the importance of increasing productivity and otherwise cutting costs per unit of output, with the implication therefore that some examination of nationalised industries' performance as measured by changes in productivity would be valuable. Nothing came of this. In its report on ministerial control of the nationalised industries,[18] the Select Committee in 1968 recommended that there should be one ministry sponsoring the nationalised industries and saw among its functions the making of those efficiency and productivity comparisons that Professor Robson had suggested as the business of an audit commission. That recommendation was turned down by the Government. For a few years the National Board for Prices and Income performed some of the functions of an audit commission. It did not systematically monitor the performance of nationalised industries over time. Neither did it make inter-enterprise or international productivity comparisons. For a few years, however, it comprised a group of experts of some size and competence who investigated some aspects of the efficiency of nationalised industries (as they did of private firms). But it did not last long. The old arguments against such independent assessment proved victorious. Just as Lord Citrine in 1951 had argued against any notion of an efficiency audit that it would undermine board responsibility and self-confidence and encourage over-caution,[19] so chairmen of public and private

[16] ibid., pp. 201, 202.

[17] *The Nationalised Industries: A Review of Economic and Financial Objectives*, Cmnd. 3437 (1967).

[18] Select Committee on the Nationalised Industries, First Report, Session 1967/8, 3 vols (HMSO, 1968).

[19] Citrine (1951).

enterprise successfully objected twenty years later to the existence of any board which criticised their activities – even though few doubted that most of the points the Board made were well founded. Opposition to the critical activities of the Board was a major factor, it would seem, in persuading the incoming Conservative Government to kill it off in 1970. So ended the closest official approach in Britain to an objective, independent assessor of the nationalised industries' performance, or rather to a body which had the competence to develop in that direction.

However, if governments did not support an efficiency audit of public enterprise, at last an academic economist took it on himself to measure the efficiency of the major nationalised industries as evidenced by changes in their productivity. After fifty years the Webbs' 'professional expert who invents, discovers, audits, costs, tests or measures' [20] was at hand to evaluate the performance of the nationalised industries from 1948 to 1968.

II

PUBLIC ENTERPRISE IN PRACTICE

The publication of Richard Pryke's *Public Enterprise in Practice* in 1971 was a breakthrough. As he himself remarked,[21] economists had previously shied away from studies of the whole nationalised industries' sector. There had been books and articles on particular industries (which happened to be nationalised), but Pryke speculated that economists avoided studying the nationalised industries' sector as a whole because of a rooted economists' instinct that ownership as such was irrelevant to economic performance. His method was essentially simple. His main calculations were of three types.

1 *Measures of Changes in Labour Productivity*

From Central Statistical Office and other sources, he created indices of production for the major nationalised industries. From these he constructed the indices of changes in labour productivity (usually expressed in terms of output per man hour) shown as Table 7.1.[22]

On this basis he argued that, contrary to popular belief, over the whole period 1948 to 1968, the growth rate of productivity was higher for the public enterprise sector (3·4 per cent) than for manufacturing (2·8 per cent); that it was only slightly lower in the first decade (1·5

[20] Webb, op.cit., p. 356. [21] Pryke (1971), pp. 2–3. [22] ibid., p. 20.

Table 7.1

INDEX NUMBERS OF LABOUR PRODUCTIVITY * 1948–68 (1958 = 100)

	Electricity	*Coal*	*Railways*	*Gas*	*BEA AND BOAC*	*Nationalised Buses*	*BRS*	*Public Enterprise Sector*	*Manufacturing*
1948	64·0	91·7	97·2	85·0	27·0	106·0	—	86·0	83·2
1949	60·9	96·6	98·8	86·5	33·7	106·2	—	88·0	86·8
1950	63·7	99·5	100·7	90·6	45·5	106·5	(93·7)	90·8	89·3
1951	67·9	99·6	105·2	90·1	58·7	106·9	98·8	93·2	90·1
1952	69·0	97·2	103·3	87·6	62·2	105·6	95·2	91·8	88·2
1953	72·5	99·1	105·0	91·8	67·3	107·4	100·3	94·3	91·7
1954	78·6	99·4	105·2	97·0	69·3	107·4	(104·6)	96·3	94·3
1955	82·8	98·6	104·8	96·6	76·3	109·0	(93·8)	96·6	97·0
1956	89·7	98·2	106·9	98·3	87·5	107·3	91·9	98·5	96·5
1957	92·9	96·8	106·5	97·4	97·0	101·6	89·4	98·3	98·9
1958	100·0	100·0	100·0	100·0	100·0	100·0	100·0	100·0	100·0
1959	107·0	105·3	103·4	103·4	115·9	103·0	105·9	105·3	104·8
1960	121·5	108·3	109·5	108·2	139·5	103·0	108·4	111·8	109·7
1961	126·0	112·9	107·3	113·0	146·7	100·2	110·4	114·6	109·3
1962	134·1	120·6	104·2	118·0	142·5	99·6	112·0	119·0	112·3
1963	141·5	126·4	110·8	120·0	163·9	99·5	117·1	125·0	118·4
1964	146·5	129·7	121·9	128·3	190·0	95·9	125·7	131·1	124·6
1865	167·5	134·4	125·1	138·3	224·0	89·7	138·1	139·6	128·6
1966	181·0	137·9	132·3	145·1	238·6	86·1	148·5	146·2	132·4
1967	189·6	143·1	136·7	158·6	238·2	84·7	155·4	152·1	135·5
1968	215·4	158·5	151·9	170·9	235·3	87·3	161·7	167·9	143·8

* Output per man hour, except for Nationalised Buses and prior to 1963 Railways where figures are for output per man year.

Source Production from Table 3 and employment from Table 5, in Richard Pryke, *Public Enterprise in Practice*. Hours worked from MLG/EPG (electricity, gas, air), BRS and for coal MPSD 1968–9, p. 41, adjusted for the reduction in shift length during 1961 (UN/ECE *Concentration Indices in the European Coal Industry* 1967, p. 4). Public enterprise productivity was obtained by combining the industry figures with 1954 and 1958 net output weights (for which see source to Table 3). Manufacturing productivity was calculated by the same method. Production and weights from *The Index of Industrial Production* 1959, pp. 26–7; AAS 1967, p. 136, 1968 p. 137; and for 1968 from CSO. Employment from AAS 1959, 1960 p. 104, 1967, p. 109, 1969 p. 120. Average hours from MLG/EPG.

per cent by comparison with 1·9 per cent), and that it was sharply higher in the second ten years from 1958 to 1968 (5·3 per cent compared with 3·7 per cent). Growth in labour productivity over the period had been particularly high in the airlines (11·4 per cent) and electricity (6·3 per cent). Even in coal, it had been as great as in manufacturing. Only railways and buses had substantially lower growth rates in productivity. Pryke also pointed out a contrast within the first ten years of nationalisation. All the nationalised industries (except buses) had had substantial gains in productivity in the first three to five years, but there had been a period of comparative stagnation until the end of the 1950s (except in the airlines and electricity).

2 *Measures of 'Residual' Productivity*

An objection to measures of changes in labour productivity is that they treat all changes in output per man hour as attributable to labour; and that no allowance is made for changes in the contribution of other factors, particularly capital. For example, if a 10 per cent improvement in labour productivity were to be achieved with no increase in capital inputs in one industry but with a large increase in investment in another, measures of labour productivity would show the improvement in labour productivity as the same in both cases and would therefore be misleading. It has been a common criticism of the nationalised industries that the increases in labour productivity they have achieved have been at the expense of more capital than was needed to get the same improvements in the private manufacturing sector. To overcome this objection, Pryke constructed an ingenious measure of 'residual' productivity – that is for the change in output allowing for changes in both labour and capital input, suitably weighted.[23] The results of this exercise are shown in Table 7.2.[24] He shows that most of the nationalised industries survive this test well. Its main effect is to reduce the growth of nationalised industry productivity from 1948 to 1958, though 'residual' productivity in the airlines and electricity grows faster than in manufacturing industry. In the second decade, all on this measure, even the railways, do as well as or better than the average of manufacturing industry. Therefore the nationalised industries on average cannot be said to have used capital less productively than did manufacturing industry.

[23] He imputed a 10 per cent rate of profit on capital as a social opportunity cost to get round the problem of low profits or actual losses. See Section III *infra* for discussion of this point.

[24] Pryke, op.cit, p. 112.

Table 7.2

INDEX NUMBERS AND GROWTH RATES FOR OUTPUT PER UNIT OF LABOUR AND CAPITAL 1948–68

	Electricity	*Coal*	*Railways*	*Gas*	*BEA and BOAC*	*Manufacturing excluding textiles*
(i) *Index Numbers (1958 = 100)*						
1948	69·9	96·4	100·6	93·6	47·0	85·9
1949	69·6	101·4	102·2	95·6	53·3	89·1
1950	73·9	104·0	103·0	100·7	65·8	91·9
1951	78·4	104·2	106·8	100·9	83·5	93·2
1952	78·0	101·9	104·8	97·0	89·0	90·9
1953	80·9	103·2	106·6	99·5	93·4	93·2
1954	86·7	103·0	105·9	104·0	92·1	96·5
1955	90·6	101·4	104·5	102·3	98·2	100·1
1956	94·4	100·5	106·7	101·2	104·3	98·6
1957	95·4	98·7	107·7	98·5	106·1	100·2
1958	100·0	100·0	100·0	100·0	100·0	100·0
1959	103·7	102·7	101·2	100·5	108·9	103·8
1960	112·8	103·4	105·6	103·1	126·7	108·7
1961	116·8	105·7	102·5	105·7	131·8	107·1
1962	124·8	111·7	98·5	111·1	132·4	108·0
1963	128·1	115·8	102·8	113·0	148·7	112·3
1964	128·7	117·2	111·9	118·3	169·7	117·8
1965	133·8	119·6	112·7	125·7	193·7	120·1
1966	130·8	121·1	116·1	131·2	213·9	121·9
1967	130·1	125·1	116·0	139·7	218·5	122·2
1968	135·9	135·2	126·3	144·0	—	126·8
(ii) *Growth Rates (Per cent compound per annum)*						
1948–68	3·4	1·7	1·1	2·2	8·4*	2·0
1948–58	3·6	0·4	—	0·7	7·8	1·5
1958–68	3·1	3·0	2·4	3·7	9·1 †	2·4

3 *International Productivity Comparisons*

Pryke also made a number of international comparisons between British nationalised industries and their counterparts overseas. While some were unfavourable, many favoured British nationalised industries. In particular he showed [25] how well the coal industry had done compared with that in other European countries. The same was in general true of railways,[26] though for some capital assets use by BR seemed substantially less intensive. On the other hand while domestically the electricity industry had one of the best records of growth in terms of both labour and 'residual' productivity, this did not appear as outstanding internationally.[27] In a particular case, though correcting for biases and deficiencies in the data reduced the margin by which output per man hour in US electricity supply exceeded that in the UK, nevertheless Pryke showed that such margins still existed and needed investigating.[28]

While the comparisons that Pryke made were methodologically straightforward (though requiring considerable statistical ingenuity), the scope, and indeed the size, of his book were enormously enriched by his command of detail. Pryke's knowledge of the economic, technical and political detail of the industries was formidable. So was his command of the published sources. His collection of relevant press cuttings must be unrivalled and was frequently put to excellent use. In the bulk of his argument he was relying not on complex statistical techniques but on the arguments of the economic historian. He used statistics well to attack many strongly held but poorly substantiated opinions on the nationalised industries. From the earliest many commentators had assumed first that there would be, and later that there had been, excessive increases in administrative staffing and other bureaucratic overheads. Pryke showed this had not happened.[29] It was a commonplace opinion that nationalised industries were particularly liable to strikes. Pryke showed that while there were rather more days on strike per worker from 1948 to 1958 than in manufacturing industry, the reverse held from 1958 to 1968.[30] Pryke also produced evidence, at least in relation to the introduction of joint conciliation schemes and occupational pensions, that nationalised industries were 'good employers', again contrary to what was often maintained.[31] Pryke examined technical progress – necessarily in a more qualitative way – and concluded that the nationalised industries had much to be proud of by comparison with manufactur-

[25] ibid., pp. 119–34. [26] ibid., pp. 140–55. [27] ibid., pp. 134–9.
[28] ibid., pp. 136–8. [29] ibid., p. 26. [30] ibid., pp. 91–7.
[31] ibid., pp. 99–102.

ing industry.[32] By showing that labour productivity had grown relatively fast in the first few years after nationalisation, he challenged the common assumption that the act of nationalisation was itself necessarily disruptive.[33] Though he showed that the growth of labour and 'residual' productivity stagnated in the 1950s, assigning blame for this – how far caused by capital starvation by Government, how far interference by an indifferent or antagonistic Government – becomes harder. In coming to an opinion on questions like this, a statistical approach is not of much value. Even on questions like this Pryke is suitably tentative,[34] as he is when he comes to his final conclusion, that public ownership may not be irrelevant to performance; and indeed his claim there is evidence that public ownership may actually be superior to private enterprise.[35]

The significance of Richard Pryke's contribution to British debate on public ownership is:

1 He has made the measurements of efficiency and the productivity comparisons that the Webbs and Professor Robson called for. He has done this on a much more comprehensive and careful basis than anyone else has attempted. It should be the point of departure for future analysis which should become still more detailed and sophisticated. It is not sensible to rely on a lone individual – whether Pryke or another academic – devoting his own resources to continue and develop this work. Much more could be done than Pryke attempted, particularly in international comparison. This is a useful method of testing the efficiency of our nationalised industries and suggesting possible improvements. Neither do analyses of efficiency have to be tied to productivity comparisons. The need for permanent organs remains and will increase as the nationalised industries' sector expands. If for various reasons it is felt the scrutiny cannot be official, then there is a case for funding one or more academic institutes whose permanent duty it should be to make such investigations.

2 His findings have given a fillip to those who believe in nationalisation politically and to those who work in the industries. He has provided prima facie evidence that the nationalised industries have done comparatively well since 1948 (excepting the railways). In the process he has upset many canards about their poor performance. Thus he has shown that if it was fear that they would be found wanting which inspired past board chairmen to fight off efficiency audits

[32] ibid., pp. 64–77.
[33] ibid., pp. 21–35.
[34] ibid., ch. 3.
[35] ibid., ch. 3.

and other such investigations, for most of them that fear was unjustified.

3 Though he does not draw this conclusion, his findings could be interpreted as showing a weak connection between the boards' independence and their performance. In general he shows their productivity improved considerably during the late 'forties and the beginning of the 1950s when the Morrisonian concept of the independent board was dominant and the boards were in most respects 'independent'. The improvement fell off during the 1950s when the independence of the boards was no less. It improved again during the 1960s at a time when relations between central government and the nationalised industries were changing towards more interference by the former.[36]

4 Pryke did argue that his concentration on the measurement of efficiency and on productivity comparisons was sensible; and that the attention that economists had earlier paid to pricing and investment criteria was misplaced, not because theoretically wrong but as practically unimportant. He further argued that the popular attention given to low profits and actual losses had been mistaken. A nationalised industry could be efficient and yet make a loss. To eliminate a loss might be a trivial, even a negative, contribution to efficiency. It was more useful to improve productivity and worry less about profits and losses. This view was heartening to many because it suggested that the relatively poor profits records of nationalised industries did not matter. It also heartened those who had believed it anomalous that a nationalised industry should be concerned about its profits – as if it were a private firm in disguise. To this fourth question – of allocative versus X-efficiency as it is sometimes called – let us now turn.

III

ALLOCATIVE EFFICIENCY

A very large part of the economic literature on public enterprise has been on what economists call allocative efficiency. It has been concerned with exploring the consequences of prices that diverge from marginal cost and recommending the correction of this on the grounds that if prices are substantially above or below marginal cost, there must be a loss of allocative efficiency. This was the argu-

[36] Not that up to the late 1960s, the practical effect in increasing central government financial control was necessarily great. See Foster (1972).

ment that I. M. D. Little [37] used to try to persuade the National Coal Board to raise its prices when coal was scarce in the late 1940s and early 1950s. As coal was an increasing cost industry where marginal costs exceeded average costs, keeping prices down to average cost would only encourage overconsumption and queues. It would be more efficient if coal were priced at its marginal cost of production even if this meant that the NCB earned a substantial profit. Similarly a number of economists have argued the allocative inefficiency that resulted from the electricity failing to introduce realistic peak pricing, because the marginal cost of providing extra electricity in the peak greatly exceeded the marginal cost of off-peak prices. Analogous arguments have been common in transport. Congested urban roads are underpriced because the prices road-users pay (through fuel and other duties) do not reflect the marginal costs of congestion. In deciding the level of underground and suburban railway fares, account should be taken of the reduction of congestion on road as traffic is attracted to rail by lower fares.[38] Again the arguments for and against peak pricing in transport and telecommunications relate to propositions about allocative efficiency.

Economists have used arguments from allocative efficiency to criticise what they have seen as some of the cruder positions taken on nationalised industry profits. As has been noted, Little argued it would be efficient to raise coal prices to marginal cost though it would mean the NCB earning what some might regard as politically unacceptable profits. In the comparatively rare cases – e.g. rural roads and under-used branch railway lines – where marginal costs are less than average costs, the introduction of marginal cost pricing would imply an overall deficit. A relevant economic argument against allowing such industries to make a loss would be if the effect on the morale and efficiency of the management of loss-making are such as to result in a greater loss of allocative efficiency than would be caused by the divergence between prices and marginal costs needed for the enterprise to break even. Whatever the reason nationalised industries are required to make a profit, or avoid a loss, taking 'one year with another' economists tend to regard this as a rule or constraint imposed for non-economic reasons, and to be criticised from the standpoint of allocative efficiency.

Economists with an interest in allocative efficiency have tended to criticise the use of productivity measures of public enterprise efficiency as too crude. From the standpoint of allocative efficiency the

[37] Little (1953). [38] Foster and Beesley (1962).

correct and rational approach to evaluating a change in production – whether an investment, laying off manpower, starting a new or discontinuing an old product, or any other significant change – is to estimate the costs of the change and set them against the benefits (both discounted to allow for the effects of time). An efficient enterprise is one which makes all the changes in production open to it which collectively show a positive return. To measure changes in efficiency as if they were the same as improvements in labour productivity is crude. As has already been noted, growth in labour productivity 'may not measure the effort and efficiency of the manager, but simply the efficiency of the capital investment. It is always possible to instal magnificent equipment and thus to gain high productivity, but at great cost'.[39] Professors Florence and Walker went on to explain that the disadvantages of productivity measures of improved efficiency is that they do not incorporate an estimate of the costs of achieving the productivity gains.

Pryke's answer[40] to this was twofold. 1. As a matter of fact economists[41] had shown there was a close relationship between growth in output per man hour and changes in 'residual' productivity. This implies that in private industry at least one does not typically find very high gains in labour productivity 'explained by particularly large capital expenditures'. 2. Since an allocative economist might explain this in private industry as what one would expect when entrepreneurs have the fear of competition and take-over to stop them engaging in unprofitable capitalisation, Pryke met the counter-argument that nationalised industries might be particularly voracious and undisciplined consumers of capital, by developing his own indices of residual productivity which, as we have seen, suggested that on average the nationalised industries he had looked at used capital as productively as did manufacturing industry.

While the use of measures of residual productivity is a substantial improvement on using labour productivity, it is not a complete answer to the difficulties of the allocative economist. He may argue that no movement in a productivity index, however favourable, can prove that there were not still more efficient courses of action which the enterprise passed by. The practical answer to this is that one can never prove whether an enterprise was not capable of more than it achieved; but that it did well by comparison with comparable enterprises is nevertheless surely some useful test of achievement. One

[39] S. Florence and G. Walker in Robson (1952), pp. 198 and 199.
[40] Pryke, op.cit., p. 109.
[41] cf. Reddaway and Smith (1960); Matthews (1963).

can always argue when faced by any particular comparison that there may have been special circumstances which explain away a difference in performance. Thus one might argue during the 1940s and 1960s that the good performance of the nationalised industries resulted from an alleged fact that they were 'catching up', starting from a lower base; or that there were other 'special factors' which explained away what was interesting or heartening in any comparison. Indeed if there were to be an efficiency audit commission or public institute one would expect testing the effect of such special factors and making whatever adjustments were necessary to be a way in which it improved on the foundations given it by Richard Pryke. In the end the case for making productivity comparisons of the type that Pryke made is not that they are perfect measures of efficiency (even if efficiency is unambiguously defined) but it is better that economists should actually measure changes in efficiency than that they should simply lay down ideal criteria, or try to construct ideal measures of changes in efficiency which would be incapable of realisation.

However, in the past economists used to use another argument against the use of labour or residual productivity comparisons to measure nationalised industry efficiency. This followed directly from the argument on the efficiency of marginal cost pricing. If price was below marginal cost pricing there was a prima facie argument for altering (generally reducing) output until the two were made equal. An activity by analogy which could not cover its marginal costs was inefficient and should be altered or discontinued. This was not the same as the businessmen's dictum that one should not continue with a product which is unprofitable, but it is closely related to it. A major objection to relying on productivity comparisons was therefore that 'the physical products whose output is increased may not be the products required in additional quantities by the community'.[42] For example, one can imagine a situation in which a new form of diesel traction might greatly increase the productivity of manpower engaged in freight haulage; but if consumers are not prepared to pay a price which covers the marginal costs of providing the service then the allocative economist would argue that there is a prima facie case for not providing the service whatever the increase in physical productivity. That something of the kind is implicit in Pryke's calculations can be shown quite simply. To estimate residual productivity he weighted (or valued) the capital used by the nationalised industries as if it had earned a return of 10 per cent. In many of these industries

[42] Florence and Walker in Robson (1953).

a high proportion of capital never earned 10 per cent. Therefore in some cases the net residual productivity Pryke is measuring will be negative: that is, the value of the capital, labour and other inputs will exceed the revenue raised by the sale of the product. The improvements in residual productivity he records are therefore reductions in a negative quantity. The obvious question this posed for the allocative economist has been to ask why, if at the margin the resources devoted to the production of a commodity exceeded the amount society paid as evidenced by its price, it would not be efficient to stop production or at least alter the volume until marginal revenue equalled marginal cost. To proceed to a *reductio ad absurdum*, one can imagine a situation in which the residual productivity of, say, the railways as measured by Pryke was increasing at a rapid annual rate, but that the demand for railway services was dropping at such a rate that railway output could only be sold at prices which fall further and further below marginal costs. By Pryke's test such an industry would be efficient; but not by the test of the marketplace (or of marginal cost pricing).

Until recently the strength of the case against relying on productivity comparisons to measure efficiency would hardly have been challenged. Now it is – by Pryke who draws for this purpose on arguments by Leibenstein.[43] This is an important question for a number of reasons:

1 If Leibenstein and Pryke are right, then those economists who have argued about allocative efficiency in the context of public enterprise have been wasting their time.

2 It follows from this that the attention given both by them and by governments to pricing and investment criteria has also been misplaced.

3 In so far as these have been used as instruments of control by central government over the nationalised industries, this also has been a waste of time.

4 *A fortiori* the attention paid to the financial performance and deficits of the nationalised industries has been wasted.

[43] Pryke, op. cit., ch. 18. Leibenstein concentrates on the private sector where firms cannot increase productivity if this results in overall financial losses. One cannot infer he would agree with Pryke's use of residual productivity to measure increases in efficiency where the enterprise is loss-making. Indeed the arguments for using productivity changes as a measure of the changes in efficiency of a firm are Pryke's, not Leibenstein's.

5 In future the efficiency, and presumably the control, of the nationalised industries should be related to productivity comparisons and measurements of growth in productivity.

IV

X-EFFICIENCY VERSUS ALLOCATIVE EFFICIENCY

The reasons that Leibenstein and others have given against bothering with allocative efficiency have their genesis not in public enterprise but more generally in relation to competition and monopoly. To understand them, one needs to understand their origins.

With few exceptions economists since the nineteenth century have argued that misallocation of resources, and therefore waste, results from monopoly. By contrast they have pointed out that if there were perfect competition, there would be the most efficient use of given resources. In the past some economists have argued as if there were absolute value in perfect competiton. Now virtually all economists would carefully qualify the advantages of perfect competition. Among the most important qualifications are that if there are social costs or benefits, perfect competition will not produce the most efficient allocation of resources (and by implication the highest real income per head) and that the outcome would only be acceptable if the income distribution that resulted was, or could be made, acceptable. However, perfect competition does not exist; and the general tendency of the inter-war and immediate post Second World War period was to argue that a large and rapidly growing sector of the economy was monopolistic. While some voices were heard arguing that this tendency was not wholly bad – for example Schumpeter suggested that monopoly could stimulate innovation – it was in general difficult to argue that the growth of monopoly and monopolistic competition was likely to make firms more efficient in relation to social costs or benefits; or to result in what would generally be thought to be a more acceptable income distribution. Rather the reverse. Therefore it was widely asserted that the growth of monopoly as evidenced by growing concentration of production between a few firms in many industries was worsening the misallocation of resources without in itself improving the distribution of income or being the cause of any countervailing tendencies to improve the efficiency with which resources were used.

Also in the inter-war period, the Polish economist Lange [44] had

[44] Lange (1934, 1936, 1937).

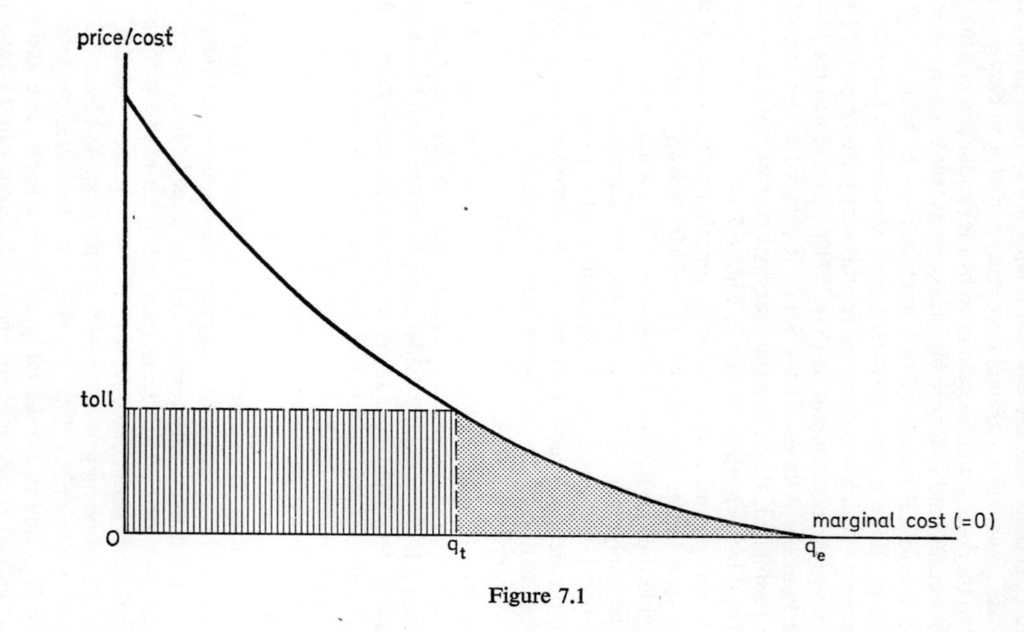

Figure 7.1

demonstrated what was efficient economic behaviour for 'socialist' public enterprise. A consequence of perfect competition was that output was sold at marginal cost. As an allocative economist Lange argued essentially that the efficient pricing policy for a public enterprise was (short run) marginal cost pricing, that is to charge a price equal to the costs actually occasioned by the production of a marginal unit of output (and to ignore historic costs as 'sunk' or byegones).

The theoretical nature of this misallocation in both the private and the public sector can be most simply shown by a diagram – and an example – which was first used for this very purpose by the French engineer-economist Dupuit in 1844.[45] His example was the building of the Pont des Arts across the Seine. It entailed a capital cost, but as he postulated, thereafter the marginal cost of using it was zero ($MC = 0$ is the horizontal axis in Figure 7.1).

This was not an unreasonable assumption as the costs of maintaining the bridge per person or vehicle crossing were probably negligible (but he neglected congestion which today we would consider as implying a positive and rising *MC* curve). Dupuit invented the concept of consumers' surplus and used it to describe the area under the demand curve (but above the marginal cost price) as a users' valuation of the bridge measured by their willingness to pay. If either a private tollkeeper imposed a toll to maximise profits or a public authority levied one, say, to cover historic costs, there would be a reduction in consumers' surplus measured by the shaded area in Figure 7.1. The vertically shaded area, however, would not be a loss but a transfer. What consumers lose, the tollkeeper gains. But the horizontally shaded area would be a deadweight or absolute loss. This would be the inefficiency from misallocation of resources that would be caused by pricing a commodity above marginal cost. If marginal cost were positive there would be a similar 'little triangle' of lost efficiency. It represents output for which the amount its consumer would be ready to pay exceeds the resource cost (in this case zero), though these consumers would be priced off by the toll.

A profit-maximising private firm will price above marginal cost unless there is perfect competition. As we have seen with the NCB, a public enterprise may price below marginal cost. As Figure 7.2 shows there is an analogous 'little triangle' that measures the loss of efficiency. If p_e and q_e are the marginal cost pricing price and output and p^* and q^* are less efficient price and output – in this case reflecting average cost pricing – then the loss of efficiency is represented by

[45] Dupuit (1844).

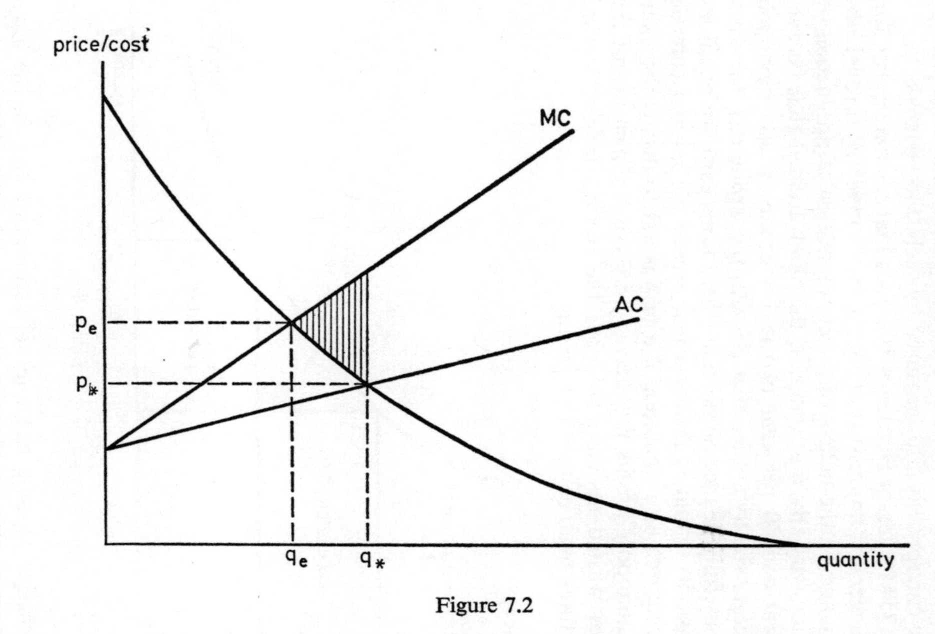

Figure 7.2

the shaded triangle. It is the range of output over which the marginal cost exceeds the consumers' willingness to pay.

It is the total of the little triangles that measures the distortion, or waste, produced in an economy by the existence of monopoly, and the waste caused by a failure to charge marginal cost pricing in a public enterprise is also measured by such 'little triangles'.

In 1954 Professor Harberger [46] argued that economists had formed an exaggerated impression of the extent of monopoly through observing changes in the indices of the concentration of production within each industry. By that criterion they had decided that between 20 per cent and 40 per cent of the US economy was monopolised. Harberger rightly argued that this was the wrong test. Monopoly is more usefully defined as existing where firms earn abnormal monopoly profits – that is profits which exceed the normal competitive level required as a minimum if a firm is not to depart the industry. The monopoly profits themselves were not the measure of the resources wasted by monopoly but the 'little triangles' caused by departures from competitive pricing.

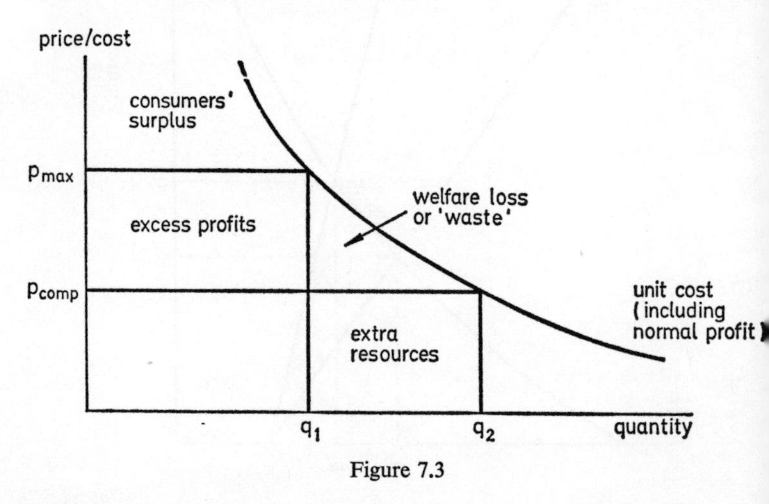

Figure 7.3

Harberger made a not unusual assumption that in the long run industries operated under constant costs. Hence unit or average cost equalled marginal costs. As the firm was monopolistic, it faced a downward-sloping demand curve. As can be seen the monopolist makes 'excess profits'. If he were to sell at the competitive price

[46] A. C. Harberger (1954).

(p_{comp}) he would sell more (q_2) but his excess profits would disappear. This is not an absolute loss to the economy since again what he loses is exactly matched by a gain in consumers' surplus – which is defined by the difference between the price they pay (which was p_{max} and has now been lowered to p_{comp}) and the maximum they would pay as shown by the slope of the demand curve. The 'little triangle' represents what those who have been priced out of the market would have been ready to pay above the unit cost of production if the price had been competitive rather than monopolistic. This measures the loss of inefficiency caused by price being not equal to marginal cost for any firm; and the sum of these 'little triangles' throughout the economy measures the misallocation of resources that results from the existence of monopoly. Or to put it another way, the sum of these measures the amount by which the actual gross national product falls short of the maximum possible gross national product that could result from given national resources.

Harberger's contribution was that he went on to try to measure the actual loss of US GNP that could be attributed to monopoly. The best data available to him related to the 1920s.[47] This showed the amount by which rates of return in some industries exceeded the average. On an *a priori* basis he argued that the industries with abnormal profit rates had low demand elasticities. He assumed unit demand elasticity for all monopolistic industries. On this assumption he argued that about 4 per cent of the resources of the manufacturing industry, or $1\frac{1}{2}$ per cent of all national resources would have to be transferred from the low profit to the high profit industries to equalise rates of profit in all industries so as to eliminate all (manufacturing) little triangles. He then calculated that the sum of the benefit of doing this would be less than one tenth of 1 per cent of US national income, or translating it into 1954 figures, the advantages of eliminating monopoly would have amounted to no more than $1.50 for every American. Harberger's study was followed by a number of others which also seemed to show how slight was the burden of monopoly.[48]

[47] Epstein (1934).

[48] Schwartzman (1960) improved on Harberger's procedure by (*a*) taking census data on profit and direct cost, (*b*) comparing data on concentrated industries in Canada with those in the same unconcentrated US industries, and (*c*) employing −1 and −2 demand elasticities. Otherwise he used Harberger's assumptions on constant costs and method of calculating welfare losses. His estimate was that the burden of monopoly was 0·1 per cent of national income (in 1954). Kamerschen (1966) used data for 1956–60, included calculations for non-manufacturing industry and tried to allow for capitalised profits, royalties and advertising expen-

In his 1966 article, which introduced the phrase 'X-efficiency', Leibenstein [49] referred to the contributions of Harberger, Schwartzman and others. But he drew a more complex set of conclusions. He extended Harberger's argument to point out that it therefore seemed relatively unimportant to improve allocative efficiency: the return from investment to improve such efficiency 'in a great many instances . . . is trivial'.[50] It would have been in the spirit of his argument if he had added that when making an investment it probably mattered very little from the standpoint of overall allocative efficiency whether a firm missed profit maximisation by even a substantial margin.

Leibenstein then pointed a paradox. While the findings of Harberger and the others implied low returns from improved allocative efficiency, a vast number of empirical studies suggested far larger returns from investment. He cites work on the return to consultancy services which suggested a return of 200 per cent to the firms that used such services. As well as micro-economic studies, he referred to the work of Solow, Aukrust, and Denison who showed that only a small proportion of growth in GNP per head is the result of capital investment. Fifty per cent to 80 per cent of growth in advanced countries is explained by technological change, education and a number of other possible changes.

The only way he saw of reconciling these is to postulate that most firms are not profit maximisers in the classical sense. 'The simple fact is that neither individuals nor firms work as hard, nor do they search for information as effectively as they could.' [51] '. . . where the motivation is weak, firm managements will permit a considerable degree of slack in their operations and will not seek cost-improving methods'.[52] Thus he sees that the important improvements in industry yielding high returns reflect progressive cost-reducing forces within firms overcoming institutional inertia against change. This also can be

---

ditures. In spite of these changes which increased the aggregate welfare losses, he still estimated these at less than 2 per cent assuming a unitary demand elasticity. Scitovsky (1958), Johnson (1958), Wemelsfelder (1960), and Jannson (1961) calculated changes in welfare losses resulting from forecast increases in competitiveness from a free trade area.

[49] Leibenstein (1966).

[50] ibid., p. 413.

[51] ibid., p. 407.

[52] ibid., p. 408. Leibenstein later (1969) formalised this argument by introducing the concept of 'inert areas' in the firm defined as 'a set of effort positions where associated levels of utility are not equal but in which the action required to go from a higher to a lower utility level involves a utility cost that is not compensated for by the gain in utility' (p. 607).

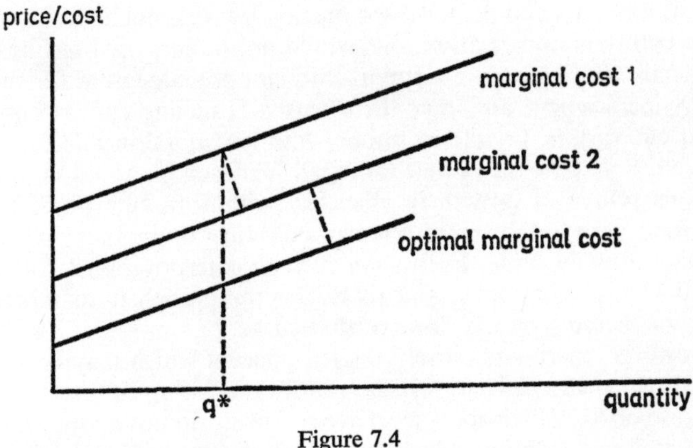

Figure 7.4

represented in Figure 7.4. Optimal marginal cost represents the cost path of a firm without inertia and with a perfect ability to take account of every cost-saving innovation. Such a firm would absorb any new idea instantaneously and if it were also allocatively efficient would not be able to increase its profit rate through investment. But marginal cost curves 1 and 2 represent the cost curves of firms which are not optimal in that sense. The dotted lines represent the overcoming of inertia in one firm as its output expands past q^* so that it moves on to a lower marginal cost curve. The implication of Leibenstein's argument is that cases of high reported rates of return on investment are of this last kind.

This formulation of X-efficiency is not entirely satisfactory. Leibenstein's exposition relied heavily on the notion of 'inert areas' within an enterprise which 'explain the degree to which actual output is less than maximum output (for given inputs)'.[53] By definition then the costs to the owners of the firm of overcoming the inertia outweigh the prospective gains in efficiency. Nevertheless the general proposition that gains in X-efficiency are the most important cause of growth in efficiency presumes that firms (and public enterprise) do overcome inertia. This must explain, for example, the high returns to the use of consultancy services found by Johnston.[54] It is not implausible that firms do from time to time overcome the resistance of managers, the inertia of labour practices, etc., and move from one cost curve (as in Figure 7.3) to a lower one. Given the history of low investment, bad

[53] Leibenstein (1969), p. 600.
[54] Johnson (1963), cited by Leibenstein.

labour relations and demoralised management in much public enterprise before nationalisation, one would not be surprised to find that nationalisation created an opportunity and a momentum for reducing X-inefficiency; and that there was a 'catching-up' process on other enterprises, private or public, with less initial inertia.

What is impossible is that falling X-inefficiency should be a continuous source of growth in efficiency within an enterprise. When one inert area is galvanised one can only turn to another; and their number must be finite. Eventually such an enterprise must find itself on its lowest cost curve; and thereafter the growth in its efficiency must be dictated by the slope of that curve.

However, there is a closely related concept which may be simply called technical efficiency which is more promising in the long run. Because of X-inefficiency – inert areas – firms do not adopt immediately every innovation which would result in significant efficiency gains. We may suppose, however, that instead of *the* important factor governing efficiency growth being the overcoming of inert areas *per se*, what matters is that at any point of time there are a number of innovations an enterprise can adopt. These may be new techniques, or more practical innovations – e.g. in labour practices. In some cases their genesis may be within the enterprise – e.g. the NCB's Anderton shearer – or they may amount to the adoption of innovations initiated elsewhere. The enterprises's growth in efficiency depends on the rate at which it adopts innovations. If it tries to innovate too fast, it may do worse – through increasing the inertia of its inert areas – than if it innovated more slowly. If it happens to reduce its X-inefficiency, it may be able to absorb more innovation in a short time. It may even be able to maintain a higher rate of innovation in the long run. But in the long run what must be important is not reducing X-inefficiency in itself but the interaction between the ability to absorb or create innovations, and X-efficiency.[55]

On this basis the main causes of the growth in efficiency of the nationalised industry best performers would seem to have been technical, though it may also have involved reduction in X-inefficiency; in the airlines, technical progress in aircraft design as well as other

[55] What is here called technical efficiency, some writers have tried to incorporate in X-efficiency. But this soon becomes a semantic argument. See Jameson (1974) and Leibenstein (1974). In this controversy Leibenstein (e.g. p. 328) would seem to be denying meaning to 'dynamic X-efficiency' except as X-efficiency having effects on growth. He would also seem to be making a distinction between X-efficiency and the kind of efficiency effects in the long run, I am calling technical efficiency; and incidentally denying reductions in X-inefficiency as a long-run cause of economic growth.

economies of scale; in power generation, technical progress in generating station design; and so forth. On the other hand, the reason for the low growth in bus productivity is the very great technical difficulty of increasing output per man hour, especially when traffics are falling but becoming more peaked. (The only new technique is 'one man operation' and in some cases the total costs of this – including the effect on waiting time – outweigh the gain in efficiency.)

We therefore have two causes of growth in efficiency:

1 There may well have been falls in X-inefficiency which help explain the greater productivity growth of the nationalised industries relative to manufacturing (as well as difference in productivity growth between nationalised industries). We do not know what proportion of productivity growth is to be explained in this way.

2 There has been the absorption of innovation. A greater rate of innovation – X-inefficiency aside – may also help explain the higher productivity growth rate of the nationalised industry sector (and of particular industries within it). As always, the greater availability of innovations to some industries than others is itself difficult to explain.

Even with this amendment, both forms of efficiency are distinct from allocative efficiency. Both are important for economic progress; and Leibenstein and Pryke were right to point out that very substantial improvements in efficiency can be achieved without considering allocative efficiency. A process of efficiency audit or control should recognise this, and until Pryke far too little attention was paid to non-allocative efficiency in public enterprise. However, both Leibenstein and Pryke went further than this. In Pryke's [56] words, 'economists seem unprepared to face up to the fact that one of the most important discoveries of economic science is the unimportance of allocative efficiency. Nowhere is the recognition of this truth more overdue than in discussion of the nationalised industries'. It is one thing to recognise that other forms of efficiency are important, another to assert that allocative efficiency is unimportant.

[56] Pryke, op. cit., p. 396.

V

THE GENERAL CASE FOR ALLOCATIVE EFFICIENCY

As it happens, the Harberger and Schwartzman calculations are vitiated by a fallacy, and so therefore are the Leibenstein and Pryke conclusions that depend on them. Leibenstein's proposition that the evidence shows the unimportance of allocative efficiency has been challenged by Bergson,[57] who developed an early point made by Stigler.[58] As a glance at Figures 7.1 or 7.2 shows, the size of a 'little triangle' depends on (*i*) the elasticity of demand – the higher the elasticity the greater the inefficiency of an allocative distortion; (*ii*) the ratio of price to cost – the greater the ratio again the greater the efficiency loss; and (*iii*) the slope of the marginal cost curve – if it slopes upwards from left to right, the triangle will be smaller than if it is horizontal (as drawn in the three diagrams) or if sloping downwards from left to right. It will be remembered that Harberger assumed a unit demand elasticity. Schwartzman considered demand elasticities up to 2. Leibenstein assumed an average demand elasticity of 1·5. Stigler argued against Harberger's assumption that one would expect the longer-run elasticities faced by monopolistic industries to be higher than this.

Bergson criticised more fundamentally the validity of the procedures used by Harberger and the others. They had all assumed it valid to lump together all the monopolistic firms and industries in an economy as one sector in contradistinction to an undifferentiated competitive sector; and assume a single demand elasticity for the monopolistic sector. By a well-known proposition in elementary demand theory, the more goods and services are lumped together, the lower the demand elasticity (because the few close substitutes remain). Bergson argued that this was wholly inappropriate. One should use separate demand elasticities (or elasticities of substitution) not merely for each firm or enterprise, but for every product. On this basis a nationalised industry like electricity or rail becomes the producer of many products which are close substitutes for each other or the products of other industries. If one were to disaggregate in such a manner one would measure larger efficiency losses principally because the elasticities of substitution would be greater. Similarly one should assume different price/cost ratios for different products. Bergson argued that a dispersion of these would also increase the

[57] Bergson (1973).

[58] Stigler (1956).

net sum of welfare losses because of their effect through elasticities of substitution.

On these bases he developed hypothetical calculations to show that on quite plausible assumptions, allocative inefficiency in consumer goods markets was sensitive to (*a*) the share a good had of the market for all goods and services; (*b*) the price/cost ratio for each product; (*c*) the dispersion of these around the mean; and (*d*) the elasticities of substitution. He calculated what he called the Net Compensating Variation coefficient for alternative combinations of (*a*), (*b*), (*c*) and (*d*). The NCV coefficient he defined as the amount which would have to be paid to consumers of a product priced above marginal cost to make them as well off as if all prices were competitive, expressed as a fraction of full employment national income. These more complicated calculations make a very great difference to the result. Instead of the less than 1 per cent of national income of Harberger, Schwartzman and others, Bergson calculated that with elasticities of substitution of from 4 to 8 and with a large number of products, as well as a range of price/cost ratios, the loss of allocative efficiency might vary from 1½ per cent to more than 15 per cent of national income.

While hypothetical calculations do not settle the extent of allocative distortion, Bergson has restored the possibility that the existence of monopoly (and in general of departures from marginal cost pricing) may result in non-trivial losses of efficiency; and that therefore as a corollary the adoption of efficient pricing could in some cases result in significant returns relative to the cost of adopting efficient pricing. This conclusion is reinforced by two further points which Bergson mentioned but did not try to quantify.

1 All the calculations by Harberger and the rest assumed that there were divergences between price and marginal cost pricing only in the production of final consumer goods; but there will also be distortion in the production of intermediate goods which will lead to further distortions in the production of consumer goods.

2 The existence of distortions at a point of time will distort investment choices which lead to further intensification of allocative inefficiency over time.

Bergson's most significant point, that the amount of allocative inefficiency is generally increased by calculating the loss of allocative efficiency in relation to each product, can be most easily illustrated by taking the example of an intermediate and a final product as is done in Figure 7.5. Let us assume a product 'electricity generation'

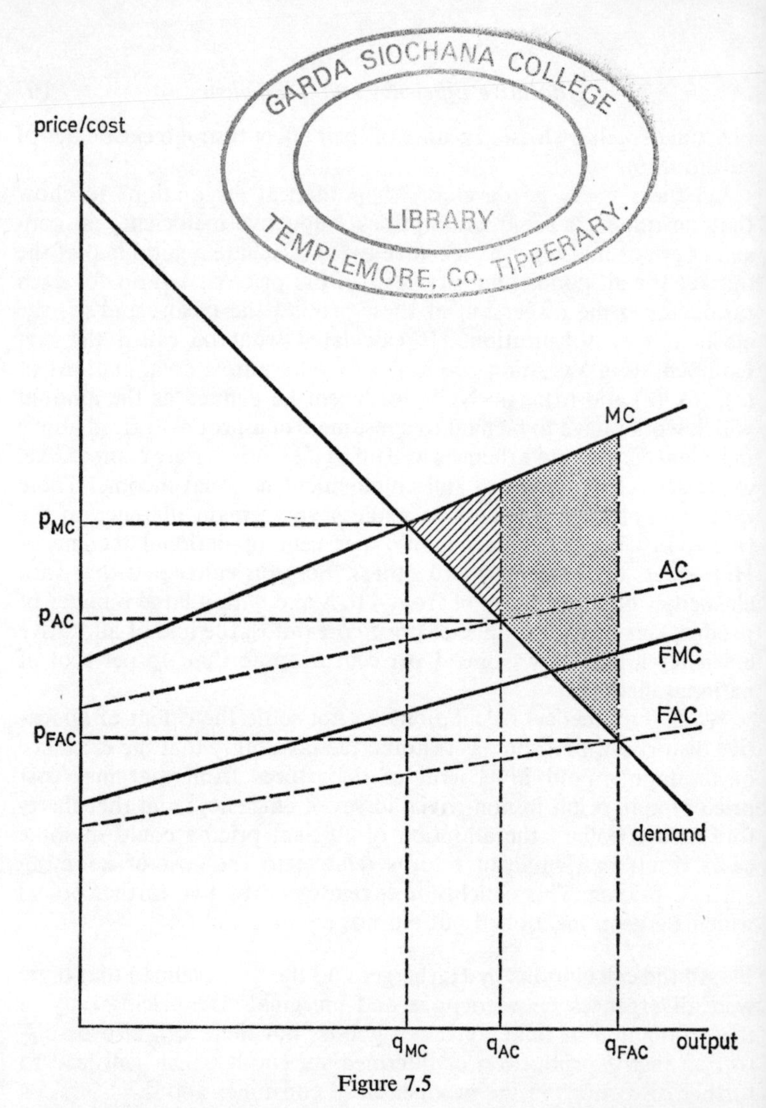

Figure 7.5

into which there is one variable input 'coal'. The 'coal' industry's marginal cost curve is *MC* and it should determine the offer price of coal; but it is assumed that the coal industry supplies coal at a lower price illustrated by the (false) marginal cost (*FMC*) curve. In its turn, we assume the electricity industry supplies power at some price below marginal cost, say average cost (*AC*). If it was working on a true marginal cost curve (*MC*) it would produce q_{AC} amount of electricity at a price of P_{AC}. But as it is working on a false *FMC* curve, it uses the corresponding false average cost curve (*FAC*) and produces q_{FAC} electricity at a price p_{FAC}. If the only distortion were the electricity supply's underpricing, the loss of allocative efficiency would be measured by the diagonally shaded little triangle; but when the coal pricing distortion is added in as well, the relevant little triangle expands to include the dotted area too.[59] It was because Harberger and those who made similar calculations tended to ignore this kind of point that they greatly underestimated the waste caused by allocative inefficiency.

Therefore there is strong presumption that Harberger, Schwartzman and the others have underestimated the importance of allocative inefficiency. That this is so seems likely when one considers that where partial measures have been made of inefficiency that results from the existence of non-marginal cost pricing, these have frequently come up with far from negligible quantities. What this should do is to put all forms of inefficiency in perspective. X-inefficiency, what has here been called technical efficiency, and allocative inefficiency may all be important. Concentration on any one and neglect of any other may result in unnecessary inefficiency. However, while this general argument seems good against Leibenstein, Pryke could nevertheless still be correct that allocative inefficiency could be unimportant in UK nationalised industries.

VI

ALLOCATIVE EFFICIENCY AND THE NATIONALISED INDUSTRIES

Pryke's major demonstration of the unimportance of allocative efficiency refers to the railways deficit. In 1968 BR's working deficit was £91m. He assumes an elasticity of 2 and argues that to break even, it would have had to raise its charges by 20 per cent, losing 40 per cent of its revenue. There would have been a reduction of £183m. in revenue from those priced off the railway. However, the relevant 'little triangle' in Figure 7.5 would only be £18m.; and as 3 per cent of total working expenses, Pryke argued that to take action to eliminate the deficit for so little gain would indeed be 'trivial'.

1 The first point is that Pryke is assuming that allocative efficiency

[59] This is not the case if the monopolists collude so as to maximise joint profits. If a monopolist discriminates in its pricing to increase its profits, this will reduce the welfare loss. I am indebted to Professor Yamey for these two points.

implies that BR should in 1968 have covered their working expenses including depreciation. Since Pryke elsewhere argued [60] that in 1968 rail depreciation provisions should have been enough to provide for capital expenditure to maintain the then level of activity, Pryke is in fact assuming that marginal costs equal average cost – that is, that the railways are properly regarded as a constant returns industry. This is the position argued by Joy,[61] but it is worth noting that allocative efficiency implies marginal cost pricing, not the elimination of the financial deficit as such; and that if marginal costs were to be below average costs, raising revenue to cover working expenses could reduce rather than increase allocative efficiency.

2 But what is a significant amount of allocative inefficiency? Harberger and those who made similar calculations were talking of the whole burden of monopoly being no more than from a fraction of 1 per cent to 2 per cent of national income. Bergson suggested that it might amount to a much higher fraction of national income. But practically it only makes sense to talk of the benefit of achieving an improvement in allocative efficiency in relation to a cost of achieving that benefit. One crude way of regarding Pryke's 1968 figure of £18m. is to say that (at a given interest rate) it would have been worth spending up to a Net Present Value of £18m. per annum to get rid of it. (If, as is the case, the deficit, if not corrected, and therefore the allocative inefficiency are expected to deteriorate over time, then it follows it is worth spending something more than this.) Of course it is always possible that X-inefficiency – inert areas which cannot be overcome – impose such a cost that to attempt the increase in allocative efficiency that would follow from adopting marginal cost pricing would not pay. But this kind of point can only be decided in particular instances.

3 The most serious objection to Pryke's procedure is Bergson's. Namely he assumed one demand elasticity for the industry; but very different demand elasticities apply to different traffics. Some probably have high elasticities of substitution – e.g. long-distance passenger traffic which competes with rail, freightliner traffic which competes with road, and, by Pryke's own showing, a high proportion of traffic on unremunerative branch lines. The demand for other traffics is relatively inelastic – some trainload freight and long-distance commuter services. There are also services where costs of congestion are such that marginal social cost prices should be lower than the

[60] Pryke, op. cit., pp. 187, 188.
[61] Joy (1964/5); Foster and Joy (1967).

marginal private cost prices. And the ratio of price to marginal cost varies greatly between services. From this it follows that on the lines suggested by Bergson, one should get a substantial measure of allocative inefficiency if one were able to estimate the 'little triangles' for the various railway 'products' separately. That it is very difficult to estimate elasticities of substitution in such detail does not mean that one should therefore assume that rail allocative inefficiency is as low as Pryke's calculations suggest. Moreover if one thinks of the cost – whether related to X-inefficiency or not – of achieving the gains in allocative efficiency related to specific traffics, it is likely that the returns in some cases will be much higher than others. Similar arguments apply to other nationalised industries; and one should not forget that many of the outputs of nationalised industries are intermediate products so that any distortions may be carried over and intensified at later stages in the productive process.

VII

CONCLUSION

Pryke has shown the importance of reductions in X-inefficiency (and increases in technical efficiency) in explaining productivity growth in the nationalised industries and has corrected an earlier tendency among public enterprise economists to concentrate almost exclusively on allocative efficiency. By measuring changes in productivity, despite the inevitable limitations of such measures, he has been the first to attempt to measure comprehensively nationalised industries' performance. But he has not proved the case that allocative inefficiency is unimportant or even relatively unimportant. It follows that pricing and investment criteria remain worth attention, though it is also important that there should be policies and methods of control which will stimulate greater non-allocative efficiency. Pricing and investment criteria need supplementing by policies to increase non-allocative efficiency.

REFERENCES

Bergson, A., 'On Monopoly Welfare Losses', *American Economic Review* (December 1973), pp. 853–70.

Citrine, Lord, 'Productivity and the Nationalised Industries', *Public Administration* (1957), pp. 325–6.

Dupuit, J., 'On the Measurement of the Utility of Public Works', *Annales des Ponts et Chaussées*, vol. 8 (1844), reprinted in *International Economic Papers*, no. 2 (1952).
Epstein, R. C., *Industrial Profits in the United States* (NBER, 1934).
Foster, C. D., *Politics, Finance and the Role of Economics* (George Allen & Unwin, 1972).
Foster, C. D., and Beesley, M. E., 'Estimating the Social Benefit of Constructing an Underground Railway in London', JRSS, Series E (1963).
Harberger, A., 'Monopoly and Resource Allocative', *American Economic Review* (May 1954), pp. 77–87.
Hicks, J. R., *Revision of Demand Theory* (Oxford, 1956).
Jameson, K., 'Comment on the Theory and Measurement of Dynamic X-Efficiency', *Quarterly Journal of Economics* (1974), pp. 313–26.
Jansson, L. H., *Free Trade, Protection and Custom Union* (Leiden, 1961).
Johnson, H. F., 'The Basis from Freer Trade with Europe', *Manchester School* (September 1958), pp. 247–55.
Johnston, J., 'The Productivity of Management Consultants', JRSS, Series A (1963), pp. 237–49.
Joy, S., 'British Railways' Track Costs', *Journal of Industrial Economics* (1964–5), pp. 74–84.
Kamerschen, D. R., 'Welfare Losses from Monopoly', *Western Economic Journal* (Summer 1966), pp. 221–36.
Knight, F. H., 'Some Fallacies in the Interpretation of Social Cost', *Quarterly Journal of Economics* (1929), pp. 582–606.
Lange, O., 'Marxian Economics and Modern Economic Theory', *Review of Economic Studies* (June 1934).
Lange, O., 'On the Economic Theory of Socialism I and II', *Review of Economic Studies* (October 1936, February 1937).
Little, I. M. D., *The Price of Fuel* (Clarendon Press, 1953).
Leibenstein, H., 'Allocative Efficiency versus X-Efficiency', *AmericanEconomic Review* (June 1966), pp. 392–415.
Leibenstein, H., 'Comment on the Nature of X-Efficiency', *Quarterly Journal of Economics* (1974), pp. 327–31.
Leibenstein, H., 'Organisation or Frictional Equilibria X-Efficiency and the Rate of Innovation', *Quarterly Journal of Economics* (November 1969), pp. 600–23.
Matthews, R. C. O., *Transactions of the Manchester Statistical Society* (November 1964), pp. 19, 20.
Morrison, H., *Government and Parliament* (1954).
Nelson, J. R. (ed.), *Marginal Cost Pricing in Practice* (Prentice-Hall, 1964).
Pryke, R., *Public Enterprise in Practice* (McGibbon and Kee, 1971).
Reddaway, W. B., and Smith, A. D., *Economic Journal* (1960), p. 29.
Robson, W. A., *Public Enterprise* (George Allen & Unwin, 1937).
Robson, W. A., *Problems of Nationalised Industries* (George Allen & Unwin, 1952).
Robson, W. A., *Nationalised Industry and Public Ownership* (George Allen & Unwin, 1960).
Schwartzman, D., 'The Burden of Monopoly', *Journal of Political Economy* (December 1960), pp. 627–30.
Scitovsky, T., *Economic and Western European Integration* (Stanford, 1958).
Stigler, G. J., 'The Statistics of Monopoly and Merger', *Journal of Political Economy* (February 1956), pp. 33–40.

Turrey, R., *Optimal Pricing and Investment in Electricity Supply* (George Allen & Unwin, 1968).

Walters, A. A., 'The Theory and Measurement of Private and Social Cost of Highway Congestion', *Econometrica*, vol. 29 (October 1961).

Webb, Sidney and Beatrice, *A Constitution for the Socialist Commonwealth of Great Britain* (Longmans, 1920).

Wemelsfelder, J., 'The Short-term Effect of Lowering Import Duties in Germany', *Economic Journal* (March 1960), pp. 94–104.

8

Administrative Law and Policy Effectiveness

J. D. B. MITCHELL

All the world is free. Editors are entitled to choose the titles for thei contributors. The contributors [1] remain free to make what they can or will, of the title. This title was chosen by the editor. Some change are needed in interpreting it. For the words 'administrative law' wil be substituted the phrase 'public law', which is shorter, and avoid the narrow connotation of the former words with their penumbra o drains and planning law. For 'policy effectiveness' one might sub stitute 'the efficiency of the administrative or governmental process' 'Policy effectiveness' is an ambiguous phrase. If the policy be wrong it does not follow that it should be made effective, in the sense o overriding all obstacles. 'Efficiency' is used in a broad sense whicl includes elements of the generation of contentment, or at least of a acquiescence which is not too grudging; for efficiency in governmen is certainly not a simple concept of maximising production, it involve the feelings both of those who are (in a variety of ways) on the pro duction line, and of those who are the consumers or recipients of th product. In all cases those feelings are specific to the processes whicl are called administrative or governmental. Apart from these mino changes, the title remains that chosen by the editor.

Even thus defined, it would be easy to convert this essay into facile plea for law and order, either in the generalised sense in whicl those words are often now used, or else in the sense that state powe is the enemy of the rule of law.[2] The abuse of that power is certainl an enemy to be fought, but the existence of that power is not inimica to the rule of law and the efficiency in the correct use of that powe is of increasing importance. Clearly, to take an obvious example, once the costs of effective medicine had reached a certain level, the intervention of state power in the organisation of the provision of medical treatment became a human and economic necessity, and in that organisation law must play its part. Indeed, even at the outset, it is as well to emphasise that public law can exist to ease the exercise of state power, and to do so for the benefit both of those who exercise the power, and of those who are the objects of that exercise, or are affected by it. The citizen has a real interest in the efficiency of the governmental process. Otherwise he suffers in general from the enhanced social costs, just as he may suffer, as an individual, from detailed inefficiency. Planning in its delays and in particular hardships can afford examples of both. Clearly, therefore, the individual gains if law can help to achieve that efficiency. If in the performance of his functions law can also produce a better framework for his action, the administrator also gains.

This is the primary reason for substituting the adjective 'public' for 'administrative', though, as will appear, there are others. It is not so much the subject matter with which administrative law has been concerned with us which tends to falsify the argument, it is rather the almost exclusive connotation of control in a negative sense which has come to be associated with those words which make them unhappy ones in this context. They are unhappy because they thus conceal the positive or creative role of what should be called public law. That role has many aspects. Wordsworth, in his preface to the *Lyrical Ballads*, wrote of 'the effects of great national events which are daily taking place, and the encreasing accumulation of men in cities, where the uniformity of their occupations produces a craving for extraordinary incident which the rapid communication of intelligence hourly gratifies'. The result, he asserted, was to reduce the mind to a state of 'almost savage torpor'. Believing that man could react without the application of 'gross and violent stimulants', he chose to write of the events and circumstances of common life and to do so in common language. The gap between poetry on the one hand and politics and law on the other may seem vast, but is not as great as it seems. Politics, and particularly bi-polar politics, tend to stimulate that craving for extraordinary incident, generating a climate in which essentially political controls of administration result inevitably in distortion. The error of administration becomes, if not a matter of high politics, at least one of heated politics. On the other hand, the law in this area has assumed all those qualities of extravagance and unreality which Wordsworth saw in the decline of writing. The late Professor de Smith, citing one who described British government as a 'rich Byzantine structure through which few can pick their way with any degree of certainty', was forced to admit that administrative law shared that quality, the circumstances in which judicial relief was obtainable had to be stated in minute detail (which is confusing) or at a high level of generality (which is misleading), general principles were lacking even to define the title to sue.[3]

The common events of life deserve emphasis. An administrative act, which many would regard as unimportant, can assume for the individual a very great subjective importance, and the cumulation of the same sort of acts can have a considerable social significance. The sense of frustration becomes generalised. At one stage in France, to be inscribed as a *résistant* or as a *déporté* mattered greatly to some individuals. That the whole process could be regulated evenly and acceptably, as it was under a system of public law, mattered to the fabric of society. It is true that at that period a similar need was not felt in the United Kingdom. Yet, leaving on one side the issue that no society can be certain that events of that sort will not occur, what mattered was that there existed a machinery, already respected, which had the capacity to deal even with such unforeseen events. It mattered as much that it could deal with the small things. The example should not be taken as typical. Clearly the circumstances were not. It is used simply because it is extreme.[4] The one significant element in it was the existence of the machine capable of dealing with 'minor' matters in which officialdom and the individual met. The irritation with government, or the sense of the remoteness of government, does not for many citizens arise from the great events, but rather from routine matters in their daily lives. These need to be dealt with adequately if government is to be acceptable. Without pushing the analogy too far, one could also underline the point of language. The language of public law, with us, has become such that it not only confuses the citizen, it also conceals from the practitioner (judge or advocate) the substance of what the dispute is about. Such a concealing word is 'prerogative'. To take one example, the Burmah Oil Case,[5] which was concerned with the destruction of the oil installations in Burma during the retreat. The essence of the argument was, as the French would have said, the problem of *égalité devant les charges publiques*, equality in sharing public burdens. Thus it would have been debated there, and a rational solution could have emerged. The essence could not, with us, appear through the mass of inapt terminology, and so a legislative intervention became inevitable. That intervention was nevertheless unhealthy for the law, and, in the long run, for the process of government, which lost respect. The problem was that 'prerogative' had merely become a concealing word used to talk about the necessary and inherent powers of government whatever form government may take; but the word and not the nature of the power governed debate. Indeed like powers, though not thus called, were formerly possessed by boroughs,[6] they too were in the business of government and, in more limited ways, felt the same need.

To break from analogy, it must also be said that this discussion is not about law and order in general, nor even about the rule of law in general. Some elements may be appropriate to other facets of such debates, to the role of law in social or domestic affairs, or even to the debate about law in industrial affairs, but those are not matters of present concern. That concern is with government, and with government both in its relationships with individuals and in regard to its internal organisation. What must be emphasised is the specific quality of government as a process. It is specific in its purposes, and that quality affects all aspects of it. Recently, the chief executive of the Property Services Agency wrote: 'so the aims and objectives of the Property Services Agency which are the basis of accountable management cannot be defined in exclusively quasi-commercial terms', and added, 'I see dangers and disadvantages in a thoroughgoing commercial approach to Government operations.' [7] In the same article he emphasises the effect of the concept of a public service on the management and deployment of staff, even terms like 'job-satisfaction' require redefinition. This appeal has been re-emphasised by the last report of the Civil Service Department.[8] Yet by training that writer's views might have tended in the opposite direction. Sir Samuel Goldman has emphasised the way in which the conditions and attributes of government affect expenditure control.[9] This specific quality obviously affects equally relationships between government and individuals. Essentially a government agency of whatever size distinguishes itself from a private corporation, however large, because of the overriding concern which must exist in government for the public interest. To say that is not to deny that 'mixed' bodies do, and should, exist, bodies which have characteristics of both worlds. The public corporation, whether in the form of a nationalised industry or in its older forms, is an obvious example, and such bodies are universal, they are not peculiar to, or perhaps even peculiarly important in, this country. The Mersey Docks and Harbour Board had governmental attributes even in the nineteenth century. There is a point of balance in function which changes structures – at a certain point the East India Company had to become, or be replaced by, the Government of India. That change is not inevitable, and the existence of this grey area does not invalidate, or essentially change, the argument. The problems which it presents are susceptible of relatively easy solutions.

It follows, then, that if government has this specific quality, so too the law relating to it in its governmental aspects must also be specific. It was one of the fallacies of the Crown Proceedings Act, 1947, to attempt to produce identity in rules of liability between the Crown and private individuals. The attempt was, of course, built on the Diceian view of the 'ordinary law of the realm' and the 'ordinary tribunals'.[10] Simple illustrations will demonstrate the fallacy. We chose, for our own social purposes, to create open borstals, or open prisons, which obviously create risks for their neighbours, or even for those further afield, when for proper purposes of treatment the inmates are sent or taken upon expeditions. Safety cannot be guaranteed, some degree of risk-taking is inherent in the system. The rules by which the burden of those risks should be shared by the community cannot be the same as the rules which govern my liability should I, for example, turn my land into a zoo or a pleasure park. Even the concept of negligence may be badly in conflict with the purpose of treatment. A different basis of liability needs to be found because the borstal is serving our purposes, as is the speeding policeman in hot pursuit and thus the liability of the police authority for the accident needs to be regulated in the light of the public functions being performed. Thus also the problem of allocating loss has to be differently worked out. These examples have been chosen since they have a relevance to a later stage of the argument. The non-contractual liability of Article 215 of the Treaty of Rome is built upon such a specific concept of liability and it owes (happily) far more to the idea of *faute de nature à engager la responsabilité des puissances publiques* than to ideas of tort or reparation under private law. The word 'happily' is used because it seems that these other ideas are much wider and more fruitful and more realistic. It would be easy to continue these examples into the field of contract. One aspect will suffice to indicate the problem. It frequently happens, and the Blue Streak affair is only one instance, that the Government does not command the electronic or other expertise. In making its contract it is in a weak position. It may also be in an overwhelmingly strong position, for among all contractors government bodies are in the unique position of having the lawful capacity to change the rules of the game half way through a contract, by changing the law, and they may indeed be under a social or public duty so to do, because of the pressure of other desired ends or necessities which are also in the public interest. Two things will be noticed. First, that properly understood the issues of public law are not confined to the relatively simple questions of the control, annulment (or not) of administrative acts (or of failures to act which present more difficult problems), as it has been conceived in this country. Indeed experience shows that that control can only be efficient if it is combined with the issue of liability. Second, that the problem is not simply the overpowering might of government. The particular weakness of government in certain situations is there too.

Perhaps a third more important thing emerges, that finally the distinction between public and private law, and between the British and the continental systems, is a philosophic one, or at least a jurisprudential one. Private law remains a jurisprudence of rights; public law one of interests. It is concerned predominantly with the balancing of public and private interests, whereas even in my dealings with ICI the rights on either side remain of the same nature – private. Of course the distinction can be too baldly stated, but for the moment baldness will suffice. It will follow, therefore, that the creation of a specific court and hence of specific techniques is necessary. It is unreasonable to suppose that a judge can jump from divorce to company law, to the problems of government and deal with each with equal facility. This is not professionalism, it is amateurism of an injurious sort; but it exists. What is required is a jurisdiction which can produce appropriate general principles, for in detail the elements of what has earlier been said can be found in our system. Yet to break through to principles of the type that have been mentioned, a breach with the past is necessary. That breach is also necessary if one is to gain an appropriate degree of specialism and knowledge of government. Knowledge both of the strengths and weakness of government is needed. The nature of the Court may be left for the moment.

That the individual can gain should be clear, but it is also true that the administration can do so too. There is within any system of public law a respect for the autonomy of the administrative process. It is not for a court to assume the tasks of the administration, but only to insist that it performs them well. There is no escape from administrative discretion. The belief, which emerges from time to time in Germany, and which influenced so heavily the report of the Franks Committee,[11] that if only one could make the administration behave more lik a court all would be well, and the citizen find happiness, has been demonstrated to be false by the subsequent history of inquiries. The increase in the length and cost of them has not produced any equivalent satisfaction, rather the converse. Indeed it may well be the function of an administrative court to maintain and to insist upon the exercise of a discretion.[12] The more an administration seeks to behave like a court, the more it will seek the comfort of a precedent. There are many pressures working towards forms of automatism. Uniformity is often easier to defend politically, reliance on habit or precedent may be an excuse for thought, and a relief from the burden of choice, yet equal treatment of things which are unequal is bad administration. Thus while a jurisdiction and the administration remain distinct in purpose, and should remain distinct in techniques, there needs to be an awareness by the former of the needs of the latter, and an acceptance by the latter of the former as being in a sense a keeper of a conscience. There should be no animosity. That situation is certainly not unattainable. It is in broad terms not unlike the situation in which the Comptroller and Auditor General lives with the administration in a different context. The effects of such a keeper of conscience should not be regarded as simply restrictive. In the absence of the possibility of such external control an administration may, in fact, become too timorous. If it lacks a tribunal of standing, in which it can justify itself, then it may hold back, or else it may create suspicions against itself which it cannot rebut, and that circumstance can also inhibit. Indeed there are instances, even in the field of security, in which the existence and use of that possibility have eased the task of administration. Finally, whatever is claimed by Members, that control cannot come through Parliament in general or the House of Commons in particular. Two reasons may be given as illustrations. The first is the nature of the forum. It is, and must remain, a political one. Decisions of the type here envisaged are of course in one sense political, there is little in government which is not automatic, which has no political overtones, but to debate a matter which is essentially administrative in terms of politics is to falsify the debate. Indeed one of the problems of British administration at the moment is that because of the lack of a valid alternative control system we have almost lost a sense of what is a true political decision. The second is that of practical impossibility. Members of Parliament are free to delude themselves, but in so doing are not entitled to deny to citizens appropriate protections. With the present size and complexity of government and of departments, reliance on the myth of ministerial responsibility can no longer be defended as an instrument of detailed control. The doctrine has had some virtues, particularly its effects internally in a department, and those it will retain, but it is no sure foundation for a claim for holding control within the arena of politics. The House could not manage. The evidence is there. The Parliamentary Question did emerge as a detailed control, in the absence of any other. But already in the early years of this century, when government was much simpler than now, restraints had to be imposed, restraints which have grown stricter while the width of government has grown. Reliance upon such detailed control as the primary method is not only impractical in, it is inappropriate to such a body; it distracts it from its true political purposes. On the other side it becomes injurious to the administration.

Those, then, are the general principles. The full effect on the administration will be elaborated later. It is worth adding that unless one takes an extremely short view of tradition, as did the Kilbrandon Committee,[13] there is nothing antithetical to the British system in such courts. Nor indeed is there anything undemocratic in any real sense of the word. The reasons why we have no such court relate to the accidents of history. Important among them was the late upsurge of the administrative state in the second half of the nineteenth century at a time of an upsurge of Parliament. Again as a result of accident, too much of our constitution-making has been left too exclusively in the hands of politicians, and they have fashioned it in their own way. One consequence has been that never has the whole machinery of government been looked at as an entity.[14] Changes have come when forced by the pressure of events, but each change was seen in isolation. Thus the modern state crept up, in a sense unobserved, upon both politicians and lawyers. Certainly the latter in early cases like *Local Government Board v. Arlidge*[15] or *Institute of Patent Agents v. Lockwood*,[16] cases in which things started to go wrong, showed little perception of what was happening in the constitution or in the administration. One result has certainly been a current distrust of lawyers in this field, a feeling which, in some quarters, both fed and was fed by the place of lawyers in the Civil Service. A more serious result was a general sense of malaise. Resort was had to a series of piecemeal measures, none of which proved to be a cure. The Tribunals and Inquiries Act, 1958, brought alleviation but no cure. The Parliamentary Commissioner for Administration has had scarcely that modest success.[17] These measures were symptomatic of differences between a true system of public law and British ideas of administrative law. A philosophic distinction has been mentioned, a more practical one is that the British systems have concentrated on ante-natal measures, hence the emphasis on procedural safeguards which themselves congest administration. Indeed, at the start the Parliamentary Commissioner had to be diverted from an excessive concern simply with procedural rectitude. The alternative system, a true one of public law, exercising a control *a posteriori* can be much more concerned with substance. Thus with such a system procedure can be simplified, and hence preliminary stages accelerated. The problem is one of balance, but without a reasonable control *a posteriori* we will remain with a system which cumulates procedural safeguards, which in the end of the day do not satisfy individuals, but which delay and encumber the administration and thereby create heavy social costs. Indeed, the situation can and does arise in which these delays have to be short-circuited out of practical necessity. Such is the primary cause of the Petroleum, Off-Shore Development (Scotland) Bill, 1974. If the process becomes too complex, seemingly draconian measures may have to be taken because of the necessities of government, and administration falls into further disfavour. The question is not one of either or, but of getting an appropriate balance, but if administration is to be able to act with appropriate speed a shift to a system of *a posteriori* controls, which differs from the one we have, is needed.

Thus internally the question is already important. It will become more so because of internal and external causes. Internally, further pressure will result from any implementation of the Kilbrandon Report.[18] It is unreal to suppose that, without substantial change in the political framework, any attempted devolution of real power would endure. One of the greatest factors in the high degree of centralisation in the United Kingdom is that caused by the organisation of political parties and of the other major political actors which are themselves centralised in their structures. Those structures are themselves both a cause and a consequence of the centralisation which results from the place of Westminster in the control system. This is an uncertain time at which to write of the structure of parties, but it would seem likely that the United Kingdom parties (with some modifications which might be short lived) would seek to maintain or return to that pattern. For the others the problem will present itself in a different way. For the Highlands it is doubtful if centralisation in Edinburgh is more welcome than that in London. Moreover, those other parties will be affected by the need to act where strategic decisions are taken. Apart from such matters there are questions about the nature and style of any 'assemblies' which may be created. If they behave, administratively, like blown-up local authorities, they will command little support and do little good. Even for the new local government authorities a radical change of style has been urged,[19] with delegation and devolution within them. The need so to do is important, though it is uncertain whether in present circumstances the response to that need can, or will, be adequate. Delegation of real authority will require a different style of control, which can be supplied by public law. At the level of assemblies that need will be even more pressing. Moreover, it will, again, be quite unrealistic to suppose that there can be a delegation of legislative power on the scale contemplated by some members of the Kilbrandon Commission [20] without providing for judicial review. Bye-laws are relatively inert economically (even when they do not follow national models and are thus more or less uniform). At this level of legislation there is a real economic or social interest to challenge – as indeed one recent challenge to private legislation promoted by British Railways demonstrates.[21] The alternative to providing such relief would be the invocation of the overriding powers of Westminster with relative frequency, a solution which would merely exacerbate present ills. It was one of the illusions of that Commission to assume that legislative powers of that order can be defined with such precision as to exclude argument.[22] The whole history of such distribution of legislative powers (even including Northern Ireland) [23] is against them; the definitions change in scope with changing circumstances. One wonders for example where a frontier is to be drawn between 'succession' and a 'wealth tax' when each reacts on the other.

One other element relating to that Report deserves mention. It was not only concerned with Scotland and with Wales. Much of the malaise felt in those parts of the kingdom is also felt elsewhere in England. All that was lacking in those regions were those elements which cause that malaise either to be more sharply felt or to be more strongly expressed as it is in Scotland and Wales. There is, for such regions, too, a need for devolution. Regional structures in England have been denied strength because, once again, of a centralised system of control. If a local means of effective and ready challenge of administrative decisions can be created, the authority can go to the regions. Thus law, which will be essential for significant devolution in either administrative or legislative terms, can also be the means for real decentralisation. This view of the basic weakness of the present system is not simply the distorted view of a lawyer. Professor Beer has written: 'A system which by the very extension *and centralizing* of power undertaken to deal with modern problems has set in train political consequences that make it exceedingly difficult to deal with these problems.' [24]

There are two external pressures which tend in the same directions. Only one of those will now be mentioned, the other will be left to the conclusion. Our insular confidence of the perfection of our system is shaken once it is exposed to international scrutiny. In fact the original structure of immigration appeals, leading to that part of the Immigration Act, 1971, was in substance forced upon us by the European Commission of Human Rights (with the Court behind it). Without change the domestic system was regarded as insufficient. Indeed, if the matter is pursued, it seems that, political pressures having failed to achieve the result, it was only the threat of that system of law which eased the lot of boy-servicemen and perhaps convinced the Admiralty that powder-monkeys were no longer essential. Within the system of the international protection of human rights in the European scale there is likely to be a continuing need to extend judicial protection.

There is, then, at least one external pressure, though as will appear it is not the most important. The phrase 'insular confidence' may legitimately be used, for the Kilbrandon Commission did, briefly, widen its scope of enquiry. It looked at the French system of prefects (and an efficient prefect can be a considerable instrument for decentralisation; he has regional power) but in the absence of any alternative system of control no solution could be found to the problem raised by a side effect of the doctrine of ministerial responsibility, and thus having a civil servant who might serve two or more departments of state. [25] Indeed the Report reinforces what has just been said about authority in the English regions.[26] The Swedish model, which, it seemed, found favour at first, was rejected because it was found that in Sweden Members of Parliament were concerned with policy, but here Members could not be expected to divest themselves of an interest for detail,[27] and moreover the Swedish system depended upon a fully developed system of public law (not, it may be noted, upon the Ombudsman). The experience of Germany, which was found in general to have much to commend it, had also to be rejected. The reasons were of mixed value. The first was that statutes were, in Germany, drafted with more generality – which is only partially true and not in this context of great significance. The second was the existence in Germany of a system of public law which made the system, with its desirable results, workable.[28] All this was rejected on the grounds that 'it might be thought to be alien to our tradition'. It should not, of course, be overlooked that the French system was equally dependent on public law. It is as if observing the incidence of a disease one noted that if you kept your windows open then beneficial results followed, but it was not your habit to open windows. Thus let them stay shut. (Law is not among the experimental, or even observational, sciences.) The story could of course have been carried further. The post-war emergence of the Belgian Conseil d'Etat as a court could have been noted. Its place will not be without significance in the working out of cultural devolution there, which could be planned on the basis of its existence. The Dutch, who were for long perhaps closer in style in this matter to the British, but have been moving away, have determined finally to make of their Council of State a full-blown jurisdiction unifying at the same time the techniques available against local and central government authority.[29] The last instance may be particularly relevant to that other 'external' pressure which we will feel, that of the Communities, which is for the moment left over.

What has been attempted so far is to indicate in the broadest terms the sort of law and the sort of jurisdiction which is at issue, and to indicate that there lies within this sort of law the possibility of helping at the same time both individuals and the administration. There is evidence, passed over by the Kilbrandon Commission, to that effect, as was indeed admitted in the cases of Sweden and Germany. The solution has never yet been properly examined in this country. It clearly was not by the Franks Committee, and indeed was, perhaps, excluded by the terms of reference of that Committee. By its nature it was not examined when proposals for the Parliamentary Commissioner for Administration were proposed. It cannot be said that the creation of that office eased the task of the administration, any more than it can be claimed that it helped towards a generalised and creative solution of admitted problems. It is improbable that the extension of the system of local government will in the long term have any more beneficial results. Among other reasons is the simple one that the two systems, whatever notional links are created between them,[30] conserve the distinction between the two levels of government. Yet the process of government, at whatever its level, remains intrinsically the same. Not least of the weaknesses of the present law is that it perpetuates a distinction as do these palliatives.

From that level one must turn to the nature of the court, the nature of its law and the nature of some of the techniques. It is evident that there is no one system of public law. Within those that have been mentioned there are considerable variations, and other systems should be added. Nevertheless, certain general principles emerge. It should also be said that techniques in themselves are not necessarily of significance. They only assume significance when they have a bearing which is important upon the end result. Perhaps it would be as well to add, at this stage of the argument, that the views expressed are not based upon a single acceptance of the maxim of Sterne's Sentimental Traveller, that 'They order this matter better in France', but upon observation and consideration.

To such requisites as those of a specific law and a specialised jurisdiction one adds a presupposition that law does not exist for lawyers, whatever place a lawyer may hold in the hierarchy or whether he may hold a post in a court or not. It is not essential in any change to conserve their cherished habits, if these are found to be too costly or inappropriate. Law exists for citizens both in their individual and generalised capacities. What is required here is a system which can deal, with understanding, with both the problems of government, and the proper claims of individuals within the sort of framework which has been indicated. It should be a system which is both easy of access and cheap to the individual. In a modern State, with all its complexities, it is reasonable that within broad limits access should frequently be at the cost of general funds, though that cost may take the form of support of a court rather than the form of legal aid. The first step is to ensure a professionalism of judges. That is not a professionalism, in the sense in which it involves the appreciation of the realities, including the strengths and weaknesses of government, that can be gained at the Bar. A specific recruitment and training has the advantage that it is then in fact possible to engage youth and middle age in the process of judging. This degree of specialisation is perfectly consistent with the essential neutrality of a court, provided above all that a collegiate character of the institution is maintained. That characteristic is also important as forcing a dialogue which happens at the right time. As has been pointed out, our present form of judgment produces, in public, a debate among judges precisely at the point at which debate serves no real purpose.[31] Within the collegiate setting there can be a real debate at appropriate stages which can produce the evolution of the law. This is certainly true at two levels within the French Conseil d'Etat.

Among the techniques involved, perhaps the most important is the intervention of a figure akin to the *Commissaire du Gouvernement* in the French Conseil d'Etat of the Advocate General in the European Court of Justice. That figure is not universal. In Germany for instance it is at the choice of the *Land* whether he exists or not. Yet comparison of results in jurisdictions in which such a figure is present or is absent suggests that that role is of major importance for two reasons. First the role is that of the representative of the public interest. Thus the idea of this sort of litigation as being the traditional private battle between Tweedledum and Tweedledee is broken. That idea unfortunately dominates in the United Kingdom, even in matters of public law. However the case for the administration is conducted, in that situation the administration inevitably becomes simply a litigant, such as any other. Yet, in such disputes beyond the interest of each side there is also a public interest, which may be clear to neither side and which in such circumstances the administration cannot express with conviction. It is *parti pris*. Through such a *Commissaire* that interest finds a reasonable place in public argument, and at a point in the whole debate when it can have effect. The second reason for the importance of that role follows. It is that it is the task of the *Commissaire*, or his like, to synthesise and to advance the law. In a sense that follows from the representation of the public interest, but it has its own importance. It is above all by this means that general principles are brought out and coherence of the law maintained, and indeed that the law may be advanced, or, if need be, redirected. Thus emerges a compromise with the common law system. Essentially these other systems are of the 'common law' type in evolving law by decisions, but this office removes the disadvantages of the random nature of that process. Each case without losing its identity becomes a part of the whole.[32] One could compare that situation with an extreme but not untypical case, *McWhirter v. Independent Broadcasting Authority*[33] – an attempted challenge by an individual of the proposed showing of a certain film. In such cases the right to make a challenge is a major matter. It was scarcely debated and different views were adopted by the court on different days. The court, it would seem, wanted to express certain opinions, whether or not the action were properly raised. There was no proper debate about this key issue, for in public law the matter of title to sue is of great importance if the system is not to get out of hand. It is as a result of such episodes that there arises all the uncertainty of which Professor de Smith wrote. Without the intervention of such a figure a coherent body of law does not easily emerge.

Since the nature of the law is so tied to the public interest, one other technique is important. The court has an inquisitorial role, both as to facts and law. It is important to emphasise that inquisitorial is not the same thing as investigatory. The contrast is made by the comparison with the Parliamentary Commissioner for Administration, who does investigate on behalf of the party. The inquisitorial role does indeed mean that the court asks questions, but in a different style. They are asked in the interests of justice and not on behalf of a party and thus the process is not inconsistent with the role of being a keeper of conscience. On the side of law this aspect is equally important. It is, with us, by no means unknown in this field for key matters not to be the subject of debate because of this concept of a 'private battle'. That concept has little place in this field since both the public and the administration have a general interest in the result. One illustration of this defect has been given, many others could be added. Under the alternative system it is for the court itself to raise questions of law which it regards as essential to the proceedings.

There is another consequence of this inquisitorial aspect, which is more apparent, for obvious reasons, in national courts than in the European Court of Justice. It eases the task of the litigant. Indeed, in France, in many of the most significant proceedings for individuals the individual is not obliged even to use a lawyer. If procedure is kept to its essentials the individual can then, in a sense, rely upon this inquisitorial role.[34] Clearly there is an effect on costs, but more importantly there is an effect on the sense of directness. There is no intermediary, as there is with the Parliamentary Commissioner for Administration, between him and the body which judges.

Linked with this matter is one other difference. That is the much greater use of written procedure, which can even have the effect (in substance) of making an oral debate superfluous. This is not a minor matter, nor is it totally alien. Lord Devlin in the Restrictive Practices Court, for reasons of efficiency, made moves in that direction. This not the place to elaborate the argument; it is enough to say that those who have not experienced this technique in practice should not be too quick to condemn it, even, in the field of present concern, as a means of finding fact. The advantages are numerous. It is a procedure which greatly shortens hearings, with an equivalent consequence on the bill of costs, but it can have an effect on the decentralisation of justice. At lowest there is no significance in all the preliminary stages, in the facts of where the litigant is and where the court. It is easy to construct a system whereby the final hearing is, if need be, held regionally. The advantages when issues are becoming increasingly technical in their subject matter are obvious, particularly when this procedure is combined with an inquisitorial role. Technical subject matter fits less and less easily with oral procedures. The combination of written procedure with the inquisitorial technique is particularly helpful, for it is the extreme orality of British procedure which often presents difficulty for the administration. Publicity of justice is, of course, important, but the question arises of publicity for whom? It is publicity or openness to the litigant or his advisers, together with publicity of judgment and of the reasons for it which are the only essentials and these are conserved.

To go into detailed rules would be beyond the scope of this essay. Nevertheless some indication can be given. On one side, there has emerged, granted evidence which suffices for the purpose, almost a reversal of the burden of proof in favour of the individual. This is reasonable since in many instances it is the administration which is the real possessor of information. On the other side, since concern is with substance, it does not follow that a mere procedural error will suffice. Hence the problem of the true administrative error or slip can be dealt with, and the solution is helped by another matter mentioned below, particularly the rules about compensation. It is in the application of such rules that the expertise of the court can lead to flexibility which we lack. It is that flexibility and their procedures which have enabled such courts to grapple much more successfully than we have been able to do with the problem of what we call 'Crown privilege', but which is the hard problem of balancing a necessary degree of administrative confidentiality with the interest of the individual.

The problem of balance runs through the whole discussion and it would seem that the form of debate with the intervention of a *Commissaire* or his like is the most likely to attain it. One issue may perhaps illustrate this. That is the question of liability to compensate. It has been forcibly and well argued that the determination of that liability must lie with the jurisdiction which is responsible for annulment. It does not always do so, for example it does not in Belgium. It does in France and in the European Court. The importance of conjoining the two issues is that the decisions on both must be informed by the same principles and that by thus conjoining the court gains added flexibility. Thus it does not follow that where it is necessary that a decision should be annulled, *pour encourager les autres* the individual should necessarily be compensated. To do so would be to give in effect an undue enrichment. On the other hand, it is by using that instrument that the court can respect the autonomy of the administration. This principle, when combined with the principles of compensation, has gone a long way to finding solutions to the problems presented when the real fault is a failure of the administration to act, and not an improper act. In neither case will the court tell the administration what to do. It will annul or condemn and leave it to the administration to draw appropriate consequences, including in suitable cases the payment of compensation. If the administration does not so act, then, of course, fresh recourse to the court is open. An admirable illustration is the case of *Bréart de Boisanger* [35] involving a wrongful dismissal of a director of the Comédie Française. That is, however, only one aspect. In practice in both jurisdictions the action for compensation has become an autonomous head of jurisdiction.[36] There has been a great expansion of the idea of *faute de nature à engager la responsabilité des puissances publiques*. The circumstances which have caused this were indicated at the start of this article but that expression has also its effect upon the administration. The latter is liberated and can act with requisite speed because if need be the individual can be compensated. In effect this is necessary compensation for a diminution of the pre-natal procedural safeguards and the substitution of a more substantial control *a posteriori*, but it also makes acceptable to individuals those social experiments, of the sorts mentioned, which have become part of the task of government. These experiments may cause loss to individuals, but under such a system they become acceptable. The ideas have even stretched to compensation (at times) of individuals for the consequences of laws needed for the general good but which work particular hardship. So, the freeing of the administration is coupled with a remedy which makes its actions more acceptable. It is in that sense that efficiency is also enhanced. A study of the cases shows the rising importance of this distinct concept of public liability, and it must be remembered that annulment is often an inadequate or, for reasons of the public interest, inappropriate remedy. Thus this combination of remedies both governed by the same ideas becomes an extremely flexible instrument.

No system of law can be claimed to be necessarily perfect. All that can be claimed is that one system is likely to be more helpful than another. It is at this point that the elements of professionalism and of living with the problems of government assume their significance, when combined with the nature of the process of debate. What is observable in the systems under discussion is that overall there is a real endeavour to keep step with the evolution of the activities of government as these change. Thus there is a need to follow government activity not merely into fields of planning but also into fields of economics. It is notable how far we in the United Kingdom have fallen behind in regard to the latter, despite the fact of the increase in governmental economic activity. Advance requires the sort of approach and of dialogue here discussed. Once the simple element of 'control' in its purely negative or restrictive sense is removed the law can evolve, it can even become creative. It cannot be said that in this respect our modern law has been successful, though formerly in a simpler society it was. The advance is possible because instead of a particularisation of remedies, which has been the road which we have followed, the other system has driven back to the general principles which are capable of adaptation to changing needs. Of these some examples have been given.

It is at this point that the other external compulsion becomes apparent. It arises simply from membership of the European Communities. We enter a world which is highly legal, but not legalistic. A grain importer, if levies are miscalculated, will not be content with such half relief as the Parliamentary Commissioner for Administration can offer. He will expect full relief from a court, and indeed be entitled to it. The law of those Communities is based on the general background which has been discussed. It illustrates this creative role of law, and it illustrates the concern of that law for individuals. For the first time we have, within our system, a general enforceable concept of fundamental rights within the ambit of that law. We have it as a result of a case called *Nold*,[37] in which the European Court declared that such rights were part of the law of the Communities, having direct effect in Member States. Of that decision our courts must take note both by reason of community law itself, and also because of the European Communities Act, 1972. The illustration suffices to show that law can enlarge, and it suffices to indicate that Community law, derived from the patterns of law discussed above, is as concerned with the individual as the original systems. The full significance of the pressure exercised by this new force is appreciated if two factors are borne in mind. First that the administration of Community law turns out to be highly decentralised. For most matters affecting individuals it is administered through national courts. Second, there has evolved the linked concepts of the direct effect and direct applicability of Community law, that it creates rights in favour of individuals which national courts are bound to protect. The reasoning behind this is simple, the regulation of economic activity requires a degree of uniformity over the economic unit concerned. Taxation has to be uniform over the whole United Kingdom, and it is only against that background that the desired variations can be made. Granted the decentralised system, it followed that national courts had to play their part in ensuring uniformity. This role has to be played not merely when the issue is between individuals, as where one abuses a dominant position, but also (and perhaps more frequently) where the issue is between the individual and his own government. The circumstances in which that government may deny (in effect) to individuals rights to which they are entitled under Community law are various. A political crisis may prevent the passage of national legislation, administrative action or non-action may prevent the attainment of that result or the national authorities may wrongly interpret or apply Community law. Moreover, increasingly activities are mixed, that is to say that national authorities act as 'agents' for, or under, powers conferred by Community law. It is, for example, difficult to see in what sense the Intervention Board for Agricultural Produce is 'responsible' to Ministers when it is exercising functions on behalf of the Community and both it and those Ministers can only act in ways which are thus appropriate. In such circumstances the validity of administrative action by national authorities must be tested in terms of Community law. One could add that this is only true where private individuals are concerned. The Dutch State railways have thus challenged the Dutch Government. Indeed, there is no reason why, within the framework of regional policy, a regional authority should not thus act. Immediately there is raised the question of the availability of suitable remedies in the area of public law in the United Kingdom. As has been seen, even in the field of human rights existing possibilities in this country have been found wanting when tested by international standards. The gap is even greater in the area now under discussion, and yet must be filled. To give one example, where both levels of authority have acted, but have acted wrongly, the problem of compensation for non-contractual fault arises. Liability must be shared between the two levels on the basis of responsibility, yet the concept of liability, at the community level, is not only different, but much broader. A reconciliation of concepts becomes essential if the individual is not to suffer. It is perhaps, as a result of such pressures that, as was earlier mentioned, the Dutch are after long debate finally intending to replace their Administrative Appeals Act, 1973 (which was already in advance of our system), by a new law extending the remedies open to individuals against administrative decisions and creating an ultimate jurisdiction.

Indeed the effects of the new situation will not only be felt in courts. Recently the European Communities Committee of the House of Lords remarked:

'Because of the great difference between the approach of English courts to the *vires* of United Kingdom subordinate legislation and the approach of the European Court to the legality of regulations and directives made under the Treaty of Rome, it is very difficult for any English or Scots lawyer to give an informed opinion as to whether any particular provision in a regulation or directive is within the powers conferred by the Treaty of Rome.'[38]

The statement is of interest. It reinforces what has been said of the need for reconciliation, but it is in a sense false. It is, of course, true that an English or Scots lawyer, as such, if he remains within a narrow tradition, would have difficulty, but there is no absolute difficulty. All that is needed is for the lawyer to lift his eyes and observe, and thus understand, a system of public law that is purposive and susceptible. Because of the purposive element it is less technical and more creative than the law that we have come to know, and for that reason is helpful both to administration and the individual. It is concerned with the rationality of government. Yet the statement has a wider interest, for it indicates that there are consequences upon elements of the political process. The whole of the Report in question shows clearly that without this wider comprehension the Committee will be unable to perform its proper task; and will chance to delude itself that it can perform another – that of the lawyers – with finality, or even with authority. There underlies the tenor of the Report the assumption that if only in one way or another the Committee could deal with the matter, that was, or should be, the end of it. It is in the old tradition, the weakness of which is now apparent, that if only all forms of control can be confined within the political process then things work best. It is even curiously typical that the Committee even invites resort to two fall-back provisions of the Treaty of Rome as a general rule, in the spirit of the old recital 'and any other powers thereunto enabling'. It is as typical that the Committee should equate the validity of a regulation with *vires*, neglecting the significance of form, which in this context can be important. All Community regulations are required to be reasoned, and if they are inadequately reasoned or if the reasoning does not justify the content, they will fail. That rule is again, in one form or another, general in the systems here discussed. It is not simply a technical rule, for finally it leads to a genuine form of 'open' government, whereby the administration in acting is forced both to explain itself and to stand by the explanation which it has given. It follows, though, from what has been said, that the approach to the reconciliation of content and reasoning requires the sort of understanding which has been emphasised by the court of the nature and necessities of governmental processes, or else this control can also become one which is either empty or of great technicality. Risks there are, but experience shows that they can be overcome.

The learning of this other pattern of thought becomes more important in the light of the report just mentioned, when it is remembered that it is not only national acts which can be challenged in national courts. So too may the validity of Community acts be there challenged, through the mechanism of Article 177 of the Treaty of Rome. There are other means of challenging such acts directly in the European Court, but for sound reasons of policy that court has chosen to keep these possibilities narrow, compensating for that choice by opening much wider the door to challenge by individuals through Article 177. There are differences in the consequences of a successful challenge by either route, but they are not of immediate concern, and do not affect the consequences for a successful individual. The reasons for the choice thus made relate in fact to the background of ideas here sketched. But what is clear is that unless lawyers and judges are familiar with that background individual litigants before our courts will be denied protections to which they are entitled.

On this larger scale two elements in the operation of this law may be emphasised. One is the creation of immediate links between the individual and government, at whatever level, which is clearly important in avoiding the sense of remoteness or of over-centralisation, or even of impotence. The other is the effect upon the acceptability of government. It is true that hitherto (but not of necessity) the democratic element in the Communities has been too weak. Yet despite that, because of the alternatives open to individuals the system has been acceptable and accepted. (In parenthesis it might be added that much of the law has been built not out of great affairs, but even out of the 'minor' affairs of migrant workers.) Even though it was not protected by a sheltering wall of politics the Commission was open to attack, and in that sense was not a remote bureaucracy. Indeed the possibilities of attack have conditioned its activities. Even when the democratic element is strengthened as it must be, the need to conserve the alternatives will remain or else there will start a process which tends in fact to closing up government and to centralisation. Hence the need for adaptation here will also remain.

That 'external' pressure exists, and will I believe continue to exist, but it should not be regarded as distinct, so that did it not exist change would not be needed. The other pressures suffice in themselves, as do the benefits which change could bring, to justify at least serious considerations. Indeed recent events in government tend to add their own pressure. Government by White Paper is becoming increasingly apparent. At the outset it was said that the simple theme of law and order was not the subject of this essay. At the end it is necessary to distinguish the argument farther from others that have been recently raised. Sir Leslie Scarman in his Hamlyn Lectures [39] has touched upon some of the same ground, including the influence now apparent of international or external factors. Moreover he is not the first judge to underline that the common law has failed to meet modern challenges. Lord Devlin preceded him.[40] But again many of these arguments are insufficiently specific. The case here argued is not, as Sir Leslie argues, one for 'entrenched provisions' (including a Bill of Rights) and restraints upon administrative and legislative power, protecting it (scil. the new settlement) from attack by a bare majority in Parliament.[41] There probably is a case for a written constitution, and for a constitutional court, though that case is not argued here. There may well be a case for a Bill of Rights, but neither is that argued, for such a Bill must deal not only with public power, but also with private power, whether or not those who wield the latter cloak themselves with the semblance of public office. The case argued here is specifically related to administrative action and distinguishes itself by a concern, which tends not to find expression in those other arguments, with the efficiency of the administration. It may be noted that the German system of administrative law is independent of the basic rights guaranteed by the federal constitution. The richly formative principles such as that of *égalité devant les charges publiques* in French administrative law, though philosophically linked with the Declaration of the Rights of Man, are independent of that declaration. The European Court of Justice in its extension of the protection of individuals has not been dependent upon any such declaration. Each has evolved those protections on the basis of general principles nowhere precisely formulated. In effect each court has evolved its law in a way closely resembling the way in which the common law worked in a different context, during the period in which it retained a formative capacity. It is in fact this background of generality which has enabled that law to move with the times and to accept that the modern State with all its complications is our creation, as citizens, and thus to accept that State but nevertheless contend with the problems which it presents. Therein lies the essence of the comprehension of government, which has been underlined and which finally allows the administration to perform its tasks easily, provided that it performs them well. That difference in argument should be noted since it affects equally the Solicitor General's response to Sir Leslie Scarman's challenge.[42] The creation of such a system is clearly not to enshrine for all future generations our own cherished ideas, as he suggested.[43] Indeed, as reported, the Solicitor General posed a false antithesis. There is no conflict between giving an individual effective and rational remedies through the law against administration and the responsiveness of Parliament to changing expectations of society. The only conflict is with the view that individual redress should be found through the political mechanisms. It is that view which is as injurious to administration as it is unhelpful to the individual. Indeed the process of separation of distinct arguments which is involved in the case here advanced is even finally helpful to politicians, who are freed for politics. There is a very good case to be made for having a framework within which politics is conducted. It is the existence of such a framework which has enabled the European Communities to advance despite the difficulties which have faced them. It is that framework which makes both government and politics acceptable to the ordinary citizen.

Two things should be added. In one way the antithesis between a government of men and one of laws is in a sense false. Men make the laws, men administer them for other men, and men adjudicate upon their results. Concluding one of his essays on the Supreme Court, Professor Archibald Cox wrote: 'That the institution of constitutional adjudication works so well on the whole is testimony not only to the genius of the institution but to the wisdom and courage of individual justices.'[44] That wisdom can best be found through training, which cannot result from normal practice at the Bar. Hence the insistence here on specialised recruitment to a particular jurisdiction. That courage must be fostered by techniques of debate and judgment, and particularly of collective or collegiate judgment used in so many of the courts here discussed. Both are important if right results are to be attained.

Finally, Raymond Aron, commenting on the size of the gap between rights that are proclaimed and those which are actually respected, remarks, 'l'optimiste pourra objecter que jamais les hommes n'ont été aussi ambitieux: ils veulent concilier les idéaux de régimes ennemis; tour à tour ou simultanément, ils font confiance à l'Etat ou se méfient de lui. Par impatience ou par nécessité, ils préfèrent souvent la violence aux réformes. Faut il s'étonner d'advantage que, dans un âge révolutionnaire, les Etats violent aussi souvent les droits de l'homme ou que les représentants de ces mêmes Etats affectent d'en garder le souvenir et le respect.'[45] Clearly in such circumstances there is need for a susceptible system of law as a regulator or gyroscope.

NOTES

1 At the outset this contributor would like to pay tribute to one of his masters – Professor Robson, who (years ago) first opened up to me the world of French administrative law, the extension of which is the subject of this essay. The master cannot be blamed for the faults of the student, but the gratitude of the latter must be acknowledged.
2 'State power is the great antagonist against which the rule of law must forever be addressed,' wrote H. W. Jones in 'The Rule of Law and the Welfare State', 58 *Columbia* L. R. at 144.
3 *Judicial Review of Administrative Action*, ch. 1, p. 24. It is true that in the third edition of the work he saw signs of better times. He was perhaps an optimist.
4 Even if it be extreme, nevertheless the capacity of public law to contribute to the stability of society, while not obstructing desired change, is well illustrated in post-war France. To add an illustration of a great event one could cite C. E. 19 October 1962 *Canal* R. 552.
5 1964 S.C. (H.L.) 117, [1964] 2 All E. R. 348.
6 Hume, *Lectures*, III, 205. He was talking of burghs, but the principles are the same; see to *Phin v. Mags of Auchtermuchty* (1827) 5 § 690. The British use of the word 'Crown' has proved to be one of the most destructive to any rational development of law.
7 'The Commercial Approach to Government Operations' in *Management Services in Government*, vol. 29, no. 3 at 127 and 129.
8 Third Report 1971–3, particularly ch. 3.
9 *The Developing System of Public Expenditure Management and Control* (1973).
10 Dicey's second meaning of the rule of law in his *Law of the Constitution.*
11 Cmnd. 218.
12 See, e.g., Odent, *Le Contentieux Administratif*, vol. IV at p. 1248.
13 Cmnd. 5460, para. 850.
14 In no real sense can the Kilbrandon Commission be regarded as a constitutional one. It dealt with a single aspect detached from much that was relevant even to that one issue. The Franks Report looked at Tribunals and Inquiries detached from the whole administrative process. The Committee on Ministers Powers was similarly isolated. The Wheatley and the Redcliffe-Maud Commissions divided local

government over most of the United Kingdom between them, but their work (and its implementation) was divorced from what was happening about devolution. There is no reason to believe that the technique of making a layer-cake is appropriate to making a constitution, nor that the cooks of the cake should be exclusively politicians. Each of these bodies was simply a quick political response to a particular problem. The complex of problems indicated that the whole machinery needed to be looked at.

15 [1915] A.C. 120.

16 [1894] A.C. 347.

17 Consider the figures in H.C. 72 (1972–3), H.C. 379 (1973) and H.C. 106 (1974).

18 *Royal Commission on the Constitution*, Cmnd. 5460.

19 See the report *The New Local Authorities: Management and Structure*, prepared under a steering committee presided over by Sir Frank Marshall.

20 para. 744.

21 *Pickin v. British Railways Board* [1974] 1 All E.R. 609.

22 para. 745.

23 Where the problem was much affected by the practice of conscious parallelism, a practice which goes against the apparent hopes of the Kilbrandon majority.

24 In 'The British Legislature' in *Essays on Reform* at p. 91 (italics supplied); and see Apter, 'The Premise of Parliamentary Planning' in *Between Sovereignty and Integration* (ed. Ionescu) at p. 5. By analogy similar results can be attained within the Civil Service, by creating a system of 'accountable management' which is in governmental and not in quasi commercial terms. Cf. note 7 (supra).

25 para. 999.

26 para. 986.

27 para. 849.

28 para. 854.

29 The Bill was first moved in summer 1974.

30 As to which see the *Annual Report of the Parliamentary Commissioner for Administration* for 1973 § 47 (1973–4) H.C. 106, and see the Report of the Select Committee on the Parliamentary Commissioner for Administration (1974–5) H.C. 268.

31 See the article by Professor Simpson on the common law in the volume *Then and Now 1799–1974*, published by Sweet and Maxwell.

32 e.g. § 36 of the Criminal Justice Act 1972; which can be regarded as also attempting such a correction.

33 [1973] 1 All E.R. 689.

34 It was for this reason that it was earlier suggested that public support might above all be focused on the court, and not upon legal aid. Internally, if it is to support these burdens the court needs a more elaborate structure than ours has.

35 C.E. 13 July 1962, R. 484 and its sequels.
36 Aff. 4/69 Lütticke XVII Rec. 325.
37 Case 4/73 *Nold v. Commission of the European Communities* [1974] E.C.R. 491.
38 *Special Report* (Session 1974–5) H.L. 38.
39 Sir Leslie Scarman, *English Law – the New Dimension* (1975).
40 In particular *The Common Law, Public Policy and the Executive* (1956), 9 *Current Legal Problems* 1 at p. 14. As did Lord Reid in *Ridge v. Baldwin* [1963] 2 All E.R. 66 at 76, though perhaps his opinion in *Malloch v. Aberdeen Corporation* S.L.T. 1971 L. 245, [1971] 2 All E.R. 1278 underlines as much as anything the fundamental need to re-think philosophy.
41 Scarman, op. cit., pp. 75 et seq.
42 *The Times*, 14 December 1974.
43 Though indeed any reading of the history of the American Bill of Rights would demonstrate how false, overall, is such an interpretation.
44 *The Warren Court – Constitutional Decision as an Instrument of Reform*, p. 134.
45 'Pensée Sociologique et Droits de l'Homme' in *Etudes Politiques* at p. 234.

9

Justice and Administrative Law Revisited

J. A. G. GRIFFITH

The first edition of *Justice and Administrative Law* was published in 1928 and I suppose I bought a copy in 1939 when I first sat at the master's feet as an evacuee undergraduate in Cambridge.

How typical of Robson that he chose Whitehead as the source for a quotation on the flyleaf of his book and that the words should be: 'The period has been one of unprecedented intellectual progress . . . We do not go about saying that there is another defeat for science, because its old ideas have been abandoned. We know that another step of scientific insight has been gained.'

Robson was thirty-four years old when the book was published and could say without being daunted: 'The most fertile field of investigation in the social sciences appears to be presented by the ground which lies between law, economics, political science and psychology, a territory which so far has been almost unexplored.'[1] Not being daunted by the dimensions of the tasks he has set himself has remained a characteristic. Unlike Hewart's *The New Despotism* which first appeared in 1929, Robson's book was not a polemic. Its aim was

'to examine in detail the nature and scope of the judicial functions exercised by government departments and other public and private bodies; to analyse the causes which have led to such power being conferred on informal tribunals of this kind; and to evaluate the

[1] William A. Robson, *Justice and Administrative Law* (1st edn, 1928), p. xiv.

advantages and disadvantages which result therefrom . . . I have attempted rather to understand the reasons which have led to the setting up of these Administrative Tribunals, to comprehend what services it was felt they could render beyond the power of the courts of law, and to ascertain whether they in fact perform their functions in a satisfactory manner.' [2]

And this has been his manner and style throughout, as it was with so many of his contemporaries. But like them – especially the Webbs – strong political feeling kept breaking through, not necessarily or even often to damage the objectivity of the analysis but to provide its motive and to inform it. He is the last of the Fabians.

Rereading Robson's essay on administrative and judicial power in Chapter 1 of that first edition, I was brought up sharply to find that he tried a definition of the primary characteristics of 'pure' judicial functions, so as to distinguish them from administrative functions. Admittedly this was done apologetically ('It is, however, necessary for practical purposes to have some kind of a classification' [3]) but I had forgotten he had some responsibility (though he might dispute paternity) for the notorious conceptual analysis of the Committee on Ministers' Powers – to which body he gave evidence and on which sat his friend and colleague Harold Laski.

Robson gave two primary characteristics to pure judicial functions: 1. The power to hear and determine a controversy. 2. The power to make a binding decision (sometimes subject to appeal) which may affect the person or property or other rights of the parties involved in the dispute. Far less useful or practical was his classification of administrative functions as consisting of 'those activities which are directed towards the regulation and supervision of public affairs and the initiation and maintenance of the public services' [4] if only because one such activity may be the making of a binding decision on a dispute.

More important than the analysis and description of administrative tribunals in Robson's book was its emphasis on what he calls the Judicial Mind (the capital letters are his). He claimed a great deal when he said that, without it, our body of law 'would disintegrate in a year and society relapse into savagery'.[5] Perhaps a little carried away by his own rhetoric (as are all good Jews and all good Welshmen), he thought we would be in danger, like American Indians, of 'a return to the blanket'.[6] Under this rubric of the Judicial Mind,

[2] ibid., loc. cit.
[3] ibid., p. 12.
[4] ibid., loc. cit.
[5] ibid., p. 36.
[6] ibid., loc. cit.

Robson lumps together our aesthetic and moral judgments, our scientific theories arrived at according to the weight of evidence, and even our disapproval of 'injudicious speculation' on the Stock Exchange. I confess to being a little unhappy about this. I doubt if my responses to the Goldberg Variations or to Edith Piaf have much to do with the Judicial Mind, and the gambler who loses is likely to be given less or more than his due by being called injudicious. At this point in the argument (for we are still in the first chapter) the Judicial Mind looks like the Rational Mind and somewhere H. G. Wells seems to have crept in. 'This, after all, is the vital question. For the predominant virtue of the judicature lies only in the fact that it thinks and acts judicially and is recognised as doing so . . . What society needs is the operation of the judicial spirit far more than an insistence upon the mere outward features of a formal court.' [7] There is too much tautology here for comfort. He must, I think, be asking for more than that reality of judicial process which lies behind judicial procedures. It is perhaps surprising that Robson accepts so easily the claims for judicial excellence so often made by and on behalf of the judiciary.

The idea of the Judicial Mind is developed towards the end of the book under subtitles like consistency, equality, certainty, the rule of reason, and impartial thought. By this time the reader has been introduced to administrative and domestic tribunals at some length and the point has been made many times that the judicial function is exercised not only in the courts. The emphasis now is on the judicial *process* which consists in 'the application of a body of rules or principles by the technique of a special method of thought, and in the presence of certain psychological elements'.[8] Hence the 'judicial spirit' which has a number of attributes.

The first of these is the need for consistency which results in the making of rules. This need for consistency is seen to be at the bottom of the respect for precedent but Robson accepts that it is not confined to those who perform judicial functions. The second attribute of the judicial spirit is the need for, or the tendency towards, equality before the law, which is seen as close to the notion of impartiality. Again Robson accepts that these notions are not confined to judicial proceedings. The third attribute is the need for the law to be certain and ascertainable and Robson notes the great reluctance on the part of government departments to announce publicly the principles which they apply – a defect found commonly enough nearly fifty

[7] ibid., pp. 36–7.

[8] ibid., p. 186.

years later. The publication of the reasons for decision is more frequently required today but the advance disclosure by departments of their criteria, which taken together is often all we have by way of policy, is no less difficult to extract.

Robson ended this section of his book with what I take to be an attempt to provide an intellectual foundation for the establishment of a *system* of public law. He emphasises the technique of impartial thought and the artificial reason of the law, drawing heavily on Whitehead but recognising the limitations of the legal–scientific method. This attempt to relate the approaches of modern science and of psychology to the legal process was very ambitious and only partly successful. Today we are not much nearer to breaking down the categories and structures of legal thinking.

So we come to the problem of judicial discretion.

'What is needed at the present time is that the administrative and other tribunals whose decisions at present enjoy an absolute immunity from review by the courts (assuming that certain superficial and elementary procedural requirements are complied with) should be required to display a judicial discretion in making those decisions . . . We cannot endow all men with the judicial mind; but we can at least prevent them from behaving in a manner which makes sound judgment impossible.' [9]

Judicial review of administrative tribunals has undoubtedly expanded since those words were written. But the kind of judicial discretion Robson is here speaking of may still be absent from many administrative and domestic tribunals – and is not always present in the courts themselves.

No doubt many truths pointed to by Robson in 1928, now become platitudes, were not discovered by him. But none of them had been related to the context he provided because he wrote the context for the first time. We know well enough, for example, that administrative and judicial functions were for a very long time not distinguished in English government. But Robson made clear that one result of great growth of governmental activity in the late nineteenth and early twentieth centuries was to fuse these functions yet again. So he was able to avoid the conceptualist wrangling about the categories and institutions of powers. He saw that the need was for the evolving of new standards in 'untrodden fields of legal and

[9] ibid., pp. 236–7.

administrative activity' and that administrative tribunals had evolved to perform this task.

Some institutions do look as though they had come out of a forge, pieces of machinery put together to perform a new task. Neither the civil service nor the courts were well suited for the job which administrative tribunals came to perform.

Robson's memorandum to the Committee on Ministers' Powers (which had been set up in October 1929) restated some of the main arguments of his book. He called the Separation of Powers a legendary conception:

'All our constitutional arrangements are only provisional attempts to satisfy the needs of the community; and all claims to monopoly of jurisdiction must be tested by expediency . . . It should not be assumed that the mere existence of legislative enactment conferring powers which preclude review by the Courts of Ministerial determinations is evidence of executive tyranny. Nor must we assume that access to the Courts is inevitably a guarantee against ministerial oppression . . . Again, another dangerous and unscientific assumption is the belief that immunity from control by the Courts of Law involves an anarchical absence of all effective restraint whatsoever.' [10]

In 1930 all this must have been heady stuff to many members of the Committee. It was not so much that they would be shocked by the ideas themselves for Robson was, after all, stating facts in accordance with which so many of them lived the public part of their lives. It was rather that Robson was breaking a long-standing British tradition which insisted on there being two levels of presentation. It is a tradition no less strong today. On one level was advanced the view of the constitution handed down from Blackstone to Bagehot and Dicey. This consisted of a series of comfortable, liberal–democratic doctrines about the nature and functioning of the constitution, and disregarded the close political, social and class linkages between the different groups of public authorities, the inaccessibility of the courts to all but a handful of people, the gross inadequacies of judicial control over the Executive, the absence of Crown liability, the inefficiency of the courts to deal with questions involving, in part, executive policy, and other major defects. The other level was that of day-to-day reality. The 'what actually happens' constitution. This reality was not to be written about. Time and again, it was usual to hear learned

[10] Minutes of Evidence, p. 52.

exposition about 'the theory of the constitution'. And occasionally when the lecturer had closed his bible it was possible to persuade him to speak a little about the reality of power in a capitalist parliamentary democracy.

Hewart's attack on the civil service in *The New Despotism*, published the year following Robson's book, stumbled helpfully across these two levels and spoke of the power of the Civil Service in ways which no decent Britisher, least of all a lord chief justice, was supposed to speak. Robson saw the reason behind the attack as an opposition between the idea of 'law' and the idea of 'government', a heritage from the seventeenth century.

Hewart and Robson, with opposed political positions, opposed philosophies, and opposed remedies, were both breaking the tradition and were talking about power and its exercise in the real world. Neither was easily forgiven. Indeed, because Robson persisted in this theme for many years, I think he was never forgiven.

Robson gave oral evidence to the Committee on Ministers' Powers on 10 and 26 March 1930.[11] After the chairman had taken him through his memorandum, Sir Leslie Scott (then a KC) embarked on his 'cross-examination', as lawyers seem compelled to do even on such committees:

'760. Will you assume with me in my questions that it is the duty of the Committee to approach the whole subject with an open mind, unprejudiced by theoretical ties of any kind? – I very warmly accept that.
761. I do not say it is their view. I merely ask you to assume that it is so . . .
762. You do not dislike justice?'

At which point, I scream silently inside my head and wonder if Robson did. After his colleague Harold Laski had enabled Robson to elaborate some parts of his memorandum, another KC, Sir W. Ellis Hume-Williams, took up the questioning about Robson's scheme for administrative tribunals:

'858. What you would be doing then would be, would it not, to establish in Departments an entire judicial system? – That is my aim.
859. Considering the experience of the Courts of Law, and that they

[11] ibid., pp. 53–66, 81–91.

are already in existence and functioning, is there any objection to the appeal at any rate going to a Court of Law, except that you fear they may be wanting in administrative experience?'

Robson, having perhaps gulped somewhat as a man will when he hears his elaborate syllogism reduced to the level of a minor premiss, replied at some length. His questioner then asked about the relative expense of High Court proceedings and that likely to arise before the proposed administrative tribunals. The dialogue became somewhat bogged down though perhaps without Robson quite answering the problem of the cost of legal representation before tribunals – thirty-five years later the problem is still with us in an enlarged form and it will not wholly disappear if legal aid is extended.

Sir Claud Schuster (yet another KC but also Permanent Secretary to the Lord Chancellor) pushed one line of questioning hard. Robson began by saying that he understood the judicial function to be the power to hear and determine a controversy and the power to make a binding decision, sometimes subject to appeal, which might affect the person or property or other rights of parties involved in the dispute. Then the dialogue proceeded thus:

'943. The Board of Education determines that a particular site shall be taken for an elementary school. Is that a judicial decision or not? – No.

944. Why not? – Because it is not a dispute between two or more persons.

945. It very often is. It very often means that some person appointed by the minister hears people. Supposing that a school ought not to be put on that side of the canal because, for example, it will touch the local people's pocket, or it will be inconvenient for their children? – Where there is a dispute between citizens and a local authority as to where a school shall be that is a judicial matter, because it is between parties . . .

951. The person who is dealing with this particular thing has to ask himself whether in law he has power to decide anything at all – Yes.

952. When he has once decided that, there is nothing left but the fact whether such and such a site is suitable; to that question he has to address himself no doubt in an impartial spirit. Is there anything else? – There may be in many instances, though, in this particular instance there may be none . . .

959. Now we have disposed of the question of law, what is left on

which there should be an appeal to somebody else? – The substance of the decision.

960. To whom better than the Ministers can an appeal lie, assuming of course that the Minister is responsible to Parliament? – I think there are what one might call wider aspects of justice between the State and citizens, and it may well be that the ministerial tribunal may take a narrower Departmental view of what is desirable in the interests of good administration.'

It seems to me that Robson does not come unscathed from that examination, confusing though it must have been to answer a questioner who (during the parts omitted above) jumped on to different points without warning and then jumped back to his main theme.

The reason why our hero had his armour dented was, I think, a failure to distinguish the kind of case which we nowadays accept is proper for administrative tribunals and the kind of case which goes to a local inquiry conducted by an inspector from the Department. Robson appeared to say that the decision whether or not a particular site for an elementary school should be compulsorily acquired was a judicial decision appropriate to be taken by an administrative tribunal rather than by a minister. Today a distinction is made between those decisions which are wholly or largely policy-free and so appropriate for tribunal decision and those where policy is important (like many compulsory purchase orders and most planning decisions) which should be taken by ministers – or local authorities. Sir Claud had a point.

Sir John Anderson (then Permanent Under Secretary of State at the Home Office) pursued it.[12] Was the grant of a certificate of naturalisation to an alien a judicial or an administrative function? Robson's reply was that it was not possible to bring that type of case within any formal definition of the judicial function but was a function which it was necessary to perform judicially. He gave a similar answer to the power to deport which, he said, was not a judicial function 'because there are not two parties'. But the exercise of the prerogative of mercy he thought was 'very definitely judicial'. Now policy and the amount of discretion clearly entered the dialogue. Robson suggested 'the conventional line of demarcation between judicial and administrative functions' broke down if things were looked at in a realistic way. But Sir John thought that this was not so.

[12] Q. 1107–1294.

He developed the concept of a judicial function in much the same way as Robson had indicated when replying to Sir Claud Schuster: that it must involve a conflict between parties.

But it was when the argument about definitions was abandoned and the rights of individuals affected by ministerial decision were examined that the real differences emerged. In what circumstances were oral hearings, public hearings, cross-examination and reasoned decisions necessary or desirable? To what extent should they be insisted on when they inevitably slowed down departmental work? It is not surprising that different views were expressed by questioner and questioned.

With hindsight it is possible to see the embryo in Robson's evidence, and in the views expressed by members of the Committee, of the attitude more frequently adopted by the courts in later years. Alongside the insistence that so-called judicial functions should be conducted in accordance with the rules of natural justice has arisen the sort of principle that even 'purely administrative' functions should be conducted fairly and judiciously, even though it may not be possible to bring conduct within the already established categories of bad faith, unreasonableness or improper purpose, etc. (On the other side, it is true, the courts have shown themselves willing not to insist on compliance with those rules when unsympathetic to the activities complained of – for example, by students.)

But before that development there intervened the Report of the Committee on Ministers' Powers.[13] Rereading Sir John Anderson's questioning of Robson after many years, one wonders how it came about that the Committee advanced so dogmatically those definitions of judicial, quasi-judicial and administrative decisions for which it became famous.

According to the Committee [14] both a 'true' judicial decision and a quasi-judicial decision presupposes an existing dispute between two or more parties. The essential difference is that a true judicial decision involves a decision which disposes of the whole matter by a finding upon the facts in dispute and an application of the law of the land to the facts so found, including where required a ruling upon any disputed question of law; whereas a quasi-judicial decision leads to administrative action the character of which is determined by the minister's free choice. In the case of an administrative decision, there is, according to the Committee, no legal obligation upon the person charged with the duty of reaching the decision to consider and

[13] Cmd 4060 (1932).

[14] ibid., pp. 73–4, 81.

weigh submissions and agreements, or to collate any evidence or to solve any issue; the grounds upon which he acts, and the means which he takes to inform himself before acting, are left entirely to his discretion.

All this is old stuff and reads even more oddly today than it did over forty years ago. In the second edition of *Justice and Administrative Law* published in 1947, Robson strongly criticised the Committee for suggesting that a valid distinction could be based on the amount of discretion. He argued that the courts frequently exercise wide discretions; and that government departments and administrative tribunals were not free 'to follow any whim of the moment' [15] under the guise of calling it policy. These criticisms overreach themselves. No doubt the Committee's formulation of 'finding upon the facts in dispute and an application of the law of the land to the facts so found' implies an automatic operation of the judicial process which is false. But it is not clear that the Committee meant to deny the existence of all discretion in the courts. And they did not come near to asserting that ministerial discretion was exercisable whimsically. It is surely true that judges in all but a handful of cases (important though those few may be) have a far narrower range of choices open to them than ministers and civil servants taking decisions in the ordinary course of their duties. But of course this does not mean that the difference in the amount of discretion is a firm basis for distinguishing judicial, quasi-judicial and administrative functions.

Still Robson must bear some responsibility for he did, as we have seen,[16] in the first edition of his book (retained in the second) classify the primary characteristics of 'pure' judicial functions as the power to hear and determine a controversy and the power to make a binding decision (sometimes subject to appeal) which may affect the person or property or other rights of the parties involved in the dispute. He was a bit of a conceptualist himself.

The second edition was much larger than the first, mainly for the best reasons: the chapter describing administrative tribunals had more than doubled in length because of the increase in number and scope of those tribunals, proving that young Robson in 1930 was wise in his generation although he had to wait until 1957 for Lord Franks's Committee [17] to make an honest woman of him. I had almost written 'to make him respectable', but he has managed magnificently to avoid that kiss of death.

Only once did I fear that the great man might be slipping. That

[15] William A. Robson, *Justice and Administrative Law* (2nd edn, 1947), p. 352.
[16] Above, p. 201. [17] Cmnd 218.

was when I bought my copy of the third edition in 1951, three years after I had taken over his administrative law teaching at LSE and twelve years after I had sat at his feet. Rereading the chapter on the Committee on Ministers' Powers I knew at once that something I had loved was missing. I tracked it down. The following appeared in the second edition but not in the third:

'Sir Ellis Hume-Williams, K.C. stands out in my memory of the committee's proceedings as a distinguished member of the Bar honestly struggling to understand an approach to the subject which seemed to lie beyond his comprehension . . . Sir Claud Schuster K.C. gave me the impression of being the member of the committee who had given least thought to the problem, and the one who was least able to express himself coherently. It was almost impossible to keep to the point with him, as he was always going off at a tangent. After a long and rambling interrogation, the drift of which it is impossible to discover even from the printed record . . . Obviously no light could emerge from a discussion in such loose terms as these. To talk about applying "an honest mind" under the "guidance" of someone who has no idea of what is being done and no personal knowledge even of the officials engaged in the work; but who is "responsible" for seeing that "a certain policy" is followed – remarks of this order are a mere substitute for thought.' [18]

Those were the days.

Despite these sad and serious deletions, the third edition was some 120 pages longer than the second. This resulted from a considerable further enlargement (to 227 from 95 pages) in the general descriptive chapter on administrative tribunals. By 1951 the major achievements in the social services of the Labour Government had to be analysed and so new or much enlarged treatment was given to tribunals concerned with national insurance and industrial injuries, national health service, family allowances and national assistance, children's homes, rent tribunals, the Transport Tribunal, town and country planning, the nationalised industries compensation tribunals, and agricultural land tribunals.

Of the health service tribunals, Robson commented: 'The complexity of this labyrinthine system of adjudication is fantastic. It is difficult to discover any intelligible principles which would justify, or even explain, the existence of so many different tribunals . . . each

[18] William A. Robson, *Justice and Administrative Law* (3rd edn, 1951), pp. 329, 330, 331.

nook and cranny of the profession is accorded its own judicial autonomy.'[19] And detailed criticisms followed. Robson sounds a little as though he felt himself to be a latterday Frankenstein considerably alarmed that his ideas could assume such forms.

He reacted somewhat similarly to the procedural requirements of the Transport Tribunal.

'There are 67 rules and they occupy (with the schedules) twenty pages. They deal with matters which are part of the stock-in-trade of common law procedure, such as summons for directions, amendment of pleadings, interrogatories, swearing of affidavits, production of documents, dismissal of applications for want of prosecution and so forth.'[20]

'One wonders,' he adds coldly, 'if some of these technicalities are well adapted to the settlement of the price system in a nationalised industry. Many of them appear to have been adopted without sufficient thought being given to the purposes the Tribunal is intended to serve.'[21] Robson has more than a touch of the mandarin in his character, as 'without sufficient thought', here and very often elsewhere, indicates.

On the other hand, the national insurance and industrial injuries tribunals are well thought of and it was with these that Robson had the greatest direct experience as a member of the National Insurance Advisory Committee. No doubt he was greatly influential in framing the procedural regulations which have stood unchanged in their essentials for nearly thirty years. It is a pity that he was not similarly placed when the national assistance and later the supplementary benefit tribunals were created. A Robson in the hand is worth more than one council on tribunals in the bush.

In the third edition, Robson also extended his discussion of the attitude of the judicature, particularly by dealing at length with pension appeal and rent tribunal cases. From the former, appeal lies on a point of law to a nominated judge of the High Court. This has always appeared as a halfway house between no appeal to the courts and full appeal (on questions of law, in both cases). It avoids the criticism that appeal lies from an expert to an inexpert tribunal as the nominated judge will acquire special knowledge from dealing with all the cases (which, however, may admittedly be few). Mr Justice Denning was the nominated judge in the early days after

[19] ibid., pp. 143–4. [20] ibid., pp. 102–3. [21] ibid., p. 103.

1945 and showed a considerable willingness to review the decisions of the pensions tribunal to the advantage of the applicant. Robson seems to have approved of this attitude – he calls it 'liberal'.[22]

No appeal lies from rent tribunals on fact or law so the jurisdiction of the High Court rests on the general supervisory powers of the Queen's Bench over inferior tribunals. These powers are limited to quashing decisions on the grounds of excess of jurisdiction or procedural defects or (as later established) error of law which appears on the face of the record of the tribunal.

Rent tribunals, which were for furnished lettings only, therefore normally came under the scrutiny of the Lord Chief Justice sitting with two other judges. And in the period between their establishment in 1946 and when Robson was writing in 1951, the LCJ was the redoubtable Lord Goddard. Some of the tribunals undoubtedly made mistakes, as did some of the local authorities concerned. But the period was one of considerable housing shortage and the purpose of the legislation was to protect tenants from exorbitant rents. Robson commented on the attitude of the courts thus:

'Beneath the perfect propriety of judicial utterances such as these one can discern a deep-seated dislike of the rent tribunals; a distrust of their ability to do their work properly without legal knowledge; and a firm intention to keep them strictly within the letter of their jurisdiction. The passing reference to the personnel of the tribunals implies a criticism that no member is required to have legal qualifications; although, as we have seen, a large proportion of the chairmen are lawyers. The supposition of what Parliament would have done if it had intended to allow the tribunals to interfere with the standard rent is based on a major premiss which in this instance is scarcely inarticulate.'[23]

Later he says[24] that the control exercised by the courts over the pensions and rent tribunals was beneficial. For the former, he bases this opinion on the view that the applicants got better treatment as a result of the courts' intervention. For the latter, Robson said there was a need, which the courts provided, of 'a clear-headed supervisory authority'[25] to lay down and maintain the lines of demarcation between the functions of the county courts and the tribunals. He goes on to criticise in general the working of judicial review. First, because it is limited to procedural matters and does

[22] ibid., p. 504. [23] ibid., p. 514. [24] ibid., p. 526.
[25] ibid., p. 527.

not extend to the substance of the decision. 'There is an immense difference between the limited scope and effectiveness of the supervisory jurisdiction and a statutory right of appeal to a higher tribunal.'[26] Secondly, Robson considers that the rules of natural justice (which the courts can enforce) have become a very frail defence against arbitrary or oppressive action or mistaken judgment. He develops his theme of the decline of judicial control by going outside the area of administrative tribunals into that of subjective determination by ministers.

Yet he does not wish to increase the power of the courts, for 'the ordinary courts are not generally qualified to scrutinise and control the work of administrative tribunals or of public authorities'.[27] This leads him to conclude that what is needed is 'a comprehensive higher administrative tribunal'[28] which would be a court of appeal from lower tribunals and also enjoy jurisdiction over disputes with, and claims against, public authorities in respect of their administrative functions. And this idea, along with others for the improvement of the systems, he develops subsequently.[29]

The chapter[30] in which Robson first sets out this solution for the control of administrative tribunals did not appear in the first edition, though the idea itself is there[31] in the form of 'higher Administrative Tribunals' (in the plural).

The Committee on Ministers' Powers in their report[32] in 1932 were cavalier in the terms of their dismissal:

'Mr W. A. Robson has put before us detailed proposals for the establishment of a system of administrative Courts and administrative Law independent of Ministers as the best remedy for the defects of the existing system to which our terms of reference are directed. We have considered their expediency, but interesting as they are, we cannot recommend their adoption; in our view they are inconsistent with the sovereignty of Parliament and the supremacy of the Law . . . A regularised system of administrative Courts and administrative Law, such as Mr Robson proposes, would involve the abolition of both the supervisory and the appellate jurisdiction of of the High Court in matters pertaining to administration; and we believe that it would result in the withdrawal to a great extent of

[26] ibid., p. 529.
[27] ibid., 540.
[28] ibid., p. 541.
[29] ibid., pp. 616–20.
[30] 'The Attitude of the Judicature' (ch. 7).
[31] Robson, op. cit. (1st edn), pp. 308–9.
[32] Cmd 4060 para. 19.

those judicial activities, which are inseparable from administration, from the influence of public opinion.

We therefore, without hesitation advise against its adoption.'

Much of this is meaningless incantation, in keeping with the general attitude of the Committee. But Robson did open himself to the accusation, true or false, that his proposals would set up tribunals, which were genuinely independent of ministers, for the making of decisions which were essentially political. Robson would, I am sure, have been reluctant to vest in judges of the High Court decisions which were controversial in policy terms. He did not altogether cover his rear from the attack that his administrative tribunals might also be concerned with decisions which ought to be taken by ministers responsible to Parliament and the Press. Perhaps it was because of this that neither Harold Laski nor Ellen Wilkinson departed from the recommendation of their colleagues on the Committee on this point.

Some twenty-five years later the wheel came full circle and in June 1956 Robson submitted the third edition of his book, an article on local inquiries, and a separate memorandum to the Committee on Administrative Tribunals and Enquiries. The memorandum shows no decline in temper over the years.

'The Courts have been unable to provide an efficient and acceptable system of judicial review of public administration in the context of this expanding universe of executive power. They have been gravely handicapped by their own limitations, many of them self-imposed; by the common law rules of evidence and the canons of statutory interpretation; by the doctrine of *stare decisis*; by the excessively high cost of litigation; and by the reluctance of the legal profession to accept drastic reforms – or indeed, any reforms at all.' [33]

Robson proceeded to make positive proposals for a 'more orderly system' of tribunals, with many amalgamations. And as part of this he again urged that the most satisfactory form of appeal was that which lay to a higher administrative tribunal rather than to the High Court. The administrative appeal tribunal should be separate from the High Court.

When he turned to local inquiries, Robson specifically urged their replacement by administrative tribunals to cure their defects. These

[33] Minutes of Evidence, days 13–14, p. 487, para. 20.

defects were: the absence of a 'frame of reference' indicating what were the relevant considerations and facts; the failure to make explicit ministerial policy; the abrogation of the principle that he who hears should decide; the failure to publish inspectors' reports; the failure on occasion to give reasoned decisions.

It may be that all of these defects could be cured by the setting up of administrative tribunals, though that is not self-evident. But all could be cured – and some have – while retaining otherwise the local inquiry.

This difficulty of the rival merits of local inquiry plus ministerial decision versus administrative tribunal was not clarified during the oral evidence. But Robson once again displayed his gift of opening out questions which others often do not want opening out – not because there is anything to hide but because of the deep and understandable wish to prevent already large matters from making contact with their neighbours.

Robson's main contribution was contained in paragraph 57 of his memorandum – which was also taken up indirectly when Lord Justice Parker questioned him. That paragraph stated:

'The Welfare State has come to stay. It is unrealistic to expect any diminution in the powers of the Government. Indeed, further growth both in their scope and depth is more likely to take place. It is all the more necessary, therefore, to provide some regular machinery for the investigation and redress of any instances of maladministration, or misuse of powers, unfair or harsh treatment, for which a *prima facie* case can be made out. I submit there is a real need for an administrative appeal tribunal (or tribunals) of general jurisdiction before which complaints can be brought for investigation by a body imbued with the judicial spirit which will weigh the reasonable needs of the Executive against the interests of the citizen.' [34]

In their report [35] the Committee referred to Robson's advocacy of the establishment of a general adminstrative appeal tribunal, with jurisdiction to hear not only appeals from tribunals and from decisions of ministers but also appeals against 'harsh or unfair administrative decisions'. The wider aspect of this, the Committee decided, was outside their terms of reference. On the narrower aspect, they considered first that the general tribunal would be a relatively inexpert body hearing an appeal from an expert body;

[34] ibid., p. 494, para. 57.

[35] Cmnd 218, para. 120–3.

secondly that it would be a departure from the principle whereby all adjudicating bodies were in matters of jurisdiction subject to the control of the superior courts; and thirdly that under Robson's proposal points of law would be decided, for administrative tribunals, by the general administrative tribunal and, for ordinary courts, by the superior courts of law – and this would give rise to an undesirable dichotomy.

It has been a long war, this struggle for the establishment of part of a system of public law. And so far as it has not been won. For fifty years (he was appointed a lecturer in law at LSE in 1926) Robson has been first recording the growth of administrative tribunals, then forecasting their further expansion, and all the time pleading for rationalisation not only of their internal structure and procedures and of their relations with one another, but also of their place in the whole judicial system. There have been improvements but there has also been a firm refusal, aided and abetted by leading members of the legal profession, to remedy the major defects in the system. It is possible that legal aid will be extended to some tribunals. This will attract the interest of the profession at large and may result in some procedural improvements. Although a necessary reform it will also threaten some of the virtues of tribunals. So a new series of battles may be about to be entered upon.

When first published, *Justice and Administrative Law* was a remarkable work of academic scholarship and political perception. Because it challenged some major assumptions of the system, and not merely some defects which needed remedy, its arguments were and remain part of one of the few great controversies about the matter of the government of Britain.